FORBIDDEN KNOWLEDGE

The Paranormal Paradox

Bob Couttie

Lutterworth Press
Cambridge

Lutterworth Press
P.O. Box 60
Cambridge CB1 2NT

British Library Cataloguing in Publication Data
Couttie, Bob
    Forbidden Knowledge: The Paranormal Paradox.
    1. Psychical research
    I. Title
    133 BF1031
ISBN 0-7188-2686-8

Printed in Great Britain by
St Edmundsbury Press Ltd, Bury St Edmunds, Suffolk

CONTENTS

INTRODUCTION
The Reluctant Sceptic

No book about the paranormal, no matter how objective its intentions, can be entirely free of the personal dimension. In the absence of reliable, testable evidence, one's belief or disbelief in the paranormal is a matter of personal choice. And that applies, of course, to this collection of essays and investigations. This is neither reprehensible nor surprising. After all, whether or not the psychic component occupies space in objective reality, the experiences that imply the existence of it are certainly real enough.

My own research into the paranormal began in my early teens. In those days it seemed to me that the evidence was incontrovertible. The newspapers, magazines and books that I read and the radio and television programmes that I listened to and watched made it staggeringly obvious that telepathy, precognition, tele- and psycho kinesis, clairvoyance and mediumship were a part of our everyday lives. But sceptics scoffed at the whole idea, while 'orthodox science', whatever that might be, ignored the awkward questions entirely. Or, at least, so claimed the information sources available to me. Psychical research is one of the few areas of study in which the amateur can still make a contribution to science, which was not the least of its attractions to a working-class teenager with an obsessional interest in the way the universe worked and a strong desire to know more. I looked forward to gathering together hard, bomb-proof evidence, nailing it to a wall and saying to the scoffers 'Go on, pick the bones out of that.' It was not going to be that easy. Those youthful dabblings, experiments with friends and relatives, brought results that were either ambiguous or negative. What was wrong? I went back to studying the results and methods of others, including the writings of J.B. Rhine [1], but mainly the popular books available from the public library. What did they do right?

The first problem was finding the original sources quoted in the popular books in order to look at the experimental methods used by others. But the original sources seemed vague and the rigour of experimental conditions left much to be desired. I developed a sense of unease. Perhaps it is my Scots ancestry that makes me unwilling simply to accept *ex cathedra* statements by 'authorities' and willing to question, for example, the expertise of Oliver Lodge and William Crookes in fields in which they had not been trained. More important, if I was to answer the critics of the paranormal, it was clearly necessary to understand why sceptics felt the way they did. Were they closing their minds against reality? After all, if you don't understand your opponents

1

you cannot test the validity of your own arguments. Accordingly, I donned the shoes of a hypothetical sceptic, and asked myself 'Why am I sceptical?' and reviewed all the evidence I had. The answers I was getting were uncomfortable.

It became more and more difficult simply to believe in the paranormal. Often I found that experiments had been poorly designed and badly reported. Often I discovered beneath the overt evidence yet another layer of data rarely brought out for the public eye or ear. This data is the 'forbidden knowledge' of the title of this book. This suppression, by and large, seems not to be deliberate but due to certain information being regarded as unimportant. The nineteenth-century reports by Barrett, Gurney, Myers and Podmore on experiments with G.A. Smith and Douglas Blackburn [2] made no mention of Blackburn's stumbling on a carpet and Smith's search for a pencil, both seemingly irrelevant to the matter in hand but essential to the transfer of information from one subject to the other, as revealed by Blackburn himself decades later.[3] Brian Inglis confesses that in one of his books [4]he suppressed testimony from what he refers to as 'a disgruntled local lawyer' about a supposed confession by the medium Marthe Beraude, 'Eva C.' 'Perhaps the lawyer was lying; prehaps Marthe was a tease. Whatever the explanation, I did not feel it necessary to relate the story,' he says.[5]

Another reason for the apparent suppression of information is, quite simply, space. No book can cover every single case in depth. One hundred years of parapsychology generates thousands of reports in several different languages and it would be an impossible task to boil them all down into one book. Hence many fascinating reports have had to be excluded from *Forbidden Knowledge.* Then there is suppression for legal reasons. Britain's libel laws, so successfully used by S.G. Soal as a threat in order to protect his reputation, are horrendous – the innocent must prove themselves innocent and truth is not a reliable defence. This is why that the Society for Psychical Research's bank vault contains a report about a certain case, placed there on advice from the SPR's lawyers. It will be several decades before its contents can be released in Britain.

Sceptics said that certain effects could be produced by magicians' techniques, so I tried them out and developed a few of my own. I discovered, as Davey had before me,[6] that 'reliable eyewitness testimony' is often a contridiction in terms. At the end of it all, I found myself an open-minded sceptic, willing to look at the evidence but unwilling to accept self-deception, fraud, outright falsehood and downright silliness as evidence of the existence of the paranormal. However, I am by no means a complete sceptic and much to the dismay of some sceptics I still retain a belief in a God. An open mind should be willing to question its own assumptions. As one researches the paranormal and reads the literature through the years one acquires, almost without realising it a certain set of attitudes. While making the 'Forbidden Knowledge' series for BBC Radio 4 I had to question my own attitudes and scepticism. While writing this book, which includes some of the material from the radio series, I have had to repeat that process of self-questioning process. I remain a sceptic – but a reluctant sceptic. And who knows, maybe next year, or the year after, or tomorrow...

Acknowledgements : My special thanks to Robin Hicks, Alec Reid and Christine Bye of BBC Radio 4, Maurice Grosse, Dr Sue Blackmore of the Brain and Perception Laboratory, Bristol, Tom Johanson of the Spiritualist Association of Great Britain, Tony Ortzen of *Psychic News*, Uri Geller, James Randi, Mike Hutchinson of the

Committee for the Scientific Investigation of Claims of the Paranormal,Brian Inglis and Ruth West of the Koestler Foundation, Dr Robert Morris, Professor John Hasted, Professor John Taylor, Dr William Plumbridge, Dr Carl Sargent, Professor John Beloff, Professor Mark Hansel, Dr David Marks, Philip J. Klass (thanks for the beer), Clive Thompson of the British Society of Dowsers, and the many others without whose help and advice I might have remained in the dark and, above all, to Cherry, without whom I might have lost hope, as well.

PART ONE

THE MIRACLE WORKERS

1—A Meeting with Uri Geller

Uri Geller was the psychic phenomenon of the 1970s, a celebrity carefully nurtured by the sensation-hungry media, who still bends metal and minds today. A cabaret performer cum paranormal superstar who can still raise red-faced vitriolic rage among sceptics, cynics and magicians. He is also the man who taught me how to bend spoons.

In December 1938 Margaret and Itzhaak Geller married in Hungary, and then fled to Israel to escape the horrors of the war. Eight years later Margaret gave birth to Uri in Tel Aviv. The Gellers' marriage did not last and they were divorced; as a result young Uri and his mother went to the Haatzor Ashdod kibbutz where he seems to have been very unhappy. His mother met and married Ladislas Gero, a Hungarian who had once been part of a cabaret dance team and who ran a hotel in Nicosia. They moved to Cyprus, where Geller attended the American School in Larnaca, then a Catholic boarding school in Nicosia. After Gero died, and with Cyprus in turmoil, Geller and his mother returned to Tel Aviv. Uri eventually found himself in the Israeli army, fought in the Six Day War and subsequently became a counsellor in a camp for children. There he met Shipi Strang and his sister Hannah and in June 1970 began giving professional demonstrations of psychic powers.

Where did those powers come from? According to Geller's autobiography,[1] the source may have been a brilliant light that knocked him unconscious in a garden. In a slightly different version, in Andrija Puharich's book *Uri*[2] a human-like figure produced the blinding ray.

Puharich proved to be Geller's big break. An electronics expert with a taste for the unusual, a believer in the UFOs and mysterious other-worldly entities that dominate his version of his experiences with Geller, Puharich was introduced to him in 1971 and the two carried out research together. The following year, Geller began visiting laboratories in the USA and Britain and the controversy really started. Media appearances and verification of his powers in laboratories by scientists respected in their own fields placed him in the limelight and brought about the fame that Geller frankly admits was his aim.[3]

I first heard about him through snippets in the popular science journals of the time and felt that same frisson of thrilled expectancy that every believer in paranormal powers must have experienced at the time. Here was the real McCoy that would change forever the face of science. For the next dozen years or so, I followed Geller's progress and the controversy that surrounded him. I even learnt to bend metal by watching video-tapes of his television performances.

Although I was fully aware that his stunts could have been done by fraud, an overall view of the evidence showed it to be highly contradictory. The only way to satisfy myself that I was not dealing with a very clever charlatan was to meet him personally, and in the spring of 1985, while making the 'Forbidden Knowledge' radio series with producer Alec Reid, I got that chance. I heard that Geller had decided to settle in Britain and had set up a temporary base in a block of flats overlooking Hyde Park. Features written by Stuart White appeared in the *News of the World*, so Alec Reid and I decided to try and interview Geller for the series.

We were rapidly discovering that even the strictly-focused approach we were taking was producing an enormous amount of interview material, many, many hours' worth which had to be concentrated into 168 minutes of programme time. There would only be time for a ten-minute segment about Geller in one of the programmes. Or so we thought.

One problem was immediately apparent. Geller does not like magicians, and during the winter of 1984 – 5 I had broadcast a series of Geller-type stunts on BBC Radio 2's 'Nightride' which even reproduced the famous long-distance Geller effect.[4] I had been described on the front page of *Psychic News* as a magician and I felt sure that Geller would have seen that press cutting.

His dislike of magicians is certainly justified. In November 1973 a *Daily Mail* columnist, Richard Herd, asked Billy McComb, a very experienced and highly-regarded magician, to visit Geller with him. McComb's opinion was: 'That man's a fake.'[5] The American magician James Randi and photographer Charles Reynolds insinuated themselves into a Geller demonstration at the offices of *Time* magazine. Randi described Geller's attempts at telepathy as 'the saddest, most transparent act I've ever seen'.[6] When Geller bent a spoon Randi claims that both he and Charles Reynolds clearly saw him press the spoon against a table top. Jack Delvin, a British mentalist, a magician specialising in pseudo-psychic effects, saw Geller at an LBC 'Night Line' broadcast and reports seeing Geller physically bending a key as he walked through a door looking for some metal.

On the other hand, Leo Leslie, a Danish magician, concluded in his book *Uri Geller*[7] that Geller was genuine, having failed to catch him in any deception, and Artur Zorka, chairman of the Occult Investigations Committee of the Atlanta Society of Magicians, also concluded in a report to the Committee[8] that Geller was authentic. To confuse things even further, the influential British magician, Robert Harbin, at first accepted Geller then changed his mind.

But Richard Herd, in another article in the *Daily Mail* in January 1974, had stated that Geller was born in Hungary,[9] so I wondered what else he might have got wrong. Abb Dickson, who was involved in the Artur Zorka investigation, is said to have given a significantly different account of what happened during the meeting with Geller and, in view of Leo Leslie's book, one can wonder about his bias in favour of Geller's powers. On the other hand, I was not out to expose Geller, unless he was clearly a fake.

Several magicians have written and published books of varying practicality on what has become known among conjurors as 'Gellerism'[10] on.

At first, we tried to contact Geller through Stuart White, who discovered my conjuring connection, knew that I had accurately reproduced some of Geller's effects and became very suspicious. Letters and telephone calls directed through White came to nothing. Eventually, through another source, I was given a telephone number. When I tried it Geller answered and passed me over to Shipi Strang, his right-hand man. Strang has remained a close friend and associate of Geller since his kibbutz days in Israel and is now his brother-in-law. Sceptics have often implicated Strang in Geller's effects.

I told him, truthfully, that I was writing and presenting the series and wanted to interview Geller. Strang insisted that we should meet Geller at his Kensington flat. Over lunch on the day of the interview I briefed Alec Reid on the possible effects and methodology that might be used if Geller was a fake. We also took some precautions to ensure that we would be able to tell if any of the experimental material available was interfered with.

A drawing had also been prepared and placed between two pieces of black card, the edges bound with adhesive tape. To add a second level of security, the adhesive tape was scored so that, if removed, it would be difficult to replace. This assembly was put into an ordinary envelope. I also took a spoon and a set of keys. Ideally, the metal objects should have undergone metallurgical examination beforehand, but there had been no time to do this as the examination would have taken several days, possibly weeks. But if something really strange was going on, then it ought to become evident in later examinations.

Outside Geller's apartment building we met Rod, the sound engineer. Rod looked at me closely and said, 'I've recorded you before. You did a recording with Anna Rossi,' referring to a series of short interviews I'd had with Anna about magic and the paranormal. 'Do you remember what the recordings were about?' I asked. If challenged, I would have had to admit to being a magician, and that might have set up an unpleasantly negative atmosphere which I felt might detract from the interview. 'Oh, no,' he said, 'can't remember a thing.'

The receptionist telephoned Geller's flat. No answer. He tried again. Still no answer. The three of us began to get tense. Someone was sent up to the flat and reappeared a couple of minutes later to lead us through a double door with remote-control locks leading to the lift. We were to be met at the top, he told us. The lift stopped at the sixth floor and Shipi Strang was waiting, looking plumper than in the photographs I'd seen of him. He took us into one of the two apartments Geller rented. It was as soulless as a hotel room. As we entered, I noticed an office area with a circular table covered with papers, a calculator and a telephone close at hand. One wall was lined with a reflective, mirror-like corrugated surface. Potentially useful to a would-be mind-reader. On the other side of a slatted room-divider was a sparsely furnished area with a low couch and armchairs against one wall and a television and video equipment lining the opposite wall. At the far end of the room was a window bay with two exercise cycles in it. 'Uri will be with you in a minute,' said Strang as he left. None of us spoke.

I looked around to see what would be useful if I wanted to cheat. In front of me was a glass-topped table on a hefty metal base. It appeared not to have been wiped properly as there was a white smear across it. I had already warned Alec about the possibilities offered by glass-topped tables and it was soon covered with recording equipment Then Geller came in. He looked older than he should have done. At thirty-nine, there were white flecks in his hair, now cut short, military style. He seemed almost painfully thin – he is a vegetarian – but with a wiry muscularity. Geller works out for ninety minutes every day and his body looks hard. More than anything else, however, I was struck by a deep sense of tiredness. He seemed to carry an enormous, weary burden.

I liked him immediately. He has a boyish vulnerability and charm. It would, indeed, be difficult to blow the gaff on someone as friendly and charming as this. He came in barefoot, wearing shorts and a sports shirt. As we shook hands, I noticed the scars on his arm left by Egyptian bullets in the Six Day War. Rod switched on the Nagra and, as the tape hissed through the recording head, the conversation I'd waited fifteen years for began.

Uri Geller talked about how he wanted to give his children a British education and why England was his favourite country. 'Let's not forget that England made me. It was David Dimbleby and Jimmy Young many years ago.' If he had not succeeded the way he did, Geller believes: 'I'd probably be a general in the paratroopers in Israel or maybe an airline pilot.'

He discovered his power to bend metal at the age of four. 'I always knew that somehow I'd incorporate it into my existence. But, strangely, when I started appearing all around the world I saw that it is very hard work to appear every night in a different city on a different stage. I was young then – I'm talking about nine years ago. I wanted fame, I wanted money – that was in my head. Then I diversified my powers. I totally dropped the show-business side of it and I started using my powers for business purposes.'

What made the major change in his fortunes, claims Geller, was meeting Sir Val Duncan, chairman of Rio Tinto Zinc, who introduced him to the world of mining and minerals. 'I retired six years ago. I really don't have to work anymore. I was very successful – when I say very successful, out of ten times, for example, I would find [something] three times. Most of the time I would fail, but if I strike one time, if I find an oil well or a diamond pipe or coal, you're talking about big money.'

Indeed he is. According to a report in the *Financial Times*[11] Geller's terms are for £1m advance against royalties, non-returnable. He is reported to have carried out eleven projects in the past ten years. The report claims that Peter Sterling, then chairman of Zanex, confirmed Geller's prices and that Geller had found 'diamond-type Kimberlite rock' in 1985. However, Kimberlite is not especially rare, although diamond-bearing rock with exploitable diamond content is. But nearly a year later no diamonds had come from the site identified by Geller. In June 1986 the *Australian Skeptic*[12] reported that Geller had been paid A$350,000 for his work and granted an option of 1,250,000 Zanex shares at 20¢ each until 5 June 1987. Two Australian magazines reported, falsely, that Geller's biggest client was RTZ. A geophysicist I spoke to told me that Kimberlite has a characteristic footprint and can be spotted on aerial photographs.

I asked Geller if his children had shown the same sort of powers. 'With my son, Daniel, I can actually do a little telepathy,' he said. 'Maybe before you go I'll call him in and we'll write something and I'll transmit it to him.' Later, after we had finished recording, Geller called in his son, four-year-old Daniel. Uri wrote 'Lufthansa' on my notepad while Daniel stood, his hand on his father's leg, looking intently at Geller's face and said 'Lufthansa'! Geller then went on to show how many airline

names his son could remember. 'They see me bend a spoon and they imitate me.'
Geller says:

> I'm still very controversial. There are still people who do not believe in what I
> do and they think that the whole parapsychology field is just fraud, or it's
> magic, or it just does not exist.
>
> I want to keep it that way, for my own gain. Being controversial is always
> very interesting. If I tell you how a lamp works you won't understand
> completely but you know it exists, but if I tell you that it receives some cosmic
> energy from the pyramids it will become controversial, people will start arguing,
> and I like that.
>
> For scientists that's very, very bad. But it is an in-built safety device for me.
> As long as people still do not know whether I'm real or not, I'll always be safe.

Of his critics he says:

> I have to send all these people flowers and love, because, again, they made me.
> Those people who constantly knock me, made me more famous. There is an
> old saying that goes: It doesn't matter what they say about you so long as they
> spell your name right. I hope they'll continue.
>
> If right now a guy like Randi or somebody else is sitting in South Africa or
> Australia saying, 'Ah, Uri Geller is just a magician,' my name is being
> mentioned.... The accusations are so ridiculous – *New Scientist* had a whole
> page, with a diagram, about how I have a transmitter hidden in my tooth. When
> you go to that extent of transmitters and laser beams and chemicals, it becomes
> really funny. If I had a laser beam in my belt-buckle, it would be a bigger
> phenomenon than my real powers.

In fact, the *New Scientist* piece[13] included other possible methodologies too. The
tooth radio was put forward just as a possibility, not a probability, and was based on
electronics designs by Puharich. The laser-beam idea was a flight of pure imagination
on somebody's part and the chemical is a complete invention by scientifically illiterate
journalists – no chemical, not even the mercury compounds, would bring about the
effects produced by Geller. To be truthful, none of these has been seriously regarded
by knowledgeable sceptics.

I asked him about the court case, first reported in the *Daily Mail*[14] Britain and the
Jerusalem Post in Israel, that found Geller had used sleight of hand in his performances and which resulted in an order to repay the audience admission fee. Geller
replied sharply:

> No. If there was such a court case, wouldn't it be very easy for you to fly to Tel
> Aviv and find that court case? Of course there wasn't a case. This is
> elementary. Go to Israel, and find out. These are rumours put out by negative
> people. Listen, you know very well where these rumours generate from.... What
> about the rumours that said that I was a magician in Israel? If I was a magician
> in Israel then, again, go to Israel and find me a poster, find me a leaflet, find
> me a brochure – I'll pay you £100,000 if you do that. Can I be more generous
> than that? None of these things exist saying I was a magician, because I was
> not.

We asked David McNeil, then the BBC's correspondent in Israel, to check on the story. He found the original direct court report by the Israeli News Agency, according to which a mechanical engineering student, Uri Goldstein, sued Geller in a Beersheba court for breach of contract. The court found that Geller had promised psychic feats but had delivered conjuring tricks. He was ordered to pay the court costs and to reimburse Goldstein for the cost of the ticket. Several weeks after the interview had been broadcast, Geller continued to deny the of the court case. However the case, No. 37720, was well remembered by the clerk of the courts. In *The Geller Effect*[15] published in 1986, and a year after his denials, Geller finally admitted that the case did occur, although he was not present at the hearing.

As far as being a magician in Israel is concerned, Geller certainly never billed himself as a magician. But that does not necessarily stop him from being one – a rat-catcher can call himself a brain-surgeon, but he's still a rat-catcher. In the 18 December 1976 issue of *Abracadabra*, the British weekly for magicians, in an item headed 'Uri in Hamburg', a fire-eater and magician called Stromboli, who had appeared on the same bill with Geller in Hamburg the previous year, is credited with having performed watch-stopping feats for several years. Continental magicians and other artists know this and associate Stromboli with such happenings', says the item.

Herb Zarrow, who has also added his name to the vocabulary of conjuring – he devised the Zarrow Shuffle – is said to have met a magician called Simon Ruckenstein, in Safed, Israel, who is said to have traded tricks with Geller.[16] However, there are a fair number of magicians who have made similar claims – Geller is even said to have attended meetings of an Israeli magic club. These stories remain unconfirmed, Ruckenstein will not confirm or deny his story, and it would be unwise to accept them all at face value.

A number of people of varying closeness to Geller are reported to have confessed to aiding him in fraudulent effects or to catching him cheating, including Shipi's sister, Hannah Strang,[17] now Geller's wife; a one-time agent and manager, Yasha Katz;[18] a PRO who worked for a year with him, Miri Zichrony; his ex-chauffeur, Itzaak Saban; a one-time manager, Baruch Cotni;[19] and a showman who worked with Geller, Danny Peltz.[20] Katz has since retracted his statements.[21]

During the interview, Geller was reading my notebook upside down. 'If you read all the negative books written by these magicians, 99 per cent of them are lies. Let them write; the more, the better,' he commented.

About the laboratory work, Geller says:

It's very, very hard to work with scientists. The reason that it is so hard to prove psychic power in the laboratory is that for some very strange reason psychic phenomena do not want to be proven. For instance, at Stanford I tried for two months to bend a spoon and it couldn't bend. Telepathy worked, but it worked after weeks. On the stage it works in minutes.

Russell Targ and Harold Puthoff make no mention of these delays in their reports.[22] The only reference that might be so interpreted comes in the narrative to a film of some of the experiments, in which they write: 'In the laboratory we did not find him able to [bend metal without touching it]...it was always necessary for him...to have physical contact.... It is not clear protocol, he was permitted to touch the metal, in which case the metal did indeed bend.'[23]

While Geller talks of 'erasing a computer tape' at Tokyo University, reports of the event say only that the computer stopped. The effect took several hours to occur. Indeed, Geller says that it took more than a day, so almost anything, from a slyly applied magnet to static electricity, or the usual glitches that infect all computers, could have caused the stoppage. Ronald Hawke of the Lawrence Livermore Laboratory, California, saw Geller apparently corrupt magnetic program cards in late 1974.[24] The corrupted cards had been rubbed by Geller and the highly – localised patterns of the corrupted magnetic field are, to me, strongly suggestive of the application of a small magnet. Two of the four cards used in the experiment remained unaffected – one which Geller had touched only momentarily and another which had been sealed inside a glass container.

Uri repeated the assertion that he was now working with security agencies, and there may be cause to believe him. Many magicians have been connected with intelligence agencies over the years and even if Geller is a fake it is possible that the techniques he uses could be of value to them. After all, one American magician, John Mulholland, was paid $3,000 in 1953 to write a book on sleight of hand to aid CIA agents[25]. If we accept Geller's claim to have been involved with the CIA, this does not validate him in any way. Quite the opposite, in fact. If the suited spooks of Langley, Virginia or the Pentagon had found anything useful, why does the USA still spend hundreds of millions of dollars launching spy satellites and devote vast amounts of cash to developing the Strategic Defense Initiative hardware and research when they can get it all done for a fraction of the cost using Geller? And why is so little money available for research into an area of potential military use? Less money is spent on psychic research each year than the cost of a single F1-11 fighter-bomber.

Geller went on to tell us about his inventions, a counterfeit bill detector and a gas-leak detector, and claimed that he had designed a submarine net responsible for 'catching' a Soviet submarine in Scandinavia.

The interview finished with a couple of minutes' worth of tape still left on the reel and Geller suddenly said, 'Did you by any chance bring a spoon with you?' Throughout the interview I had been careful not to pressurise him into a performance. Any offer had to come from him and now he had made it. I took the BBC restaurant spoon from my pocket and gave it to him. 'I have to be near metal when I do this,' he said, and, ignoring the metal table-support and the metal content of the recording equipment, insisted that we move to the television set on the other side of the room. Suddenly the hollow that had been there since we met seemed filled with a charismatic sparkle. He was holding the spoon with both hands as he talked and moved, the bowl in his left fingers, the end of the handle in his right. 'Come close, he said.

Alec Reid and the recording engineer moved towards the television set, taking their eyes off Geller for a couple of seconds as they shuffled for position. Then it happened. With their attention misdirected Geller pushed in and downwards on the ends of the spoon, making it bend in the middle. It took a split second to do and I've tried it myself many times since with similar misdirection. It works.

He looked up and, for what seemed an age, our eyes met. Then he was on the move again, turning the handle in behind his right hand so that the bend was hidden. Rubbing the handle, Geller angled it gradually upwards. 'There's no sleight of hand, there's no chemicals,' he assured us. 'The people who don't believe think I have chemicals or laser beams or I prepared the spoon – I can't go around the world doing this to everyone.' He gave the spoon to Alec Reid as we moved back to the couch, and several times took it back, each time bending it a little more using thumb and middle finger with the index finger as a fulcrum.

By now Shipi Strang had returned and Geller asked if I had a sealed drawing. I took the envelope from my pocket but the tape needed changing on the Nagra and he refused to continue.

To confess what I'd seen seemed pointless. Only three entities really know what happened: me, Geller and God. Geller merely denies the incident and God is, as usual, keeping quiet. There was no sense of triumph, just a dreadful feeling of disappointment, one that I exorcised later that same day by sitting alone in a quiet room, recording my account of what I'd seen on the end of a half-finished reel of tape and then forgetting about it.

For the next few days I wondered what I was going to say, how I was going to write the script. Every form of words I put together sounded bitter and vengeful and I began to realise just how deep the emotional ties of the paranormal run.

Then Alec Reid telephoned. He had discovered my private exorcism and wanted to use it. I've listened to that piece of tape several times since and wondered what it might have been like if events had been different. There still remained one avenue that might reinstate Geller as a possible genuine psychic. He had said that the molecular structure of the metal of the spoon would have changed. Had it?

2 — The Evidence of Science

When the programme 'To Geller and back' was broadcast several believers in Geller's powers wrote in to suggest that his talent had been proven in laboratories under the gaze of 'some of the world's most reputable scientists'.[1] Geller himself cites *The Geller Papers* ,[2] a 1976 compilation by Charles Panati, once science editor of *Newsweek*, and experiments with Eldon Byrd of the Naval Surface Weapons Center as scientific proof. Ruth West of the Koestler Foundation in Belgrave Square, London, quoting George Owen of Canada, says: 'If you want to consider whether Geller is a fraud or not then you must look at these papers.'[3]

If Uri Geller considers that *The Geller Papers* provides the scientific proof of his abilities, then certainly it deserves attention. *The Geller Papers* consists of reprints from various journals together with some original papers, including the first scientific paper on Geller which appeared in the science journal *Nature* in 1974. Titled 'Information transmission under conditions of sensory shielding', [4] it was written by two laser scientists, Russell Targ and Harold Puthoff, of the Menlo Park-based Stanford Research Institute in California. Rumours about the Stanford research had been flying around for several months, gaining in fantasy content every time they circulated. Real scientific papers in real science journals go through a peer review process to ensure that the information in the paper is accurate, that the research methods do what they are supposed to do, that the conclusions are drawn correctly and that the paper is important. Or, at least, that is how the system should work. It is far from ideal and there are in-built dangers. Scientists who have gained sufficient authority in a subject to judge a paper are likely to be past their imaginative prime and unable to view it with an unbiased eye. The chances are that a paper on quantum physics would never have got past Albert Einstein.

It is not easy to get a scientific paper published in mainstream journals, as the standards are usually high. *Nature* sent the Targ – Puthoff paper for peer review to three referees with the aim of establishing whether or not the paper was worth publishing in its own right, not whether or not it confirmed or denied existing prejudices.

As a result *Nature* decided to publish, but prefaced it with a long editorial. This is reproduced in *The Geller Papers* in a topped-and-tailed version. Of the three referees, one was against publication, one had no strong feelings on the matter and a third was guardedly in favour. They criticised the paper as 'weak in design and presentation' and details of exactly how the experiments were carried out were 'disconcertingly vague'. Targ and Puthoff had not taken account of established methodology in psychology research. Two of the referees felt that lessons learnt by previous researchers had not been taken into account. The method of target selection, opening a dictionary at random, was 'a naive, vague and unnecessarily controversial approach' and revealed a lack of skill which 'might have caused them to make some other mistake which is less evident from their writing'. Details of safeguards were described as 'uncomfortably vague'.

'On their own,' says the *Nature* editorial, 'these highly critical comments could be grounds for rejection of the paper.' The decision to publish was taken because the paper was, after all, written by two scientists with the apparently unqualified backing of the Stanford Research Institute; as a matter of debate and dispute in the scientific community at that time the subject was one that needed to be reported; advance publicity had led to a number of rumours and publication would put them into perspective; and it would enable other scientists to judge the quality of work coming from the SRI. So the paper was far from being a major breakthrough in parapsychology.

There have been a number of criticisms of the SRI work by people like James Randi[5] with a number of very damaging claims about how Targ and Puthoff carried out their experiments. But what can be gleaned from the paper itself?

It is very educational to read 'The record: eight days with Uri Geller' by Targ and Puthoff[6] in *The Geller Papers*, since it is even more condemnatory, in its own way, than anything written by James Randi or in the *Nature* editorial. Two other psychics were also tested in the original paper. The paper features a series of thirteen experiments in which Geller tried to receive a drawing, a further test involving 100 drawings and a dice-guessing experiment. The validity of the paper depends on three factors: the degree of sensory shielding, the precautions taken against fraud and the number and identity of people present during the experiments.

Two special rooms were used for sensory shielding in the experiments, a room with double steel walls which was used for EEG research and a Faraday cage. The latter is good protection against radio transmissions but you can see and hear through it just as you can a sieve – because that is what a Faraday cage is, a sort of large inverted copper sieve. It was used because the experimenters wanted to take advantage of the graphics capabilities of a computer at the SRI. The main shielded room, in addition to double steel walls, had two doors, an inner and an outer one. Surprisingly, considering that the whole of the research carried out in it depends for its validity entirely on the security of this room, Targ and Puthoff give no details whatsoever about it. There isn't even a plan of the room, let alone a photograph. No information is given about how they tested the room's effectiveness. This detail is essential. Was there, for instance, a mains plug socket in the room? If so, was it isolated from the rest of the circuit serving the laboratory? If the answers are yes and no respectively, then Geller could have smuggled in a mains intercom operated with an outside accomplice. Targ and Puthoff say that the only communication was a one-way audio link operating 'only' from inside the room to the outside, [7] yet in 'The record', published only two year later, they mention that the link had a push-to-talk switch to enable communication from outside the room [8]. In other words, it was a two-way link; indeed, Geller himself describes it as such in his autobiography.[9] If anyone pushed the talk-back switch outside the room, Geller could have heard any conversation or an accomplice could simply have whispered into the microphone. Since none of this is mentioned in the SRI report, we cannot assume that they protected themselves against fraud using these techniques.

What about those doors? Could the inner one have been opened from the inside? They had refrigerator-type locks and, since logically the inner door must have opened inwards (I may be wrong, but Targ and Puthoff don't mention these doors in any detail), the handle for the inner door must have been inside the room. The sensory shielding of the doors, then, may have depended entirely on the effectiveness of the one outer door. If someone tapped on the outside, could the sound be heard inside? Was it possible to hear conversations through the single door if the inner door was open? We don't know.

In other words, there is no way that anyone reading the paper can judge how effective the shielding was. Of course, Geller would, in most cases, have needed an accomplice. Apart from the experimenters themselves and Geller, no other person is named, and only other SRI personnel are referred to. Yet, from 'The record', we do know that, in at least one case, there were several people present during one experiment who were not mentioned in the original paper. [10] Who were they? We don't know.

Even to a layman it must appear that this is very sloppy science. It refers to sensory shielding, but says next to nothing about the shielding or about how the room was tested or what precautions were taken against fraud.

When Geller was tested with 100 drawings in envelopes which an accomplice could not have seen, he failed. I found this interesting because, for once, we do have some idea of how the drawings were protected – they were in double envelopes lined with black cardboard. When I presented Geller with a similar set-up, he passed on trying to guess the drawing.

Although ten dice-guessing experiments were carried out at SRI using a metal card-file box, with Geller being correct eight times and passing twice, we know nothing about the protocol from the paper. It says that Geller wrote down his guesses. What was done with these pieces of paper? Did Geller have them? Did he show them to the experimenter before the dice was rattled? Did he touch the card file? Again we don't know.

What really is astonishing about this particular series of experiments is that with a success rate of 100 per cent, the highest level of success achieved, not one single further experiment of this type was carried out. Remarkably, the paper does say, 'Although metal-bending by Geller has been observed in our laboratory, we have not been able to combine such observations with adequately controlled experiments to obtain data sufficient to support the paranormal hypothesis.'[11] Despite that, a film shown at a 1973 physics colloquium at Columbia University was devoted almost exclusively to experiments not mentioned in the paper, the only exception being the dubious dice-guessing tests. But Targ and Puthoff were decent enough to say that what was seen on the film 'should not be interpreted as proof of psychic functioning'.[12]

One of the interesting things about *The Geller Papers* is that reports of metal-bending and the like come only from short-term experiments, in which Geller was present only for a matter of, at most, a couple of hours.

Uri did not mention the SRI tests to me, but he did talk about experiments done at the Naval Surface Weapons Center at the White Oak Laboratory at Silver Spring, a few miles north-west of Washington DC. In 1960 researchers at the US Naval Ordnance Laboratory were experimenting with various alloys for use in a new generation of missiles and spacecraft then on the NASA drawing-board. They came up with a nickel – titanium alloy, NiTi.[13] The new alloy was disappointingly soft and a hardness- testing machine made a deep dent in a block of it. To see what effect heat treatment might have, two research workers, W.J. Buehler and R.C.W. Wiley, warmed up the block and, to their astonishment, the dent simply vanished.

What they had discovered was a new memory metal, a substance that could 'remember' its original shape. It was christened 'Nitinol' from the initials for NIckel TItanium Naval Ordnance Laboratory. The material can be processed into a particular shape at a high temperature and allowed to cool. It can then be bent, twisted or battered into any shape, returning with tremendous force to its original shape when heated to what is called its transition temperature.[14] That temperature can be almost anything the user desires. For instance, if it is low then the material is very hard at room temperature and takes a fine edge. Being non-magnetic it is ideal for, say, a special- forces knife. If the transition temperature is such that the material changes from soft to hard at body heat it can be used in medicine. Another use is for an IUD. The most commonly available type has a transition temperature of between 150° and 200° Fahrenheit.

Eldon Byrd, a physical scientist at the Silver Spring laboratory, decided to test Geller's effect on Nitinol at a private parapsychology laboratory, now defunct, called the Isis Center. According to writer Martin Gardner despite what Charles Panati believes, the Isis Center was not part of the Silver Spring laboratory.[15] Two other locations are mentioned in Byrd's paper, published in Panati's book for the first time[16]. In theory, Byrd's experiments had two built-in controls which made other controls against fraud unnecessary. He believed that extreme conditions were required to give Nitinol a permanent shape change, and the material itself was in restricted circulation. Byrd was wrong on both counts. For instance, by the time Byrd carried out his experiments in 1973 there was a conjuring trick available in which a spectator wrote a number on a piece of paper. The paper was secured with a paperclip and placed in an envelope which was then burnt. Among the ashes would be found the paperclip, twisted into the figure 4, matching the number written by the spectator. The clip was made of Nitinol.

At least three years before Byrd's experiments, samples of Nitinol wire were distributed with *Battelle Research Outlook*,[17] the house magazine of Battelle-Columbus, as well as with press releases distributed in Britain and the USA. According to the literature on Nitinol, and to Byrd, the metal needs to be heated to 500° Celsius (932° Fahrenheit) to effect a permanent memory change. However, Harry Rosenberg of the department of physics at Oxford University told me in a telephone conversation that he had discovered that 180° Celsius would do the trick – and it could be done with a match.

At the first session with Byrd, Geller failed to affect a block of the metal or a 1.5mm piece of wire. Byrd then cut a piece of 0.5mm wire into lengths of about 5 inches, into one of which Geller apparently put a kink. What happened to the pieces of wire not used by Geller? How long did he take? Who was present? And what precautions were taken against the switching of one wire for another? Had Byrd's original assumptions been correct, these questions would be irrelevant. Byrd says that the kink produced by Geller could not be removed, even when the wire was heated in a vacuum chamber by metallurgists of the Naval Surface Weapons Center. Unfortunately, there is no record of this stage of the experiment. Byrd may well have had it done informally, in which case there would be no official record. This would be a pity because, if true, it would certainly indicate that something remarkable had happened.

A second test was carried out in November 1973 with two pieces of wire which Geller did bend. When? Where? Under what conditions of observation? We don't know. Again, had Byrd's assumptions about the characteristics of Nitinol been correct, these questions would not matter.

In a third session, in October 1974, Geller and Nitinol got together in the Connecticut home of John G. Fuller, Solvej Clarke and Melanie Toyofuku, friends of Geller, were present. According to Byrd's account, four pieces of wire were prepared, three of which he took to Fuller's home. He says that they were physically characterised. How this was done or whether the pieces were individually identifiable he does not say. Kinks appeared in all three pieces which seemed to remain even when the wires were heated. The question of controls remains unanswered, as usual. How could the effects have been produced? First, of course, a prepared piece of wire could have been taken into the laboratory and simply switched for a piece already present. Second, during the first test one of the unused pieces could have been taken by Geller or an accomplice into, say, the lavatory and a memory shape processed in with a match flame and an improvised clamp as suggested by Gardner in his article mentioned earlier. Using such prepared pieces Geller could, after straightening them, have simply put in a kink using sleight of hand at the point where the prepared wire had its memory kink. When warmed up, the new kink would disappear to be replaced by the memory kink. Even more simply, the kinked wire could have been held so that it appeared to be straight and given a 90 degree twist (see Part 4 – How to be Psychic).

Thanks to Renate Siebrasse of the London office of the Battelle Memorial Institute I was able to get samples of Nitinol wire and discovered that a permanent memory change could be caused by making a loop and, keeping the loop flat, pulling the ends of the wire. This produces bends virtually indistinguishable from some of those produced by Geller.

In fact, the Nitinol literature actually warns against bending the metal too sharply because this induces strain on the outside of the curve from which the wire cannot recover.[18] A permanent loop can be formed by tying the wire in a knot and subjecting it to a match or cigarette-lighter. The knot effectively clamps the wire and prevents the enormous amount of force released from springing it back during heating.

These and the SRI experiments represent the strongest case for Geller's powers. Unfortunately the results are meaningless since the conditions at SRI are unknown and the controls in the Nitinol experiments were based on false assumptions.

Of the remaining papers in Panati's book, Professor John Taylor of King's College, London, has withdrawn his support for Geller[19] and Professor John Hasted of Birkbeck College remarks, 'We realise that such conditions as we have described in this paper are just those in which a conjuring trick can be carried out.'[20] Unfortunately, one of the most impressive experiments carried out by Hasted, damage to the very crystals inside pill capsules, was marred because although he had checked the crystals earlier in the day, he did not do so immediately before Geller had overt access to them.

Curiously, Geller turned down seven or eight invitations from the chairman of the Israeli Parapsychological Society, H.C. Berendt, then claimed never to have heard of the IPS.[21] Geller also chose not to be investigated by the Society for Psychical Research [22]

Science fiction writer Arthur C. Clarke was present during one meeting between Geller and Hasted. In Geller's autobiography, Uri says that he told Clarke to hold his own house-key in his hand and it bent [23]. Clarke's own recollection is that Geller did touch the key and had it on a firm metal surface while he stroked it [24]. In addition, Jack Sarfatti, who witnessed some of the Hasted experiments, said in *Science News*, 'I wish to publicly retract my endorsement of Uri Geller's psychoenergetic authenticity.'[25]

Hasted, at least, was aware of what magicians and tricksters can do. This is not the case with William Cox of the Institute for Parapsychology, Durham, North Carolina. He claims that a true psychic would be able to allow himself to be filmed making a drawing of a hidden target, while a magician would not.[26] He makes no allowances for different methodologies, and there are numerous methods, even without a tip-off from an accomplice. Cox is so wrong that there is no need even to wonder whether or not he can spot fraud. If he knows so little about magicians' techniques then he clearly cannot, despite his claims to forty years' experience in magic and parapsychology. In 'A preliminary scrutiny of Uri Geller',[27] Cox announces himself 'impressed with his general attitude and his lack of interest in details'. An essential part of misdirection is to pay little attention to important detail.

The first test applied by Cox was with a blank steel key which was placed on a glass-topped table. The key was under Geller's sole control twice, just before being placed on the table and again after it had apparently bent by 8 degrees, and Cox's observation was interrupted twice, once when he altered his viewpoint in order to look at the key from underneath the table and a second time when he obtained a mirror to help with his observations. Geller then turned down an experiment with a ten-sided dice. Then a second key was bent by Geller, but there is less detail about his actual handling of it. A third key, placed where it could be seen at all times and untouched, apparently failed to bend, as did a skeleton key in Cox's briefcase.

This was followed by three ESP tests: Cox drew the Greek letters psi and kappa, Uri suggested that he had written a word; Geller asked Cox to 'write a geometric figure', Cox drew a circle with two lines and Geller made two responses: the second, a circle and triangle, 'showed a very good degree of success' (see Part 4 – How to be Psychic); Cox presented a digital counter and scrambled the numbers, Geller guessed 332 and the correct number was 402. Geller then failed with a five-coloured dice and was given two leather rings with the suggestion they might link – they didn't then and have not done so since. Lastly, Geller was presented with a pocket watch prepared by inserting a piece of foil to prevent it working. Although Cox says, 'The watch was never out of my sight, nor was it even partly concealed by Geller's fingers,' this is clearly not true as he cannot have been looking at the watch while also observing the key bending and other effects. Cox does not say where he kept the watch but everything else came out of his briefcase. Cox gave the watch to Geller without, apparently, checking whether or not it was ticking, Geller twice held the watch to his ear and it was found to be ticking when it was returned to Cox. Not an entirely promising piece of work.

Wilbur Franklin of Kent State University discovered no difference between a Geller-bent spoon and one bent physically. Just before his death Franklin had become aware of a significant error in his metallurgical work with a platinum ring, which had seemed to present remarkable evidence for Geller's powers, and he intended to write up the new findings. He died before he could do so, but it appears that the ring, which apparently broke in the hand of an assistant and showed high-temperature melting and a cold fracture next to each other – a seeming impossibility – actually broke at the point where the ring was brazed.

After Geller had bent my BBC spoon he claimed that under investigation its molecular structure would prove to have been changed. Alec Reid contacted Dr William Plumbridge of the department of engineering at Bristol University and asked him to examine the spoon, together with several others. The spoons were subjected to a scanning electron microscope, a transmission electron microscope and a diamond-tipped hardness-testing machine. After several weeks the result came back. When a piece of metal is physically bent the hardness of the metal at the point of the bend increases, which is precisely what Dr Plumbridge had found to be the case. The only differences between the Geller-bent spoon and the within the limits that could be expected from within different batches. Interestingly, one difference, in the curvature of the bend of the spoon, tended to match what might be expected from the type of bend I saw Uri use. Admittedly, the conditions fell short of the ideal for a scientific examination. A full examination of the spoon before it was bent might possibly have produced interesting information, but, frankly, I doubt it.

All that seems certain is that whatever method Geller uses, the traces it leaves are no different from those left by simply bending metal physically. Plumbridge's conclusion was: 'What we found from this metallurgical examination is that there is no evidence that we can see that any spoon has been bent by exceptional powers.'

A few weeks after the programme on Uri Geller was broadcast I spoke with him on the telephone. 'You have done me a lot of damage,' he said. He again denied the existence of the Beersheba court case and denied that he had cheated when bending the spoon in my presence. In the meantime an article had been published in *Psychic News* in which he talked about, and admitted, the fact that he cannot perform in front of sceptics. Geller cannot deny that a spoon was bent during my time with him. By his own logic, therefore, he must have bent the spoon by fraud. Towards the end of the telephone conversation, during which he told me that he had asked his solicitors to check out the Beersheba incident, I told him that if he could produce evidence that I had done him an injustice I would apologise publicly. He promised to contact me again. He never has.

Today Geller blames his agent for the court case and for faking a photograph of Geller with Sophia Loren; he blames Andrija Puharich for the ridiculous Hoova and men from outer space who appear in Puharich's book,[28] and for an incident with a foreign currency note that was shown to be false by Guy Lyon Playfair; he blames his exposures on mysterious reactionary powers behind his critics, and so it goes on. He has hired detectives to probe the private lives of sceptics and maintains files on them. Above all, he drops names far and wide, with great enthusiasm. Perhaps he wants some of the credibility of those he meets to rub off on him, or maybe he tries to fill the evident void that I noticed in our first meeting with other people's depth of personality. Maybe he is simply the professional confidence trickster flattering and playing his victims, as a fisherman plays a trout. Or maybe he is still a Peter Pan, unable to grow up, still the lonely child unable to live up to his father's expectations. Perhaps he genuinely believes in his own powers. I don't know whether they are genuine. All I can say for certain is that the evidence I have points in an entirely different direction.

3 ← Medium-not-very-rare

For those who believe in communication with the dead, psychic powers prove the existence of life after death, particularly the evidence provided by mediums. The concept of the hereafter painted by mediums often seems to be a sort of rather faded, comfy, middle-class Frinton, complete with guitar lessons, in which the vibrant full-bloodedness and sensuality of live individual personalities seems to have been replaced by a sort of wishy-washy, all-purpose paste.

Most religions, excepting atheism, teach the existence of a life after death as an article of faith, in some cases the actual physical resurrection of the body. Spiritualists, however, claim that what they have is not faith, but proof, proof that can be verified by personal validation.

Of course, not all spiritualists are mediums, but mediums provide the evidence upon which spiritualism depends. Not just for its existence, but also to provide a sort of psychic glue between its adherents. When a medium gives messages from the platform this not only has a spiritual meaning for those receiving the messages, but also unites the congregation with a singularity of experience, much in the same way as a football team unites its supporters when it scores a goal. Or, more appropriately, it unites in the same way that the mystery of transubstantiation and the receiving of the blood and body of Christ with the wine and wafer during the Catholic Mass unite the congregation. The experience of communication, then, is not just a subjective, individual experience, but a shared experience, too. The spiritualist assumption is an essentially nineteenth-century one our senses are accurate, the interpretation of what those senses tell us is always correct, our memories are accurate and reliable, and the events and experiences in each person's life are unique to that individual. What concerns me as an investigator, however, is not the underlying psychology and sociology of faith, but the evidence presented by those who want to convince me that they have the ability to commune with the deceased. The value of the evidence rests entirely on the 'unknowability' of the information imparted by the medium to the subject or subjects.

Another band of mediums – the physical mediums – claim to produce physical phenomena such as table lifting or tilting, the linking of solid wooden rings, the production of objects – 'apports', photographs of spirits, the invocation of the actual presence of the departed in some physical form and recordings of the voices of spirits. There is, perhaps, an argument for including voice-mediumship under the physical-mediumship label since it clearly involves the production of a physical force.

In theory, transfiguration mediums should be the most impressive of all. They claim to produce the actual physical features of the spirits. There are not too many transfiguration mediums on the psychic circuit. Lee Everett, ex-wife of comedian Kenny Everett, and Queenie Nixon are just two who have made names for themselves. Unfortunately, transfiguration mediums tend to work under dim, red light, not the best conditions for making objective judgements as to the accuracy of the image. Red light produces very black, deceptive shadows. With a bit of frowning and face-creasing all sorts of effects can be produced. Not all transfiguration mediums work in red or dim light but, even so, the results are far from impressive.

Physical mediums have borne the brunt of exposures over the years, which may explain their current rarity. Tom Johanson, general secretary of the Spiritualist Association of Great Britain says: 'Today, physical phenomena...are rapidly dying away. But fifty years ago it was very, very common, in fact every medium fifty or sixty years ago was a physical medium.'[1] Of fraud he says:

> They like to be known as a psychic, they like to be established as a good, reliable psychic and it is true that if there is something they know they are not adverse to using it, especially when they are involved in a test of any kind. They know this testing can make or break them and I think under that kind of pressure most psychics will use a little bit of trickery or use the knowledge that he has, or she has, in order to prove to you that they are a good psychic. It is their reputation they are worried about and I will admit that some psychics have at times used a little bit of trickery, even the best of them.

Paul McEloney, who produced roses, used to tape-record his performances. Leading spiritualists, however, became very concerned about his activities and called in the *News of the World*. In the company of the spiritualists, the journalists discovered roses stuffed inside the tape-recorder's battery compartment. His exposure was followed by his clients leaping to his defence. Similarly, when William George Holroyd Plowright, known as William Roy, was first exposed, then confessed, it was not long before he returned to the business as Bill Silver. Among his clients were many who knew him to be Roy, accepting his claim that his previous confession was 'a pack of lies'.

Houdini's exposures of mediums are, of course, famous. The American magician himself was a complex character, as anyone would be with two different birth dates and places. Very close to his mother, he was shattered when she died and believed that spiritualist mediums could help contact her. Unfortunately for the mediums of the time, Houdini was not merely an escape artist – he never used the term escapologist – but a magician who had dabbled in most corners of the art, including what today's finger-flingers call mentalism. That sort of background makes it difficult for the fakes to get away with nonsense. After all, if you see a 'psychic' using standard conjuring techniques, then there is only one reasonable assumption to make – you are in the presence of a fake. Eventually, Houdini's disappointment became such that he became a one-man anti-medium campaign.

It is not true that Houdini attacked spiritualism, but he did go for the throats of fraudulent mediums.[2] But just how many exposures did he really make?

Reading much of Houdini's writings makes one feel somewhat unhappy.

Exposures, as such, are rare; it is more a matter of providing an explanation for the observed phenomena. A few of these seem rather far-fetched, such as black-clad acrobats imitating a drowning body.[3] On the other hand, fake mediums could earn themselves a comfortable living. And still do. And needs must when there is a penny to be made.

When Houdini died he left behind a secret message with his wife, Bess. The message, 'Rosabelle, believe', was based on the title of a popular song, and was couched in code. Messages were also left with friends and associates. That message was eventually received through the Reverend Arthur Ford, but to put it into perspective one must know what went before it. I believe that the message was actually wrong.

A century or so before Houdini, magicians like Robert-Houdin used 'second-sight' systems based on a verbal code between sender and 'medium'. Certain words used in speaking to the medium indicated certain letters. There were minor differences between magicians but in the code used by the magician Heller, exposed in *The Times* after his death and described in *Magic: The Great Illusions Revealed and Explained*, published in 1897 and reprinted in 1976, if the object to be described was a watch the magician might build into his patter the words 'Right(W), Hurry(A), Please (T) see(C) if(H) you are able to describe this to me'.[4] Put this way, the system seems very crude, but it developed into an enormously sophisticated technique. It is still in use today. Houdini himself published a system in a book released after his death on Hallowe'en 1926. A nurse attending to him is said to have heard Houdini refer to 'Rosabelle' and a code just before his death.

Towards the end of 1928 Bess Houdini withdrew her portion of a fund worth $31,000 held by *Science and Invention* magazine to reward anyone who could deliver the Houdini message through mediumship. Joseph Dunninger[5] claims that Daisy White, who knew the Houdinis and said she knew Ford as well, told him that 'a big story' was about to break. In January 1929 Ford sent a letter to Bess Houdini containing the message and a seance was arranged for Bess to get the message direct from the Spirit of Houdini. On 8 January 1929 the sensationalist *Evening Graphic* of New York reported that Bess Houdini had been given the correct Houdini message by Ford. The next day, Bess issued a statement: 'Regardless of any statements made to the contrary, I wish to declare that the message, in its entirety, and in the agreed-upon sequence, given by Arthur Ford, is the correct message prearranged between Mr Houdini and myself.' Two days later The New York *Graphic* revealed that one of its journalists, Rea Jaure, who had reported the famous seance, had a copy of the Houdini code the evening before it took place. On the evening following the seance Jaure interviewed Ford and asked, 'You didn't get it spiritualistically, did you?' and Ford replied, 'You know, Rea, I couldn't have done that.' Bess subsequently withdrew her support for Ford.

How did Ford do it? He only had to read up on Houdini to discover the code itself, so just the message remains. He had two years to research the problem and, even then, was not sure that it was correct until checking it out with Bess before the seance. Others appear to have known it, so it was hardly secure. And what of Bess Houdini herself? She was planning to take to the stage again, which raises further implications.

Another point to ponder is that it was normal for words to be abbreviated in the code to save time. Why was 'believe' spelt out in full? Surely the code would have been used as it was on stage, in a truncated form. Why was it only half in code? Whichever way one looks at it, Arthur Ford was not Harry's lockpick from the hereafter.

So impressive was Houdini's act that some contemporary leading supporters of spiritualism believed that Houdini himself was a medium who refused to admit his powers. Among those who believed this was the influential writer of the Sherlock Holmes stories, Sir Arthur Conan Doyle [6]. Doyle's second wife put on a seance for Houdini in order to try and convert him to the cause of spirit communication. But her claim to have contacted Houdini's mother failed to impress him for three major reasons: the communication was in English, a language that Houdini's mother never spoke, he was referred to as Harry – but his real name was Eric, and, under the influence of the spirits, Lady Doyle drew a crucifix, hardly a design likely to appeal to a devout Jewish woman. Of course, since Lady Doyle was acting as the intermediary, the spirit of Houdini's mother may have been forced to use the facilities available to her, such as a Christian medium who spoke no Yiddish and wrote no Hebrew. If she transmitted a strong religious emblem or image, this may have been processed into a crucifix by Lady Doyle's subconscious. Similarly, 'Erinca', Houdini's mother's pet name for him, or as 'Erie', as he was known among friends could have been processed into 'Harry'. Just this sort of *post hoc* reasoning has bedevilled consideration of the evidence provided by mediums.

While Houdini was exposing fakes, however, he seems not to have been above a bit of fraud himself. One of his investigations was of a medium in Boston called 'Margery' Crandon, one of whose tricks was to activate an electric bell while imprisoned inside a wooden box. Although Houdini made a number of alterations to the box itself, he could not stop Margery ringing the bell placed outside it. In the last of several seances, under varying conditions, Margery's control, 'Walter', said suddenly: 'Houdini, you are very clever but it won't work. I suppose it was an accident those things were left in the cabinet.'[7] Houdini asked what things. 'You were not here, but your assistant was,' replied 'Walter'. One of the other investigators went to talk to the assistant, who produced his own folding ruler. Later, a cheap folding carpenter's rule was found inside the cabinet.

Brian Inglis, the historian, claims that the man who assisted Houdini in the investigations was instructed to place the ruler in position by the magician himself[8]. Few people dispute this claim and one sceptic told me: 'Maybe he discovered that Margery was a better magician than he was.' Inglis's research does, however, tend to be rather superficial. In *The Hidden Power*, an attack on critics of the paranormal, his sourcing of a reference by Houdini to Lafayette is complex and wrong, as even a cursory reading of the history of conjuring reveals, and while he criticises every statement by magicians that does not support the existence of the paranormal, his references include not one single work on magicians' techniques.

Few sceptics really take Houdini's exposures seriously today. His book, *A Magician among the Spirits*, [9] was fiercely criticised by Dr Walter Price for containing several blunders.[10] Although his anti-medium activities did, indeed, bring Houdini much publicity, I do not believe that this was his primary aim, as it was, for him, a very expensive exercise. My own feeling is that Houdini was, in effect, challenging the paranormal, challenging the spirits to prove him wrong, in the hope that the genuine article would pop out of the ground and tap him on the shoulder. It never did.

In the USA a network of mediums has grown up over the decades. Information on clients is passed round the network, much as it was in Houdini's day when the notorious 'Blue Book' gave fake mediums background information. 'Psychics' who have left the network and confessed have been threatened – hardly surprising in an industry worth millions of dollars. M. Lamar Keene's *The Psychic Mafia*[11] ignored entirely by the pro-medium lobby, gives a disturbing account of just what can, and does, go on in the American spiritualist scene. At which point I should say that, of all the mediums that I have investigated or spoken to, the overwhelming majority are honest and sincere and truly believe that they have a particular gift with which they can help others. That, of course, does not make them genuine in the objective sense.

I have not found any evidence of a 'psychic Mafia' in Britain, perhaps because of the immense influence of organisations like the Spiritualist Association of Great Britain and the Spiritualist National Union.

What I have always found intriguing is the attitude of the pro-medium lobby towards those found cheating. Logically, one would expect a fraudulent medium to be roundly drummed out of the business. In fact, what happens is that the followers of the medium concerned gather round and say that the exposure only goes to prove that the medium is genuine. Mediums, it seems, will cheat if given half a chance. If a medium fails to perform as advertised, then this constitutes proof of validity. If a medium can perform and is not caught cheating, then that is also proof of genuineness. This is the logical conclusion to be drawn from the number of times one hears, 'Oh, we know so-and-so cheats sometimes.' Many people consider this to be very naive. By a natural extension, all magicians must be truly psychic; sometimes they get caught, so when they are not caught, they cannot have been using sleight of hand!

However, if even a small part of the evidence that mediums provide is genuine, then we must totally rethink our whole attitude towards life and death, restructure our view of the world and radically change our relationships with those around us. The chances are that the legal profession will make a killing, if you'll pardon the intended pun. For example: Mr X commits a murder. In the old days murder was regarded as the ultimate human crime because the murderer deliberately deprived his victim of life. But if life continues, then this is not the case. Mr X's charge cannot be reduced to manslaughter because his action was deliberate. The best any court could do would be to find him guilty of grievous bodily harm. At the Old Bailey, of course, Mr X's victim will be able to testify that Mr X committed the deed. But what weight can be given to his evidence? And the statements of dying individuals can no longer be given the weight they once had. But perhaps courts can be dispensed with almost entirely. Under British and American law and other legal systems a wrong-doer cannot be punished twice for the same crime. If there is hard evidence that one is going to be punished in the hereafter for one's crimes, and evil-doers do appear to suffer for their misdeeds, then it would be patently unjust to be punished also in the here-and-now. Then there is the matter of the victim's last will and testament, which is no longer anything of the sort because he can now change his mind.

And what about marriage? If your partner is in a coma, you cannot re-marry, but you can once the partner dies because the relationship itself is at an end. If the spiritualists have got it right, then death does not end the relationship. What happens if the spouse in the hereafter is against the earthly partner re-marrying?

History studies will no longer be necessary, hours of candle-bur ning can be dispensed with in favour of an hour or so with a medium. Research laboratories can shut up shop because the omniscient spirits can tell us all we need to know.

All of which is a pretty tall order, so I think it reasonable that the burden of proof should be on the medium, and that the evidence must be cast-iron.

Much of the apparently strong evidence for mediumship, especially physical mediumship, is historical, largely from the last century. The 'Uri Geller' of the 1800s was Daniel Home. Of whom it is said he was never caught cheating. Born in Edinburgh in 1833, Home claimed to be the illegitimate son of the 10th Earl of Home. He was taken to America at the age of nine where, four years later, he is purported to have seen the ghost of a family friend.[12] Significantly, this was about the time that the Fox sisters' fame began to spread from Hydesville to the rest of the world. His mother died when he was seventeen and he went to live with Mary Cook and her husband who, it is said, threw him onto the streets as a result of his psychic phenomena.

In August 1852 he appeared at the Connecticut home of silk manufacturer Ward Cheney. F.L. Burr, editor of the *Harvard Times*, was present:

> Suddenly, without any expectation on the part of the company, Home was taken up in the air. I had hold of his hand at the time and I felt his feet – they were lifted a foot from the floor. He palpitated from head to foot with the contending emotions of joy and fear which choked his utterances. Again and again he was taken from the floor, the third time he was taken to the ceiling of the apartment, with which his hands and feet came into gentle contact.[13]

He never gave a public seance, being very choosy about who was present, charged no fees, although he must have lived on something – you can't eat ectoplasm – and made no promises. He is reported to have told researchers to treat him with suspicion. The strange powers that manifested themselves through him were outside his control and quite unpredictable. Of course, something usually did happen, especially in bad lighting conditions, and the incident described above clearly took place in the dark, despite many claims that he operated only in full light.

He worked generally with people of high social standing, having become accepted by society figures of the day, and under the sort of conditions that would make life difficult for a sceptic, even if one had been allowed to be present, which was rare. His influence over Napoleon III and the Empress Eugenie was said to have been enormous.[14]

He arrived in London in 1855, at the height of the spiritist fashion, when the Fox sisters where still going strong in America. With him he brought a letter of introduction to Mr Cox, owner of Cox's Hotel in Jermyn Street, and an enthusiastic believer. Home twice married members of the Russian nobility. Elizabeth Barrett Browning, John Ruskin and Dr Robert Chambers fell under his spell, as did Thackeray. He so annoyed Robert Browning, however, that in 1864 the poet wrote 'Mr Sludge, "The Medium"', an ill-disguised attack on Home.

Home's not getting caught can easily be ascribed to the fact that sceptics were not welcome at his table, (whether it floated or not), but one needs to look closer than that. The Reverend C.M. Davies says, 'I not only saw him float but handled him above and below,'[15] but darkness or dim light seems to have been used. An Irish journalist, Samuel Carter Hall, said, 'The day will come when Daniel will float around the dome of St Paul's.' That never happened. Indeed, apart from one famous levitation, Home never performed in the open air. There are echoes here of Uri Geller's promise to bring back a camera from the moon and stop Big Ben.

In August 1860 another Irish journalist, Robert Bell, wrote in the *Cornhill Magazine*:

> Mr Home was seated next to the window, through the semi-darkness his head was dimly visible against the curtains. Presently he said in a quiet voice, 'my chair is moving, I'm off the ground – don't notice me, talk of something else,' or words to that effect. In a moment or two he spoke again. This time his voice was in the air above our heads.[16]

Again, contrary to the usual retelling of such tales, this feat was carried out in darkness. One of the investigators of his powers was scientist William Crookes, who became president of the British Association for the Advancement of Science, a man not noted for a critical attitude towards the paranormal. According to Crookes, who gave his approval to Home in July 1851, he could levitate heavy objects, himself and other people, cause raps and knocks, change the weight of objects, move heavy furniture from a distance, make an accordion play without touching it, materialise luminous forms and lights, and hands and human forms, perform automatic writing, produce information to which he did not have access, handle hot coals and much, much more. Unfortunately, most of this was observed only by Crookes. [17]

Home flourished for forty years. A wealthy widow, a Mrs Lyons whose husband had, in the terminology of the day, 'married below his station', settled £60,000 on him. She had been largely ignored by her husband's family, which may explain her unofficial adoption of Home as her son, who had the connections with the upper crust which she sought. She gave him £24,000, then another £6,000, and, finally, £30,000. She changed her mind later and sued, successfully, for its return on the basis that Home had falsely persuaded her that her dead husband wanted her to give him the money.

After the court case he joined up with a number of young aristocrats. On the bright, moonlit night of 13 December 1868 he performed his most famous stunt in the presence of three of them, Viscount Adare – who is reputed to have been considerably under Home's influence, Captain Wynne and Lord Linsay. Captain Wynne was later to become a magistrate and clerk of the peace, Linsay became president of the Royal Astronomical Society and Adare was once foreign correspondent for the *Daily Telegraph*.

Home is said to have levitated himself between one window and another, high above the street at Ashley Place in Westminster. Details of the event are disconcertingly vague and the three observers differ on a number of important points, such as whether or not there were any balconies at the windows, the address where it took place and the height above ground at which it happened. The three agree, however, that Home was either asleep or went to one room (accounts differ), leaving the three observers together. Home suddenly appeare d outside the second window a few moments later. According to Viscount Adare, 'It was so dark I could not see clearly how he was supported outside. He did not appear to grasp or rest upon the balustrade, but, rather, to swing out and in.' Captain Wynne, when asked to prepare a statement, simply said that Home had gone out through one window and come in through another. Even allowing for characteristic British understatement, that is a bit mild for such an amazing act. However, as Jarman[18] showed, this levitation is the least impressive of Home's feats and, frankly, one of the few that a sceptic can really get his teeth into. There were any number of ways in which the stunt could have been performed. Even if the balconies of the windows concerned were too far apart for Home to jump there was plenty of material nearby, such as ropes and planking, which would have enabled him to rig up some equipment.

Home's reputation sparked off the imagination of magicians of the time, just as Geller was to do over a century later. However, George Sexton, an evangelist for the spiritualist movement, compared the levitations of John Neville Maskelyne, a leading conjuror and anti-spiritualist, unfavourably with those of Home – 'As much like Home's smooth floating as is the ascent of an eagle to an acrobat climbing a rope.'[19] But Maskelyne really was operating in full lighting, which Home never did.

Home died of tuberculosis in 1886, while living comfortably in Paris, and arguments about him have continued ever since.

In the *Journal of the Society for Psychical Research* for May 1903 there is the following account of a Home seance by F. Merrifield:

> The lights were removed, and very soon the operations began. It was about 11 o'clock; the moon had set, but the night was starlight, and we could well see the outline of the windows and distinguish, though not with accuracy of outline, the form of any large object intervening before them. The medium sat as low as possible in his low seat. His hands and arms were under the table. He talked freely, encouraging conversation, and seemingly uneasy when that flagged. After a few preliminary raps somebody exclaimed that the 'spirit hand' had appeared, and the next moment an object resembling a child's hand, with a long wide sleeve attached to it, appeared before the light. This occurred several times. The object appeared mainly at one or other of two separate distances from the medium. One of these distances was just that of his foot, the other that of his outstretched hand; and when the object receded or approached I noticed that the medium's body or shoulder sank or rose in his chair accordingly. This was pretty conclusive to myself and the friend who accompanied me; but afterwards, upon the invitation of one of the dupes present, the 'spirit hand' rose so high that we saw the whole of the connection between the medium's shoulder and arm, and the 'spirit hand' dressed out on the end of his own.[20]

So, although it has been said that Home was never actually caught in outright fraud, one needs a fairly rigid sense of semantics to accept that as the case.

In order to put the lack of exposure of Home in context it is important to realise that in the circles in which he moved, making a fuss was a social sin. It would have been very difficult for anyone who saw him cheat to make his voice heard and still remain acceptable in polite society. The very authority and social class of Home's supporters would cause enormous difficulties. During a seance in Biarritz before Napoleon III and the Empress Eugenié, for instance, sitters were being touched by the 'spirits'. Two of those present noted Home's empty shoe under the table but said nothing at the time. How do you tell an emperor that he has been duped?

All the same, Brian Inglis believes that the historical evidence for Home's powers is solid. It is worth quoting him at length:

There must be reports of about a hundred sessions with him. He must have engaged in over a thousand, over the period of twenty years. He did it week in, week out. These reports show that he was able to go into a room which he had never been in before, in a house he had never been in before, and to produce phenomena like tables levitating, sometimes himself levitating, musical instruments playing at a distance.

He had no assistant and, most important of all, he did it in good light so people could actually see that he was sitting there.

Now, if there had been one report, or even three or five, you think 'well, he might have cheated', but you have a hundred, all by people who, very often, were well-known people, royal families and scientists, businessmen and journalists and so on, many of them names known even today.

And never was he caught cheating. Often, of course, people said they knew how he cheated. But no-one ever caught him or even caught him trying at a seance. How can you explain that? That is the crucial point, you could actually see him sitting there doing nothing and the stuff moving around him. This is what I call goog historical evidence.[21]

Today it is largely pointless to wonder whether or not Home was genuine. The witnesses are now dead and the investigators can no longer be questioned. The arguments will continue for decades. And no modern version of D.D. Home has appeared, no-one has matched his feats since. More than anything else, it is the lack of another Home that makes me feel unhappy about his validity. Human beings are individual, but the abilities of each person are not unique. Like the old gun- fighters' dictum that there is always somebody faster round the corner, if Home's talents were genuine then there surely should have been someone in the decades since with the same powers.

All the same, there appears to be tremendously strong evidence, in the form of testimonies from apparently impeccable and trained observers, regarding a large number of nineteenth-century mediums and psychics. That evidence is certainly plentiful enough for it to be acceptable to an historian as proof. However, there are papers, buried in the archives of the Society for Psychical Research, rarely seeing the light of day, which give an important perspective on the nature of the evidence.

4 ⊶ Seance and Magic

It can be argued, quite rightly, that the previous chapter in no way represents the range and strength of the evidence in favour of mediumship gathered during the nineteenth century. The problem with the evidence is that it is no longer testable – the wooden rings supposedly linked by Margery Crandon for Sir Oliver Lodge, a piece of evidence worth a library of arguments, no longer exist – and as with all physical evidence from the period there is nothing left but eyewitness testimony.

The value of this sort of testimony is discussed later in the book, but this would seem to be the right moment to introduce the joker of the pack. During the nineteenth century a series of seances were held by S.J. Davey, a skilled magician who had set out to examine how people reacted in the seance room and how their expectations coloured their perceptions. His results should be compulsory reading for anyone studying the achievements of the nineteenth-century mediums and psychical reseachers. So disturbing were his findings to orthodox believers in mediumship, that even today few writers on the paranormal even mention them. This is hardly surprising, for when he first reported the experiments[1] the response from Alfred Russell Wallace, made famous by his work on evolution theory, was: 'Unless all [of Davey's performances] can be ...explained [as tricks] many of us will be confirmed in our belief that Mr Davey was really a medium as well as a conjuror.[2] However, Wallace did consider scepticism 'illogical'.[3]

Davey concentrated on two types of mediumistic phenomena: spirit messages on slates and seance room materialisations.

Magicians owe an enormous debt of gratitude to psychics and mediums. Without Home levitation would never have got off the ground, before Geller who would have been amazed by bent teaspoons and the like? So it is with slates. The educated classes of the nineteenth century were as accustomed to slates as today's are to the exercise book and pencil. They would have used slates at school and would never have considered them in any way unusual. It was quite natural to use slates to try and receive written messages from the dead; after all, the very ordinariness of them implied that they were free of trickery. So mediums used slates and one, Henry Slade, turned them into a highly successful speciality.

It wasn't long before magicians followed suit, often buying their trick slates from the same suppliers as the fake psychics. Mediums have largely given up slates and moved on – I've even heard of a psychic computer! – but magicians still use them.

Magicians often have a problem knowing which century they're in. Messages, it appeared, were written by spirits on slates that had been cleaned, between slates that were 'securely' fixed together, slates with locked covers, any sort of slates, under conditions apparently proof against fraud. The methods of performing these stunts are few. Either a message is written secretly after the required nature of its contents is known, or a message is written on the slate beforehand and kept hidden. These can involve the original slate or a substitute. The actions necessary to carry out the fraud must be hidden, or appear irrelevant to the security of the experiment, or seem natural in the context of the experiment. It is essential that the performer pays no attention at all to these details. If he makes nothing of them then the observer will hardly notice them either.

But what happens if observers are told beforehand to keep an accurate record of what happens? This was the subject of Davey's experiments. He did not give his methods in his original report because he was still carrying out some experiments. He was also reluctant to give complete details because they were, in truth, irrelevant and there was a danger that researchers might consider some mediums genuine because they were using techniques not described by Davey.

After Davey's death Richard Hodgson wrote a report for the Society for Psychical Research in order to try and overcome the delusions of Wallace and others.[4]

Davey's experiments are particularly important because they were contemporary with many of the great psychic superstars of the time. The people attending his sittings came from the same sort of background as did those attending the mediums and upon whom spiritualism depends for its scientific evidence; their education was similar, as were their religious upbringing and social standing. Hence Davey's findings can be examined with confidence when considering testimonies by witnesses to other feats of mediumship at this time, particularly since Davey's observers included people like Wallace, whose opinions of mediums are still considered to be worthwhile by some writers.

The fact that Davey was able to reproduce much of the popular spiritualistic phenomena of the time is not particularly relevant to whether mediums were cheating or not. To assume that a mediumistic event is fraudulent because it can be reproduced by a magician is a double-edged error, because first, it is not necessarily true, and second, it encourages the equally false assumption that because a magician cannot reproduce an event it must be paranormal.

A father, mother and daughter, identified as Mr, Mrs and Miss Y, each wrote their own account of an experiment by Davey involving writing on slates. Mrs Y's account was as follows:

A piece of chalk was placed on one of our slates, and the slate was held tightly up against the underside of the table leaf by one of Mr Davey's hands and one of my daughter's. Their thumbs were on top of the table, and their hands spread underneath on the underside of the slate. I held Mr Davey's other hand, and we all joined hands around the table. I watched the two hands holding the slate without a moment's intermission, and I am confident that neither Mr Davey's hand nor my daughter's moved in the least during the whole time. Two or three questions were asked without any sign of response. Then Mr Davey asked rather emphatically, looking hard at the corner of the table under which they were holding the slate, 'Will you do anything for us?' After this question had been repeated three or four times, a scratching noise was heard, and on drawing out the slate a distinct 'Yes' was found written on it, the chalk being found stationary at the point where the writing ceased. As my eyes were fixed uninterruptedly on both my daughter's hand and on Mr Davey's also, and as I certainly had fast hold of his other hand all the time, I feel confident he did not write this word in any ordinary way. This same result was obtained two or three times.

Miss Y's account confirmed her mother's outline of the events:

Mr Hodgson brought us a little pasteboard box, in which were a number of small pieces of chalk of different colours. I chose two of these and placed them on one of our slates. We had all previously written our names or our initials on that side of the slate. Mr Davey slipped the slate under the edge of the table, I holding on to it all the time, and we held it flat under the table with our thumbs above the table. I held the slate very firmly against the table, and I am sure that I did not relax my hold once. After waiting some time and asking various questions, we heard, or seemed to hear, the chalk moving on the slate. We drew the slate out, and on it was written 'Yes', which was an answer to our last question. We again put the slate under the table, and, in order to be sure that nothing had been written on it, I half slipped it out again and saw that it was perfectly clean. After some more waiting, my father asked when we were to sail for America. The chalk again squeaked, and on drawing the slate out we found 'the 18th' written very indistinctly. This happened not to be the date, which was the 15th.

Neither observer added that the slate had been withdrawn during the performance and that Miss Y did lose hold of it. This was, however, noted by Mr Y: 'At the first and second examination nothing was on the slate, and it was washed afresh, and soon the word 'Yes' was found scrawled on the upper side of the slate as an answer to some indifferent question.'

For some while before the performance the slate had been put under the table and taken out several times, a factor of no importance to the sitters but essential for the effect, because it was during one of the withdrawals that Davey wrote 'Yes' on the slate. He manipulated the slate so that the sitters saw only one side of it although seeming to see both. The writing was done with a thimble pencil and the sound of the chalk on the slate was produced by trickery. Davey asked a question to which the answer would be 'Yes' and the result was as given by the sitters. The slate was again withdrawn several times before the second message appeared. During this time Davey had asked Mr Y for a question and Mr Y asked when they were to sail for America. Davey wrote 'the 18th' on the slate, secretly as before. Later he asked Mr Y to repeat the question and the answer was revealed. The first of the America questions is not mentioned by Mr Y. The sitters cannot be expected to have seen the secret writing or to have realised the true nature of the noise they heard. These were intended to deceive. But they did not examine the slates properly, which would have nullified such trickery, nor did they accurately report the events during the sitting. You will also notice differences in the two women's accounts with regard to the chalk.

The sitting continued and the following accounts were written. Mrs Y:

After a short rest, Mr Davey asked us to wash two of our own slates and put them together, with pieces of chalk of different colours between, and all of us to reach across the table and hold them all together. This we did, and then Mr Davey asked my husband to choose mentally three colours he wished used in writing. After holding all the slates closely pressed together for a few minutes, we placed them on the table, and Mr Davey and I placed our hands on them while the rest joined hands. In a few moments the same sort of electric shock seemed to pass through Mr Davey and his hand and arm which were on the slates quivered nervously, and immediately a scratching noise was heard. He then asked me to lift one slate off the other, which I did, and found one side covered with writing in three colours, the very three my husband had mentally chosen. I am perfectly confident that my hand was not removed from the slates for one single instant and that I never lost sight of them for a moment.

Miss Y:

After this experiment, we put aside Mr Davey's slate and took two of our own. We cleaned them, and placed on one a number of little pieces of coloured chalk. The second slate was put on the first one, and my mother and Mr Davey held it above the table. Mr Davey asked my father to think of three colours. We joined hands once more, and in a little while we heard writing between the slates. When we took one off, on the under one was written:

In RED, 'We are very glad to be able to give you this.'
In WHITE, 'We can do more yet.'
In GREEN, 'Good-bye.'
My father had thought of red, white and BLUE. We could not be sure by the night light whether the 'good-bye' was written in green or blue. But there was a piece of chalk on the slate that looked much more blue than the piece with which the 'good-bye' was written.

Mr Y:

We next placed small pencils, in six colours, between two of my newly-bought slates, marked by our names written in pencil, without removing them from the top of the table, and the hands of some of the party were laid upon them for some minutes, after which they were held up in the hands of two persons. I had been asked to choose the colours in which the writing should be made. I mentally chose red, white and blue, but did not tell my choice. After holding Mr Davey's hand for some minutes, with my mind strongly fixed on these colours, the slates were opened, and we found, in the order I had mentally selected:

(Red) 'We are glad to be able to give you this.'
(White) 'We can do more yet.'
(Blue) 'Good-bye.'
Left out of all these accounts is the fact that Mr Y actually brought three slates to the sitting, not just the two mentioned; that Davey had left the room while the sitters were poring over the results of a previous experiment; that the

slates had been separated on one occasion before the coloured writing was found. Yet it was these unrecorded details that enabled the trick to work.

While the sitters were looking at the result of the previous experiment Davey had snaffled one of the three new slates and taken it to another room. There he wrote the messages in the three colours he guessed Mr Y might choose. He returned to the sitters and placed the now-marked slate blank side up on the table as the sitters cleaned the remaining two slates. After the two cleaned slates had been held together for a few moments they were separated and the upper one of the pair placed on the table. When the two slates were reassembled the marked slate was picked up and became part of the pair, which were then turned over so that the writing seemed to have appeared on the bottom slate.

At other sittings the whole sequence of experiments changed in the recording of them. Sometimes whole sets of experiments were forgotten. A test would be started, then attention diverted to other experiments, leaving the original test material unguarded. The original test would then be successfully completed with the gap in the sequence ignored.

When the lights went out the fun really started. A Mr R reported of a seance mounted by Davey with eight sitters present: 'Nothing was prepared beforehand; the seance was quite casual; we could have sat in any room we wished, and we had full liberty to examine everything in the room, even to the contents of Mr Davey's pockets, which were emptied (before the seance) by him on the table before our eyes!' In every important respect this statement is wrong. Davey and his assistant had carefully rehearsed the seance beforehand. The sitters did not have a choice of rooms; if they had chosen anywhere else some excuse would have been found to guide them into the dining room. As for searching the room and Davey himself, a Mrs J says: 'We searched every article of furniture.' In fact, when the sitters got too close to examining a small cupboard containing some of the material to be used in the seance their attention was diverted by Davey emptying his pockets. The cupboard was never examined.

Mr R reported:

The door of the room was locked, and I placed the key in my pocket, it was also sealed with a slip of gummed paper; the gas was then turned out, so that we were left in darkness. A musical box was wound up, and set to play an air, with the object, as I suppose, to enliven the proceedings.

He does not record that it was Davey who 'locked' the door. All the magician did was to insert the key in the lock, turn the key one way, then the other, thus locking and unlocking it, and give the key to Mr R. No-one checked that the door really was locked. The gummed slip was placed so that the door could be opened and closed without disturbing it. No-one checked that the slip provided a secure seal.

A Mr Munro had been secretly waiting in another room. Thanks to the unlocked door, the fake seal and the noise of the music box, he was able to enter the seance room unnoticed and take his position behind Davey. The phenomena began with noises in various parts of the room, the music box levitated and Mr R felt something grab his foot. A cold, clammy hand touched those who wished to experience it –

produced by Munro, who had held his arm in a jug of iced water before entering the room. Spirit raps and a gong were heard and a bluish light appeared and took the form of a woman, This vanished and a second materialisation glowed , a man in a turban. the report says: 'In his hands he carried a book which he occasionally held above his head, glancing now and then from underneath it.'

All these effects were produced using the materials hidden in the unsearched cabinet. The account of the second figure looking out from under the book is another example of imaginative reporting. The light by which the figure was seen came from luminous paint on the open pages of the book; therefore, when the book was lifted up no-one could have seen the face of the figure 'glancing' from beneath it. According to the accounts of the seance the figure then disappeared through the ceiling with an audible noise. What actually happened is that Munro stood on Davey's chair and raised the closed book above his head. The book had become warped earlier in the day and the pages snapped apart, producing the noise.

Mr R's report then has the seance coming to a fairly abrupt end, but it did not. There was a delay before the lights went up in order for Munro to make his escape. In full light, Davey noticed that the gummed slip of paper that had supposedly sealed the door had fallen to the floor. He walked over to it, picked it up and put it back, then had the sitters verify that it was still in place!

Several years later Theodore Besterman published the results of six fraudlent 'seances'[5] which confirmed the Davey experiments and also showed that what sitters recorded was often little more than fantasms from their own imagination.

What the Davey and Besterman papers show is a) the conditions under which sittings occurred were falsely reported, b) events were falsely reported, c) the records were painfully inadequate as sources of information on what actually happened, d) sitters' perceptions were often at odds with what happened, e) sitters often disagreed among themselves, f) the sitters, accustomed though they were to observing seances, displayed a shattering naivety.

In view of this it would take a brave and foolish person to regard the apparently strong evidence for mediumship in the nineteenth and early twentieth century as anything of the sort.

5 — Mediums and their Message

The great physical mediums of the nineteenth century may no longer be with us, but psychic superstars certainly are. Instead of Daniel Home we have Doris Fisher Stokes, the most famous British medium of the 1980s, who died during the final preparation of this book. Stokes was very successful, most of her stage shows were sold out well in advance and her 'spirit voices' took her to Australia, New Zealand and the United States. Rarely a single month went by without some reference to her in the media and she was clearly aware of the value of publicity. Her series of 'Voices' books have sold well into the millions, giving her, in addition to the £5-£15 seat prices at her shows, a six-figure income.

Tragedy dogged her life. Her first child, John Michael, died a t an early age and further miscarriages left her without an earthly child, although she had an adopted son, Terry. Her husband, whom she married in a whirlwind romance, still suffers the effects of war injuries. She contributed tremendous time and money to children's charities. All of which makes any criticism of Doris Stokes rather difficult; it feels like taking Mother Teresa of Calcutta to task for the cut of her habit.

There are, of course, many, many other mediums around, but I believe that, given her tremendous success and the anecdotes that surround her, Stokes should have been capable of exhibiting a high standard of mediumship. She is, therefore, a suitable case study when considering modern mediumship. Strictly speaking, Doris Stokes was a 'clairaudient', that is she 'heard' the voices of the spirits which communicated through her. Sometimes the voices, as my grandmother used to say, came a bit previous. The spirit of Falklands soldier Philip Williams spoke through her to his parents when they believed he was dead, missing in action. Days later Williams turned up, alive.[1] Like most mediums and psychics, Stokes claimed to have been given inside information on the Yorkshire Ripper case and that the famous murderer's mother gave her his identity.[2] She also claimed to have been given the Ripper's name by the spirit of Jayne MacDonald, one of his victims. Sadly, the man effectively 'fingered' by Doris Stokes was someone called 'Ronnie or Johnnie' with 'Berwick or Bewick' in his address. The killer was someone 5ft 8in tall, slightly- built and worked for an engineering firm, aged between thirty-one and thirty-two, with lank hair which covered his ears and was parted on the right to cover a small bald patch. There was a distinctive scar on his left cheek, a mark on his right cheekbone and he had a full bottom lip. His mother, said Stokes, had died of cancer. He lived in

Tyneside or Wearside and apparently was married, but his wife had left him. All of which was rather unfortunate for Ronnie Metcalfe of Berwick Avenue, Downhill, Sunderland, who, although innocent, found himself suspected of the Yorkshire Ripper's crimes for a while.

Is the information that Doris Stokes produced so remarkable that guesswork, generalisation, research and observation can be safely eliminated? Is it really unknowable? With any medium there is the inevitable problem of ascertaining precisely the conditions under which information was given. In the case of Doris Stokes, however, there is a television recording, made for a BBC 2 '40 Minutes' programme broadcast in 1984, of both a theatre presentation and a private reading.[3] At least one television critic was enthusiastic about Doris's demonstration, some might think excessively so. Mary Kenny of the *Daily Mail* comments: 'There are only two explanations for the Doris Stokes phenomenon.' One is that she is a fraud and every seance is a put-up job. The other is that it is all authentic: she really is psychic and in touch with another plane.'[4] Relatively few knowledgeable commentators would agree with such an all or nothing analysis. Even Brian Inglis, a staunch supporter of spirit communication, has suggested that Doris often 'finished' before what he regards as the genuine information came through.[5]

More importantly, there is a third possibility: that she gathered information unknowingly through the normal five senses. Mary Kenny goes further.

> If she were a fraud, she would have to be a fraud on such a massive scale the
> mechanics of it are inconceivable: she would have to hire thousands of actors
> all over the world as 'plants' at every meeting. The only explanation, it seems to
> me, is that it is all just as it seems: Doris Stokes speaks to the dead, and relays
> their messages back to the living, giving personal details that are only
> meaningful to them.

I have quoted Mary Kenny because her comments sum up the views of many thousands of believers in mediumship. Stokes would have to hire actors, Kenny does not say. One would have thought a single private detective on the payroll would be more secure and more useful. After all, one needs only a handful of really impressive readings in each performance.

The implication is that the evidence provided by Doris Stokes was so remarkable that spirit communication is the only possible conclusion. The '40 Minutes' programme is fairly typical of mediumistic presentations generally, not only those by Doris Stokes. The presentation begins with Doris asking for a link with the name Rogers and one of the audience volunteers one. In other presentations she similarly asked for links with names and had more than one respondent. Such names seem not uncommon. For instance, in my own local telephone directory the names Rogers and Rodgers, which sound the same, occupy one page out of 712. It is reasonable to estimate that each person listed lives with two others of the same surname. If one went into the street and stopped anyone living in the area covered by the local telephone directory and asked 'Is your name Rogers or Rodgers?' the chances are about one in 237 of getting a positive response. If, to take a modest example, each person called Rogers or Rodgers knew three other people, each not known to the other two, then the chances of getting a positive response by asking 'Do you have a link with someone called Rogers or Rodgers?' are approximately one in sixty. In an audience of any size, it would be surprising if someone did not make a link with the name Rogers or Rodgers. Similar calculations on another name cited by Doris, Williams, produces odds of one in forty. Jean Carr of the *Sunday Mirror* saw Doris Stokes at the Fairfields Hall, Croydon and says, 'The names Doris conjures from the spirit world are surprisingly ordinary. At one point three Mrs Williams rushed to the stage.'[6]

Having found her link Doris then suggests that the contact is a male heart-attack victim. Her respondent tells her that the man died of cancer. Doris then asks if it was in his lungs and the woman gives a positive response, although defining the cancer as being in the victim's glands. Lungs, however, are not glands. 'But he did have a heart attack at the end,' says Doris. Then she asks the woman if her name is Rogers (the spelling is not given). Told that it is not, Doris then tells her that the man's name was Rodgers. She goes on to mention the name 'Bill', which means nothing to her respondent, suggests that Bill is still living, again with a negative response, and finally calls out three further names – John, Joan and Tony.

At this point another member of the audience volunteers a link with 'Tony' and is asked if she knows 'Mary', which she does, although no mention is made of any relationship between the two names. Doris then refers to Tony being 'in the family', again without clarification as to what this actually means. Tony 'went quickly' and 'was a very young boy' says Doris, with success, and goes on to mention 'The Green Man', to which the respondent replies: 'There probably was, he knew a few pubs.' Doris asks if Tony had a broken neck and is told that he had head injuries in a motorcycle accident. Tony then, according to Doris, refers to his head and neck and say s that he 'never went home...I was on my way home and never got there'. She goes on to ask if Tony was the 'baby' of the family and mentions the name 'Michael' which the respondent identifies as Tony's cousin. Next Doris says that Tony was 'thrown' and that his face was all right, both correct.

Of these first two sets of messages, the first is inaccurate – there was no heart attack as far as the respondent knew, he did not die of lung cancer and there was no connection with the offered names – and the second consisted of information that could be drawn from information given to Doris Stokes by the respondent herself. Tony is a young man's name, young people tend to die quickly, young men go to pubs, a major killer of young men is motorcycle accidents, victims of motorcycle accidents today rarely have face injuries. The two names offered were not rare and only the respondent, not Doris, made the connection.

In the next message, Doris refers to 'Little Daniel' and gets a response. She suggests a birthday and the names Roberts and Robinson, which are not taken up by the respondent. Doris asks if he had to go back into hospital, which is correct, and goes on to say, 'He's all right now.' 'He might be all right on your side,' says the respondent, 'but we've lost him.' Daniel would be about three years old, suggests Doris, again correctly. It is not said whether this was the age he died or the age he would have reached at the time of the message. She also states that he has auburn hair, again correct. A message comes from Daniel asking for some flowers for his mother and Doris tells the respondent to take some from the stage, asking 'Who's Lynn?' The respondent says that she is not Daniel's mother. She does not follow up the reference to Lynn. 'But you know his mum?' asks Doris. Doris then talks about a heart defect. 'They' tried to repair it and it did not work. All correct.

The next communication is for, or from, Elizabeth, which another member of the audience volunteers as her mother. Doris refers to a wall being knocked down, and to not having enough of something when laying floor tiles. The respondent tells Doris it was glue. Here again are two sets of ambiguous communications. In the Daniel section, Doris asks if he had to go back into hospital and the clear impression, in both the programme and the transcript, is that Doris believes the child is alive and that she is talking to his mother. Heart defects are a common cause of child death and auburn is the most common hair colour in the western world. As far as the Elizabeth section is concerned, most people in their lives will either knock down a wall or have one knocked down and who has not run out of something when decorating?

In the next section she refers to a woman who died of a cerebral haemorrhage or a stroke, who is identified by a woman and a girl together, and mentions the names Rachel and Rebecca. 'I think it's your mum,' says Doris, getting confirmation. But was it the mother who died? Or did one of the names refer to the mother? This is unclear. Rachel and Rebecca are two names often found together in the same family.

What we don't know is how much information was made available to Doris Stokes prior to the stage performance. We know she met and talked with some members of the audience beforehand or during a break, because they say so on the recording. For instance, Doris comes up with the name 'Andrew', which is not picked up by the woman or her daughter, but is accepted by someone who says, rather snappishly, 'Yes, I've just talked to you downstairs,' when Doris asks if Andrew is 'spiritside'. The respondent is told that she has something to do with nursing or hospitals and the response is: 'Yes. Yes, I'm a nurse.' She then offers the nurse several names – Ada, Ivy, Amy, Eva and May – without success, so goes to someone else who has responded to the name 'May' and puts forward the names Frank, Francis or Fred. She then identifies a woman in a red dress and is wrong. At this point a second woman volunteers: 'It's my dad.' This second woman says, 'It's me again....I spoke to you earlier about my mum, and now you said my father, Fredrick – Fred.' Doris asks who worked at the Co-op and is told that it was Fred and that he drove a milk lorry. She repeats that he worked at the Co-op and gets a 'Yes', then refers to Fred's illness: 'It started down here, Gal and then went up,' indicating her stomach and chest. The woman agrees but says, 'I didn't know it started down there,' confirming only a chest complaint.

After wrongly suggesting that the name Elizabeth went with Fred, the name 'Eva' is then linked with Fred's. The relationship between Fred and Eva is not mentioned. Up to this point in the programme Doris has mentioned ten women's names, six of which were not accepted, three were names allegedly mentioned by the contact, and only one was, apparently, the name of a successful contact. That name is Elizabeth and she was the mother of the respondent. Doris had already been told by the respondent that she had talked earlier with her about her mother. Stokes then says that her subject is wearing her mother's ring, again a 'Yes', and then says, 'You haven't got a lilac bush in your garden, have you?' 'Yes...beautiful lilac,' says the woman.

In another section of the programme Doris has a private meeting with a young couple called Carl and Joan Borg, mother and son. They had met her beforehand, apparently at one of her stage presentations, and wanted to communicate with 'Stephen'. As we discover during the reading, Stephen killed himself, a young, tragic death. First, Stokes says, 'He wasn't killed in a road accident,' to which the response is 'No'. She then says that she thinks he was found, which is confirmed by Joan. She then suggests that he was found on a bed. This is wrong, he was found on the floor. Stephen, it seems, doesn't know where his body fell. Doris asks if he was in his room, which is confirmed. This is followed by Doris communicating: 'I was at home and I was found,' all information which she has just been given.

The couple are then asked about 'Gary' and are told, 'Yes...one of his best friends.' Stokes says, communicating: 'Have I got something over my head?...Why can't I breathe?...He'd taken some...an overdose.' She is then told that he took his own life and that he shot himself, a method of self-destruction not suggested by Doris. She relays the message: 'It was my head,' and and Joan says that he complained to her that 'he felt as if his head...' 'He used to think...he was a thinker,' adds Joan. Stokes then says that Stephen felt 'as if the top of my head was coming off', to which Joan replies, 'Yes, I understand that.'

Strangely, Doris Stokes then asks, 'Who's Joan?' and Joan says, 'I am.' She then says that Stephen used to brood on things, to which Joan agrees, but most suicides brood, and Joan herself has described him as 'a thinker'. A name is mentioned, 'Clark', and Joan says this is the name of his grandparents. Stokes comes up with another name, 'Mary', who is the boy's mother. Doris mentions a dinner service and Carl asks, 'To me?' which indicates a connection with him. Doris then asks Carl if has bought a dinner service and is told that this connects with a new job started by Carl. Doris asks if it is connected with pottery and gets a positive response. Since Carl connected dinner service with job it is fairly obvious that a job connected with a dinner service must have something to do with pottery. Doris then mentions 'plates and things' and Carl mentions starting a job as a steward.

Stokes asks about an anchor of flowers, which Joan says connects with the funeral. 'He loved water,' adds Joan. Joan refers to a a 'military funeral'. Stokes refers to a wreath that kept falling off, with a positive response.

In this session there is absolutely nothing that Doris Stokes is not told during the session or that she could not have deduced from being given a reference to Stephen being in the Navy. Nothing in the transcript is sufficiently remarkable or 'unknowable' or unique for an assumption of spirit communication to be necessary.

None of this demonstrates, nor is it intended to demonstrate, that Doris Stokes was knowingly fraudulent, only that the record of a public performance and a private reading do not show the need to postulate any 'psychic' ability, nor would she have required 'thousands of actors' to achieve her results, whatever Mary Kenny and others might say. On the other hand, the information may, indeed, have come from departed souls, but this is not evident from objective analysis. There are numerous anecdotes in which Doris provided remarkable information, but in the absence of precise and accurate records it is impossible to validate them.

Of course, the ability to communicate with the dead could be useful in police work, and Doris's name has been connected with a number of investigations. In her 'ghosted' autobiography, *Voices in my Ear*,[7] a number of murder cases are mentioned. One involves the murder of a girl at Kirkham, Lancashire. According to Doris's version the information she gave to the police led them to useful clues that helped them catch the murderer. Later in the same chapter she refers to three children murdered in the children's ward of the Victoria Hospital in Blackpool. Again she suggests strongly that her information provided constructive leads in the investigation. Unfortunately, the detective chief inspector of the Lancashire Constabulary has a different impression: 'Mrs Stokes made no contribution whatever to the detection of either the murderer of the children at Blackpool or the girl at Kirkham.' [8]

There are also reports of her providing 'unknowable' information to the police in other countries. In June 1979, for instance, she is reported to have provided a mass of detail about the killing of Victor Weiss, a Los Angeles sports promoter. The murder has yet to be solved and, says William H. Cobb, commanding officer of the robbery – homicide division of the Los Angeles Police Department, no suspect or suspects have been identified.[9] This, is despite Stokes claim in her book that Weiss's spirit had repeatedly told her the name of one of the killers. Lt Ron Lewis, who was involved in the investigation, told one enquirer: 'All the information Doris Stokes had was available to all the media on the Sunday.'[10] In a world of twenty-four hour television and radio that information would have been available during Sunday night. The promoter's disappearance was mentioned in the *Los Angeles Times* on Saturday 16 June and the disappearance had been reported to the police the previous Thursday.[11]

His body was found at the Sheraton Universal Hotel on Sunday 17 June.[12] The coroner's report on Weiss was released on the following Tuesday,[13] but rumours had previously been circulating that he had been 'executed' by a shot through the head while his hands were tied behind him. On the Wednesday following the discovery of the body, the *Los Angeles Times* reports that Doris Stokes claimed to have been contacted by the spirit of the murdered man at about 2pm on the previous Saturday afternoon,[14] the same day that the LA Times had reported the disappearance of Weiss. Her book says that she got her impressions at the Beverley Hills Hotel. Friends recorded her evidence and took it to the police, but it meant nothing to them. The next day she heard that a sports promoter had disappeared. This means that she is claiming not to have heard of Weiss's disappearance until the Sunday, the day that the body was discovered. But she goes on to say that the body was not discovered until the day after that, i.e., the Monday, which is wrong. In her account she goes to the Sheraton on the same day that Weiss was found, in order to try and contact him. The *LA Times* reports her as doing this on the Monday.

What is interesting is that the body was not formally identified until the Monday, but since the Monday morning papers were already talking of the body being that of Weiss, the information would actually have been available up to twenty-four hours before and most likely already featured in radio and television reports. The tape-recording does not seem to have been studied by the police until the Tuesday. Lewis himself has said that he does not recall Stokes mentioning any name other than 'Jerry', Weiss's partner, although Doris Stokes is quoted in the *LA Times* as mentioning 'Louie' and Weiss's wife's name, 'Rose'.

Stokes' account also mentions a white and maroon Rolls Royce, but the *LA Times* only quotes her as referring to a Corvette, and to Weiss being abducted by five men, although only two are mentioned in *Voices in my Ear*. Weiss was last seen driving away from the Beverley Comstock Hotel on Thursday 14 June. A missing persons report was filed later on the Thursday. Missing – persons investigations are not normally carried out until forty-eight hours after the disappearance, so serious investigations did not start until Saturday, when police started looking for Weiss's car. The disappearance was mentioned in the Saturday morning papers.

On the Saturday afternoon, following reports of the disappearance, Doris claimed to have been contacted by Weiss and to have had a recording taken of her communication which was given to the police. On Doris's own admission the recording meant nothing to the police and cannot therefore have referred to Weiss in any identifiable way. Stokes claimed to have first heard of the disappearance on the Sunday. At 6.30 that evening Weiss's body was found, the media were notified and reports appeared on radio and television, which were repeated in Monday morning's papers, mentioning rumours of 'execution'-style murder. Following the Stokes chronology, the body was found on the Monday. On Tuesday the formal identification was made by coroner Thomas Noguchi – the model, incidentally, for the TV series 'Quincy'. That same day, the police were repolistening to tapes made by Stokes and she herself talked to the *LA Times*. Put it all together and, confusing though it is, the whole incident is much less mysterious than it seems. Her account is a day adrift and with that day inserted it is clear that what she is reported as producing was, in fact, common, publicly available knowledge.

It has been reported that in Baltimore police asked Stokes to help investigate the disappearance of a young student, Jamie Griffin, seventeen years old,[15] who had gone missing in April 1982. All reports concur that Stokes went with police to the Gunpowder State Park near Baltimore where an empty grave was found. But that is not the recollection of Joseph A. Shaw, chief of field operations for the Baltimore County Police Department. He says:

> Ms Stokes was making an appearance in Baltimore, and attracted the attention of Mrs Griffin [the boy's mother] whose 17-year-old son, Jamie, has been missing under suspicious circumstances since April 2nd, 1982. Mrs Griffin made contact with Ms Stokes and discussed her son's disappearance. The next day we made contact with Ms Stokes in company with, and at the request of, Mrs Griffin. Ms Stokes did not go to Gunpowder State Park. We had earlier dug up 24 acres of the park in search of the missing person's body. Ms Stokes was aware of this. She was never at the park. She visualised the empty grave. We dug numerous acres with negative results. Ms Stokes was given maps by our department. Ms Stokes did not contribute any useful or informative information, nor did she supply any new information which could not have been given to her by the Griffin family, or by newspaper articles printed prior to her visit. Everything she told us was after she had extensive conversations with Griffin relatives and had access to newspaper files collected by the Griffin Family.[16]

So, nothing very remarkable there. We'll return to psychic detective work in the next chapter, but these four cases, remarkable only in that sufficient data has been provided to allow checking, demonstrate no psychic ability. But what about the 'amazing' information that she did come up with? Well, observation, deduction and guesswork, conscious or not, could account, for everything I have been able to examine. A simple rummage through local newspaper files could also have helped, not a difficult ploy when postal ticket sales provide names and addresses. One would only need to check out two or three to form a small but impressive nucleus for a performance. Then there is foyer research, garnering data as people wait to enter the auditorium.

When I was invited by a local Essex radio station to discuss the paranormal with a local 'medium' on a phone-in show I was asked to demonstrate just what can be done by these methods. Instead of using a phone-in participant I volunteered to 'read' the medium herself and proceeded to give what she admitted, with wide-open eyes, was an accurate run-down of her character and background. 'How on earth did you know all that?' she asked afterwards.

After the programme I handed the medium an envelope containing an emotionally-loaded photograph and I was treated to an impromptu demonstration of how to detect the contents of a sealed envelope. She pressed hard on the envelope to try and make the contents more visible. When that failed she rattled the envelope, which can make things easier to read. Then she boldly peered down the tiny gap between flap and envelope. She did not resort to the alcohol wad, which makes envelopes transparent for a while and leaves little trace. The relevance of this is that Doris Stokes defended herself against claims that she got information from letters which she later used in her stage show by saying that she did not open the letters until after the shows and even took them on stage.[17] All the same, Doris Stokes did have a guilty secret, as we shall discover in Part 4 – How to be Psychic.

While researching the 'Forbidden Knowledge' radio series we talked to a number of mediums and Alec Reid agreed to be 'read' by two for the programme. The Spiritualist Association of Great Britain agreed to find two who would be willing to be recorded.

So it was that Alec and I walked into the SAGB's Belgrave Square headquarters. Alec did not know who the mediums were to be and neither did I, so no prior research was possible. Having paid our fee for the readings we lugged the heavy Nagra tape-recorder and my own Ehuer to the top floor of the building and found, tucked away at the back, a Scots medium called David Smith, a short, stocky man wearing dark-tinted glasses, who was not expecting us. He came across as a kind and gentle man. In the following hour he produced nothing that could be regarded as positively remarkable information. He did not, however, seem to feel that either my presence or Alec's was negative. My only instructions to Alec were to be honest. If the medium was correct, to say yes, if not, then no, but to volunteer no information unless specifically asked for it. At the end of the reading, however, I asked David if he was connected with ships and went on to describe accurately people and places that meant something to him, even down to the blood-spot on his father's thumb. I did not claim that this was in any way psychic. (See Part 4 – How to be Psychic.)

The second psychic, Elizabeth Vickers, also felt that Alec and I were being very helpful. What was apparent to me was that the mediums were not only giving the sort of information that I would have given under the same circumstances, but were also making the same mistakes. Alec's name is Scots and David Smith formed links with Scotland. He also, however, linked Alec with hill-walking, which was wrong but which would have been a reasonable assumption, taking into account Alec's clothing, footwear and so on. Again, even though Elizabeth felt that we were being very supportive, her reading was not sufficiently remarkable – and there are some things which would have made both Alec and me sit up rather quickly had they been mentioned – to make us consider the possibility of spirit communication.

There is, of course, a problem with trying to demonstrate this sort of skill. If you claim to be a psychic and someone is paying you, there is a tendency for the sitter to try and prove you right. On the other hand, it is rather more difficult for an admitted magician, and therefore confessed fraud, to because a magician's audience is always trying to catch him out.

I recall an attempted cold-reading, as the technique is called, with Tony Ortzen, editor of *Psychic News*, during a confrontation on BBC Radio Oxford. He vehemently denied everything I said, including a link with Greece. Later in the programme he confessed to a link with Greece. In the report published in *Psychic News*, however, he happily repeated the claim he had made during the broadcast that my attempt to cold read was a failure, while forgetting to include his admission that I was right on one matter. This, of course, would then raise the question of how accurate I really had been in the other information I gave. But perhaps he did not write the story himself.

It would certainly not be true to say that all mediums and psychics are knowing frauds – as we shall see, the human mind is a wonderful and tremendously complex thing. Someone, somewhere, may well be in touch with the spiritside, with the personalities of the dead – dead as far as we are concerned. But, despite my own desire to live forever, I still have not found convincing evidence. On the other hand, if our lives are limited to the three score and ten or so, then how wonderfully much more our lives mean to us. If you have eternity to make your mark then your existence becomes less unique, less marvellous, indeed, less human – certainly less meaningful.

If there is a life after death, then what a wonderful adventure it is going to be for us all.

6 — Misdetection

Forget the laboratory – if there is a practical application for psychic powers then it should be in police work, from finding lost dogs to tracking down murderers and missing people.

It is almost impossible to check every single psychic claim made. Claims to help the police in one way or another are made all the time. For instance, if the remains of Shergar, the racehorse kidnapped in Ireland many years ago, are ever recovered there will be at least fifty psychics all claiming either to have passed the information to the police or to have received psychic impressions that would have helped find him if the psychic concerned had realised the importance of them at the time.

Whenever a child goes missing or there is a well-publicised crime a psychic gets involved. The Yorkshire Ripper, the disappearance of Ginette Tate and Marie Payne, the Black Panther and Keighley Barton have all helped a psychic get his or her name in a newspaper. Ginette Tate and Shergar are still missing and psychics played no part in the discovery of Marie Payne or the detection of the Yorkshire Ripper and the Black Panther.

Someone who could see into the future could, of course, be very effective in crime prevention. Unfortunately, no psychic has yet managed to give advance notice of specific crimes in such a way that action could be taken because of it. Sometimes the temptation to win publicity has proven too great. Four days after John Hinckley, son of a wealthy father, gunned down President Reagan on 30 March 1981, a remarkable video-tape was shown on several television and radio stations in Washington. It featured Tamara Rand, a psychic well known in Los Angeles, predicting that Reagan would experience a thump in the chest during the last two days of March, a sandy-haired young man would be involved, from a wealthy family, with the initials J.H., possibly a name like Jack Humbley, and there would be a lot of shooting.[1]

In fact, on 3 April a *Chicago Tribune* columnist noted that no-one had got anywhere near predicting the assassination attempt, but on 2 April an Associated Press wire had gone out stating that Tamara Rand had made such a prediction on 6 January on an Atlanta station, WTBS, during a Dick Maurice talk-show. Rand claimed that the video-tape was broadcast on 28 March, but staff at the WTBS denied this. An AP reporter, Paul Simon, dug a little further and found that the tape had been recorded at the studios of KTNV in Las Vegas, where technicians revealed it had been made on 31 March, the day after the shooting. As the true facts became known, Dick Maurice confessed to the *Las Vegas Sun* that the whole thing was a hoax. He had gone along with it because Rand was a friend and he wanted to help her career.

While Rand was down, she certainly was not out. She claimed that the tape was a re-enactment of an actual prediction, apologised for taking 'literary licence' and said the whole thing was a 'screw- up'. She had predicted, she claimed, that one day she would become famous for a 'screw-up'.[2] Six months later she filed a $10m law suit against Maurice. The Tamara Rand hoax came to light only because of the ambitious nature of it – making and presenting video-tapes takes too much man-power for such an attempt to be successful for long. Considering the reluctance of the media to investigate such claims and the tiny amount of space given when they come to nothing – Rand's prediction claim received far more publicity worldwide than the subsequent exposure – it is dangerous to take reports in the media too seriously. While the 'don't believe everything you read' dictum is widely accepted among the public, the seeming veracity of broadcast media gives television and radio reports an appearance of reality which they do not deserve.

All the same, there have been some noteworthy hits: Cindi Bulak, the so-called 'white witch of Broadway', reported that Sharon Tate had been killed by the thirteenth member of a Hollywood black-magic coven, which was wrong. In 1981 United Press International reported that police were embarrassed to discover the skeleton of a girl who had been missing for ten years in a locale that matched sketches made by a man who had died in 1973. A map drawn by a psychic helped lead searchers to a 2½-year-old boy in Lake Park, Indiana. In 1977 Dorothy Allison predicted that a missing child would be found near a drainpipe, wearing a green snowsuit, with shoes on the wrong feet and lying face-down – all of which, apparently, was true.

On the other hand, when claims were made that Allison had directed police to the body of eighteen-year-old Susan Kline in Wayneboro, Pasadena, local police said she had offered only psychological help to the parents. Allison also said that a missing fifteen-year old boy was dead and would be found near an airport. He was found, alive, by a former teacher, with a group of Moonies in New York. A psychic told Mrs Barbara Rodriguez that her missing twelve- year-old daughter was dead and that the killer was dark with a Mexican accent. All of it was wrong. Her daughter, Jeana, turned up, having been held captive for five months and having talked her kidnapper into letting her go. Her kidnapper was a white American.

The whole question of psychics and the police depends on just how remarkable the information is and its effectiveness in helping solve the crime. Police certainly are interested in what psychics have to say, sufficiently so for the Los Angeles Police Department's social sciences staff to have mounted a special investigation in the late 1970s. Psychologist Louise Ludwig of the Los Angeles City College collaborated with Martin Reiser, Susan Saxe and Clare Wagner of the LAPD in a study of eight professional and four amateur psychics. Each was given an envelope containing physical evidence from four crimes and then allowed to examine the evidence. The result was that none of the readings would have helped solve the crimes and that the psychics themselves did not agree on their findings. The final report, published in the *Journal of Police Science and Administration*, March 1979, says: 'We are forced to conclude, based on our results, that the usefulness of psychics as an aid in criminal investigation has not been validated.'

A British psychic, Nella Jones, is reputed to have led police to material evidence concerning a robbery at Kenwood House and claims to have provided correct evidence in the Yorkshire Ripper case. In this case she came up with someone driving a truck with a name beginning with 'C' on the side of the cab. His name was 'Peter'. The killer was called Peter Sutcliffe, a driver for Clark Transport. 'Peter', of course, is a fairly common name and by the time Jones told journalist Shirley Davenport that he was a lorry driver there had already been speculation in the press that the killer worked as a long-distance driver. The hit with 'C', too, is not very remarkable. A vast number of lorries with a name with 'Construction' in it are on the roads every day. Besides the operation's name there is often a brand name, the name of a town and a description of the company's field of work, so the chances of a 'C' being on the lorry are very high. (I've just counted the last six commercial vehicles passing my window. Even though this is a Saturday half of them had a name beginning with 'C' beginning on the side.)

Jones said that the killer lived in a big house in Bradford. Indeed, the house was big, but so are a lot of houses in that part of the country and it was in part of the region where the police were looking for the Ripper. She also mentioned wrought-iron gates. Again, not unusual – walk down your own street and note the houses with wrought-iron, or apparently wrought-iron, gates. She also mentioned steps. And she said that the house was No. 6 in the road – which was correct. But, and it is a very big but, much of Jones' information was wrong and self-contradictory. Out of the eleven items of information, two were already suspected by police and widely mentioned in the press (lorry driver, Bradford), four were highly or reasonably probable (Peter, 'C', steps, wrought-iron gates) and one was possibly a hit. Since Jones had made a vast number of statements about the Ripper at various times, one or two guesses were almost bound to be right, and reliable records, of her predictions are not available.[3]

Appropriately enough, one young psychic who has managed to acquire a fair degree of publicity was working from premises named after Conan Doyle's most famous character, the Sherlock Homes Hotel, when I met him. 'Discover the amazing powers of Britain's most gifted psychic...Zak Martin,' barks his press release, 'Clairvoyant...healer...mesmerist,' it continues.[4] At school, according to Martin's PR hand-out, he solved problems so quickly that his teachers were mystified. In 1975 he founded the Psychic Society of Ireland and remained president for two years 'during which time he conducted hundreds of psychic experiments. In one famous test he played a game of chess with an Australian by means of telepathy.' He also claims to have given many public demonstrations of clairvoyance. He describes his healing ability as 'miraculous' and 'remarkable'.

Remarkably, he does not feature in the newspaper files of leading Dublin newspapers. It appears they have overlooked this remarkable man, who first went to London in 1979. I first heard about Martin as the president of the British Tarot Society. Later, in the early 1980s, he opened the London Psychic Centre at the Sherlock Holmes Hotel. Then he began to advertise himself in *Psychic News* as a faith-healer. In his hired room at the hotel about a dozen mediums, including the musical favourite, Rosemary Brown, were available for consultations, and lectures on psychic powers were given. I arrived with a portable tape-recorder and met Moira Tait, Martin's associate, who took the money from the visitors. One paid either £10 entrance fee, which included up to three consultations, or a mere £2.50 to get in and paid each reader seperately, about £5 each.

Money always seems to come up when dealing with Martin. On offer was Martin's postal ESP course, £42, payment in advance.[5] Or one could take a course in the Tarot, one for beginners at £12 and one for advanced students at £65. Quarterly examinations for the British Tarot Society diploma are held, costing £15 for the examination, £35 for a diploma and registration with the BTS and a £10 annual subscription fee. Total: £137.

I met Martin and we went to the lobby of the hotel. I set up the machine and Moira Tait came in to discuss a woman who wanted a personal reading from him. I left them alone with the tape-recorder for a few minutes. When I returned Moira Tait had gone. Martin suggested that we move somewhere else, but after wandering about for several minutes we came back and settled in our original seats. I started the recorder but it jammed immediately. The tape had become wrapped round the capstan, the spinning wheel that maintains the tape tension across the recording head. After some impromptu engineering I restarted the machine.

I asked Martin, who bills himself as the only western telekinetic, if what had happened was part of his skill. 'It is one of the unfortunate aspects of being a telekinetic. I tend to have an effect on mechanical instruments...unwittingly.'[6] Later, I discovered that the same effect could be produced by lifting the tape, doubling it and dropping it back in the tape guide. To be scrupulously fair, a BBC technician told me that such a fault could be caused by the jogging of the tape-recorder as it was moved around. So, even without fraud, it is not a sufficiently remarkable event to assume telekinesis, or psychokinesis, often shortened to TK and PK.

Although Moira Tait told me on the telephone that Martin had managed to levitate an egg, he told me that he had managed only 'half a matchstick'. When the *Daily Mirror* published a series on the paranormal called 'The unknown factor' it featured Martin in very complimentary terms.[7] The series finished with an ESP test in which Martin placed an object in a locked box and readers were invited to guess what it was. Since the object was defined as 'everyday' came from a kitchen and fitted into a shoe-box, there was an implicit limitation on the readers' guesses. The results of the experiment were published well towards the back of the newspaper in a tiny 2in, two-column box, quite modest compared to the hype that the *Mirror* put into the series and the experiment. It simply said that 'thousands of readers drew what came into their minds...and many got it right'.

How many sent in drawings? How many got it right? How many drew jugs? How many with flowers? Nobody was saying, and when I tried to find out I was told that all the information had been thrown away without even being passed on to one of the many research organisations which might have been interested. Not even to the Koestler Foundation – which I found strange since Brian Inglis, one of its founders, was a consultant to the series.

No entries were kept, no records were kept, no statistics were put on record. The object was a brown earthenware jug. 'Some of you even drew a jug with a flower on it – just as Zak had!' said the item on the result. How many? Your guess is as good as mine. Why hadn't somone on the newspaper interviewed at least one of the successful respondents? To run a week-long series to convince readers of the reality of psychic powers (though the paper consulted no critics of the paranormal) and then do an experiment and give the results with no data and in such a minor position is, indeed, peculiar. A journalist at the *Mirror* told me, when asked about the series, 'It was a cuttings job...we are all very embarrassed about it.' As well they might be. One might reasonably expect the newspaper's science correspondent to have been called in. In fact, the series was cobbled together by literary editor Peter Donnelly and the first that the science specialist knew about it was when it appeared. When the newspaper's editor, Mike Molloy, was asked about the many dubious claims being made in the series – even the old 'five-finger levitation' was brought out of the museum as 'evidence' – he referred to events 2000 years ago in Jerusalem. Is Martin really a Christ-like figure?

Martin's PR release says that his most notable success in detection was with the Brittas Bay murders in Eire in 1976. 'He was able to give accurate details of the killings and locations of the wanted men, who were duly captured and imprisoned.' This claim has been repeated in the *Daily Mirror*, the *Evening Standard*, *Psychic News* and the *Sunday Times* without apparently being checked. It is hardly surprising that Martin says of his treatment by the media: 'I can't complain.'

I did contact the County Wicklow Guarda, who were involved in the Brittas Bay case. Nobody, including senior officers investigating the case, remembered Martin. There were two murders, one in Brittas Bay and another on the other side of Eire in Galway. They were carried out by two young Englishmen who were wanted for violent crimes in England – not terrorism – and had been freed on bail by a Dublin court pending extradition proceedings.

They had taken a distinctive black Ford Escort and headed south to Brittas Bay where they met Elizabeth Plunkett, battered her to death and dumped her body in the bay. Her disappearance was noted by local people, who also reported the presence of the two men to the police. Three months later Plunkett's body was found some sixty miles away by a farmer taking his dog for a walk. In the meantime, the two men had headed west to Galway, where they killed another girl, Mary Duffy, and dumped her body in a lake, weighted down with a lawn-mower. It was later found by a police diver 'working on information received', information that had come from local people. 'It was a widely publicised case at the time,' says Martin. 'They didn't know whether she was dead or alive, there were conflicting stories, she'd gone to the continent, there were various stories circulating. And I became involved in that case and gave various pieces of information *which were acted upon*.' [My emphasis.] He says that he concluded that the girl was dead and gave a description of the murder and the murderers, as well as of various circumstances relating to it.

When I spoke to him in 1984 I asked how he had described the killers. 'In the usual terms of height, weight, what kind of clothing, what kind of car they were driving.' It was what Martin missed that interested me – the two killers were English. A senior investigating officer told me: 'They stuck out like sore thumbs,' and it was their Englishness that brought them to local notice.

Martin claims that there are several bodies still missing, but that he was not involved in any investigations, other than the one at Brittas Bay. He says that he got the location of the girl's body wrong, but that he had described it as being in shallow water covered in blue plastic or sacking material and beside a stake. Plunkett was found in a sleeping bag on a beach and next to a long stake that had been used to weight the body.

Did the police act on the information that he gave them? 'I never knew that,' he replied. But just a moment before, he had said that the information *was* acted upon and his own PR release clearly implies that that was the case. 'The most help I was to them, if I was of any help, was to find the two men responsible for the murders.' What was the problem for the police in finding the men? Martin said:

> They didn't have any clue as to where they were. They had actually organised a search in the south of Ireland. They didn't know who they were looking for. Initially they didn't even know there was a murder.
>
> They were just two men going around the country killing girls. There was no pattern they could identify. They did later have suspicions.

Was Martin instrumental in finding the killers? 'I located them. And I gave their location to the police who were busy searching a big forest in the south of Ireland at the time.' The men were arrested in Galway where Martin had located them as a result of pendulum dowsing. In view of the way that the two men stood out in the local community, I asked Martin if there had been anything unusual about them. 'No. They were two anonymous men,' he said.

I was unhappy after talking to Martin. He had confused the names of the murder victims, stated that the police had acted on his information, then that he didn't know whether or not they had, and his complete lack of reference to the men being English was strange. This is, after all, in his own, or Moira Tait's, words, his most notable case. A while before I spoke to him he was featured in a *News of the World* colour magazine article where the details given did not correspond entirely with what he told me.

The first senior officer I contacted at the Wicklow Guarda said that they had had no difficulty at all in identifying the men. As a double check, a copy of the interview was sent to a second officer involved in the case, Superintendent Magle. I asked him to comment on Martin's claims:

> There could have been six people who professed to have some skill in locating bodies of people and living people. None of the assistance they gave was any value to us, and certainly not in the finding of the body of Elizabeth Plunkett. It was found on the south coast of Ireland, almost hundred miles away from the scene of the murder.[8]

And Martin's claims that he helped find those responsible?

> That is completely untrue. There was a routine police inquiry operation which went satisfactorily. There was difficulty initially in locating their whereabouts but we knew from the enquiries we made about them, and from our colleagues in the United Kingdom, that they were actually wanted to be extradited to England were they were wanted on other serious charges. So we knew they had no refuge in the United Kingdom, that they were still in this country. From the normal police enquiries and the circulation of description we made they were arrested in Galway one Sunday night.
>
> They were living a very secluded life down in Tipperary, operating under assumed names. Then they went over to the west of Ireland where they carried out a similar operation there on a girl, Mary Duffy, from Castle Barr....Her body was located in a lake in Connemara, near Tripton.

Was there anything in Martin's statement that he could not have learned from newspapers at the time?

Everything in it he could have heard from newspaper accounts.
    The account...in relation to the locating of the culprits, that wasn't true, nor were we ever aware of him giving any assistance that was needed.
    It was easy for us to locate them, it was just a matter of time.

In view of Martin's claims the next statement, about psychics involved in the case, is telling. 'We did get a number of offers, but I cannot specifically remember Mr Zak Martin being involved. I do believe they do come in and offer their help, but this is the only occasion in which I have had their assistance.' Which makes it difficult to believe that Martin had made much of an impact with his most famous case.

Was Superintendent Magle aware of any case in which psychics or dowsers had been successful? He was not, but: 'There may well be instances where they have been of assistance. But I don't want to appear ungrateful. We welcomed their assistance at the time and if a similar situation arose we would welcome their assistance.'

Despite appeals throughout the police forces of Britain, I have failed to discover an instance of a psychic helping to solve a crime or locate the perpetrators. All police personnel I have spoken to welcome help from psychics, not necessarily because they believe in the powers of the psychics but because every possible avenue needs to be explored.

You cannot afford to ignore any suggestion, no matter how silly or ridiculous it may appear. Everything must be taken into account. When it is a question of life or death you don't ignore any suggestion from any quarter.
    If they offer assistance we let them do the best they can. It may be that they come up, even by accident, withor us. If they offer assistance, we graciously accept it.

These are sentiments echoed by Scotland Yard personnel and regional police officers.
    Those who fully accept the claims that psychics have helped police say that the police would say that they had been of no help, in order to protect their own reputations. All police officers with whom I have discussed the issue have been universally in favour of accepting help from psychics and sympathetic to their claims. There is a little-known factor, rarely reported in newspaper accounts of psychics helping the police. This is that it is common for the police to give a resume of the case to psychics offering help, giving information that may not be given in the media. Also, more often than not, the mediums and psychics are brought in by victims' families, who may also have information not available to the general public.
    Bear in mind, too, that the techniques of fishing and pumping for information work as well with policemen as with anyone else. It would be possible, therefore, for an alleged psychic to use these techniques to gain information known to the police but not released to the public, information that can then be fed to newspapers to win publicity.
    What about the most famous duo of psychic detectives, Peter Hurkos and Gerard Croiset? Both are Dutch psychics renowned for their police work. Even the sceptical Netherlanders, as well-balanced a race as one can find anywhere, often accept

Hurkos and Croiset as genuine. But what about the record?

Hurkos, Peter van der Hurk, was known in the 1950s as 'the man with the radio brain'. He claims to have been highly successful, for instance, in solving the theft of the Stone of Scone from Westminster Abbey in 1950, although this was vehemently denied by Scotland Yard. He described the killer of eleven women in the USA, the Boston Strangler, in terms that did not fit the man eventually arrested and imprisoned and he gave incorrect information about the Sharon Tate murders.[9] Intriguingly, Hurkos was once arrested in New York, taken to Milwaukee, indicted for impersonating an FBI agent and fined $1000.[10] Indeed, Hurkos seems generally to be far from reaching the 80 per cent or so accuracy that he claims, despite contrary publicity.

Far more impressive, at first sight, is the record of Gerard Croiset. He was investigated by Professor Wilhelm Tenhaeff, who held the chair of parapsychology at the University of Utrecht from 1953 until he died. Like the English researcher, Soal, Tenhaeff was less than honest. Piet Hein Hoebens, a journalist on the highly-respected *De Telegraff*, who died in 1984, discovered that Tenhaeff's writings in Dutch significantly disagreed with his writings in English and German.[11] An American, Jack Harrison Pollack, wrote *Croiset the Clairvoyant*, based on Tenhaeff's writings in English and this was checked for accuracy by Tenhaeff himself prior to publication.[12] Pollack seems not to know any Dutch and even got the Dutch version of 'thank you' wrong in his book.

Hoebens investigated a number of claims by Tenhaeff and Croiset, one of which was the 'boy on a raft' case. According to the version in Pollack's book, ten-year-old Dirk Zwenne, who lived in Velsen, near the North Sea Canal, disappeared on Saturday 29 August 1953. Two days later Mr A.J. Alan, an uncle, telephoned Croiset who immediately saw images of a small harbour, a small raft and a sailing boat. Dirk had drowned, according to the report. He had been playing on the raft and had fallen off and struck his head on the sailing boat, receiving an injury to the left side of the head. The boy's body would be found a few days later in another harbour.

The Pollack version, okayed by Tenhaeff, was that five days later the boy's body came to light in a small harbour separate from that where the raft and sailing boat were found and he had a wound on the left side of his head. This version of events matches that published in English in the *Proceedings of the Parapsychological Institute* of the State University of Utrecht in December 1960 and in a German journal two years earlier. Unfortunately, the notes taken by Alan at the time show that all three versions are false.

The Dutch have a saying, 'God made the world but the Dutch made the Netherlands,' and it is largely true, much of the country having been clawed back from the North Sea by centuries of damming and draining. As a result, the entire country is reticulated by waterways. Earth reclaimed from the sea is excellent farmland and this agricultural country is scattered with water-tanks, gas-tanks, grain silos and the like. If you jump out of an aeroplane almost anywhere you'll come down near water and some sort of tank.

What Croiset actually told Dirk's uncle on Monday 31 August was that he should look near some sort of tank. He 'saw' a road, a ditch, a small bridge and 'a small water'. He said, correctly and not surprisingly, that the child had drowned, there was a small jetty, and a rowing boat was near the body. 'Could it be the North Sea Canal?' asked the uncle. 'No, that is too broad,' replied Croiset. No mention of a raft or a second harbour. The police eventually went to a small harbour near a water purification plant, which was part of the North Sea Canal. The only thing that Croiset had been certain of was that the body would be found in waters that were not part of the North Sea.

On Tuesday 1 September the police dragged the harbour to no avail and were then told by one of Dirk's friends that the boy had mentioned finding a raft. Later that day Croiset started getting impressions of a raft. Nothing was found in the harbour and Croiset went to Velsen. He stated that the boy had slipped off the raft and been killed by striking his head on a hard object. Croiset then predicted that the body would not be found before 7 or 8 September, and would have a wound on the left side of the forehead. He then went to a second harbour where he received no impressions at all.

The body was, in fact, found on 3 September in the second harbour. The boy had been drowned and although he had head injuries there were none where Croiset had indicated. In short, Croiset was wrong about the location of the body, the cause of death and the date when the body would be found. He came up with a raft only after the information was known to the police.

Let us try another case reported by Pollack in February 1961. Croiset, he says, was telephoned by a family from Eindhoven on 21 May 1960. Their four-year-old son had been missing for twenty-four hours. Croiset told them that the outlook was not good and that the body would be found in three days' time in a canal close to a bridge. Three days later, according to Pollack, the body was found close to the piers of a bridge.

The known facts were that while playing with a friend on 20 May the boy, Anthonius Thonen, fell into the River Dommel. The friend told Mrs Thonen about the accident when she came to look for him. She saw something floating in the water and called the police, but it had disappeared by the time they arrived. Two days later the body was found in the river. No bridge is recorded in the police report. Considering that the circumstances surrounding the disappearance were well known, Croiset's performance is hardly world-shattering.

During an Arheim rape case Croiset concluded that the perpetrator had a large penis. When he was arrested the police checked and Croiset was wrong. This failure was explained away by saying that, as a cook, the rapist used a large red syringe in his work.

In May 1956 a thirty-one-year-old man in Rossum disappeared. Croiset said that he was alive and living in Germany. He was not – he was dead and his body was found in a canal.

In Italy, thirteen years later, Croiset attempted to 'solve' the disappearance of thirteen-year-old Ermano Lavorini and claimed that the boy had fallen into water while playing. The boy had in fact been killed in an argument and his body was found in sand dunes.

In Australia a local group financed Croiset's search for three missing children. He said that they were buried under a warehouse, which was torn down. No bodies were found, even when Croiset suggested digging further into the foundations.

Earlier, in 1957, Croiset had been brought into a search for a missing fourteen-year-old in Utrecht. He said that the boy had drowned and led the parents to the site, but a few days later the boy was found, alive and living in a haystack.[13]

People like Croiset can be dangerous to your health. In an investigation in The

Hague he fingered a Mr Senf as knowing more than he was saying about a missing man. The family of the missing man kidnapped Senf and tortured him for three hours. Senf ended up in hospital, but he had nothing to do with the disappearance.

When Mrs Essee Kupcinet asked Croiset to find the murderer of her daughter Karyn, in Los Angeles he failed, as did the other nineteen psychics involved. When Tenhaeff was asked by an investigator, Th. van Roosmalen, to provide concrete evidence of Croiset's abilities he came up with a crime that had never even been committed and, in another case, Croiset fingered the wrong man, much to the embarrassment of the police force involved. A Dutch police officer, Filippus Brink, spent a year examining psychics, including Croiset, by giving them information and evidence, with no success.[14]

Much of the blame for Croiset's over-blown reputation lies with Professor Tenhaeff who, quite deliberately, put out different versions of Croiset's cases in foreign languages. In one arson case in Woudrichem, Tenhaeff's version bears almost no relation to what actually happened. According to Tenhaeff, in November 1969 Commander Eekhoff of Woudrichem asked Croiset to help identify an arsonist. The Tenhaeff version says that Croiset claimed the arsonist was a man who some-times wore a uniform, lived in an apartment and had something to do with model aeroplanes. The information matched a quartermaster working in Eekhoff's own police group.

Eekhoff himself told Hoebens that the consultation was in 1977 and that Croiset did not mention a uniform. Although Croiset did mention aeroplanes Eekhoff was quite specific that these were not models and that they were mentioned in the first place by himself, not Croiset. Shown photographs of possible suspects, the Dutch psychic fingered the wrong man. The quartermaster was not identified as a result of the psychic's information but for other reasons entirely. And he did not live in an apartment building. 'Everything Commander Eekhoff told us was video-taped. The tapes were protocolled and the protocol was checked and signed by Mr Eekhoff,' says Tenhaeff. This is a lie.

Croiset has had some hits, however, in the many thousands of cases he has been called in on. In Voorburg, Croiset is said by a police inspector named Van Wouden-berg to have been instrumental in the search for Wim Slee, a six-year-old who went missing in April 1963. A police dog had led searchers to the bank of a canal known as De Vliet, but no body had been found. On 16 April, five days after the disappearance had been reported, Croiset was contacted by relatives. He told them that the boy had drowned and that the body would surface in two days' time near 'a bridge, a sluice, or something like that'. The body did not appear, however, and on Friday 19 April Croiset went to Voorburg with a sketch of where he said the boy had fallen in the water. He went to where the police dog had lost the trail and felt 'strong emotions'. There were significant similarities between the sketch and the location. Croiset now said that the body would appear the following Tuesday, near a bridge 800 yards downstream. Wim Slee's body was found on the Tuesday, near the bridge indicated. A hit.

However, by the time Croiset was brought in there was already speculation that the boy had drowned and a location had been identified – information that press cuttings could have provided. Croiset had not specified what sort of structure the body would be found near and his first impressions cover many things on which a body can be caught. Since most bodies that suface from drowning do so in about nine days, the odds on the Tuesday were pretty good.

This is cited as the best possible case in Holland of Croiset's talent. I'm not dreadfully impressed, I must admit, and neither is Van Woudenberg, a believer, who is quoted by Hoebens as saying, 'The weakest part of the case is that it seems pretty unique....One cannot help wondering why there seem to be so few comparable successes.'

Tenhaeff died in 1981. Before the critical information was published, however, he was asked to comment on these and other criticisms, which he energetically refused to do.

Brian Inglis cites the information that Croiset supplied regarding the disappearance in December 1969 of Mrs Muriel McKay, wife of a director of the *News of the World*. Croiset is reputed to have pointed out the route taken by the kidnappers and to have almost led the way to the farm where, it is thought, Mrs McKay was murdered. In particular, Croiset referred to an aircraft on the route, which at the time appeared to be incorrect but was subsequently discovered to be true.[15] Police at the time were not impressed by Croiset, although his claims were attended to personally by Detective Chief Superintendent Smith, senior investigator on the case. In addition to mentioning a farmhouse, Croiset also referred to, and led Smith to, a warehouse in Essex and various locations in London. The aircraft reference sounds impressive, but the aeroplane was part of a display in connection with the film *The Battle of Britain* and Croiset was actually standing outside the cinema concerned when he referred to it. True, the display had been removed by the time Croiset arrived, but there were any number of sources available from which he could have learnt about it, from the cinema itself to local newspapers.

Inglis says: 'He had so many cases where it [Croiset's information] was correct, it is very hard to attribute them all to coincidence.'[15] Quite correct. Far more can be attributed to the falsehoods of Tenhaeff, prior research and educated guesswork.

All in all, it seems, the history of psychics and the police is littered with falsehood, fraud, self-deception and not much else. Despite the considerable publicity given to those who claim to have helped the police, the record seems clear. It just isn't so.

Though perhaps, just occasionally, those jokers on the other side do get their own back. Psychic artist Malcolm Berry's painting of a man wanted by police in connection with the murder of schoolgirl Sarah Harper, apparently made before, but bearing a striking resemblance to, a drawing made by a graphic artist on the *Yorkshire Post* based on an eyewitness description, resulted not in the arrest of the wrong-doer but in the investigation of Berry by the police, who eventually cleared him.

PART TWO

HIDDEN FORCES

7—The Psychic Playground

Children have always been considered to have a special relationship with psychic and spiritual powers. In centuries past, and even in some cultures today, they are the ideal receptacles in which the gods manifest themselves to mankind, suitable channels for communication between angels and ourselves. The child's innocence, free, wild will and lack of adult sophistication have by tradition made them the closest link with the essential human nature. Their purity, it is believed, gives them a holiness that allies them with the spiritual world. These long-ingrained attitudes manifest themselves in various ways. We see in our children not merely a reflection of ourselves, but an image of our own hopes, fears, dreams and ambitions. And this presents significant dangers when adults investigate psychic phenomena associated with children.

In previous chapters we gained some insight into the dangers of deliberate fraud by those making psychic claims, outright lying by those who want to promote their own particular brand of psychic star, poor-quality scientific research and self-deception by those who believe themselves to have some psychic talent.

When it comes to looking at the evidence for children's paranorma l claims we have to ask ourselves just how objective the adult investigators are about a child's capacity for falsehood. A salutary example involves Sir Arthur Conan Doyle and two young girls, ten-year-old Frances Griffiths and sixteen-year-old Elsie Wright.[1] These two girls had seen fairies in Cottingley Dell, near Bradford, Yorkshire. At least, they believed that they had. Unfortunately, Elsie's parents pooh-poohed the girls' tales, but Elsie successfully persuaded her father to allow her to take photographs of the tiny creatures. And, in due course, photographs of fairies did appear.

Among the facts largely ignored by the investigators was that Elsie, an accomplished artist, worked as a photograph retoucher. A believer in various species of nut-ology, Edward L. Gardner, investigated, as did others, and came to the conclusion that the photographs were genuine, as did Sir Arthur Conan Doyle. Sadly, they were wrong. The photographs were fakes and it was sixty years before the two now-elderly women confessed.

What happened? First, it was considered that two pleasant young country girls of solid lower-middle-class upbringing were incapable of lying. They were not. It was assumed that to fake the photographs would require an advanced expertise that the girls did not possess. It didn't and they did. It was assumed by the adults that they themselves were far too clever to be fooled by childish tricks. They were not.

None of the 'experts' noticed internal inconsistencies in the photographs and the double exposure on one photograph. None wondered whether Elsie had simply drawn the fairies on paper, cut them out, attached them to long hat pins and stuck them in the ground, but that is precisely what the girls did. What might have remained a childish prank and become a slice of amusing family history became a major issue with the interference of Conan Doyle. He, of course, should have known better, but then, he was not Sherlock Holmes.

Doyle was not the real victim of the Cottingley affair; that role was to be played by the girls themselves. The emergence of Doyle on the scene prevented them from ever confessing. How could two young girls show up one of England's heroes as a credulous, naive fool? Consequently, Elsie and Frances maintained their story and by the time Doyle was dead, Frances had a daughter who believed the story, so again they felt unable to confess. The two girls were forced by the support of such a monumental figure as Doyle to lie to their friends, their children and their families for most of their lives.[2]

Undoubtedly, children will continue to suffer from adult credulity and confidence, and certainly are doing so now.

The Cottingley affair should be required study for anyone awed by the apparently psychic skills of children. So should Dr Harry Collins' experience.

A colleague of Collins advertised in the local newspaper for children who could bend metal paranormally. Metal-bending is a notoriously shy effect, indeed, there is no record of real bending taking place while a film or video camera is running, despite claims and popular belief to the contrary. Collins and his co-worker, Dr Brian Pamplin, wanted to catch that elusive moment on film and placed the children who had responded to the advertisement in a room with one-way mirrors. What they saw was that after a while with no success in bending spoons paranormally, the children simply used physical methods. Collins says:

> Some of the children were extremely skilful in this. In particular, in later runs of the experiment where we had 'dummy' observers in the room with the children, they would distract the observer's attention or take advantage of moments when the observer's attention was distracted, to bend the spoons by physical force. But [they] would not reveal these bends until sometime later, so that in the observer's mind the connection between the distraction and the bending was not so obvious.[3]

These eight- to twelve-year-olds had discovered one of the most basic of the classical conjuring techniques all by themselves, something which those committed to belief in psychic powers have long held to be virtually impossible. The dummy observers themselves were surprised that they had been fooled. One or two were so convinced that they had seen genuine paranormal metal-bending that it was only by showing them the recording that Collins was able to prove that they, too, had been fooled.

At least the children in these cases knew they were playing tricks. The child at the centre of a case investigated by psychologist Nick Humphrey was not so lucky. The child was discovered by Professor John Hasted of Birkbeck College, London, who assured Humphrey that genuine paranormal powers had been demonstrated in the laboratory. But two factors made Humphrey suspicious. First, Professor Hasted revealed that he had, on occasion, faked phenomena. The child apparently lacked confidence, which affected his performance in strange surroundings. To counter this, Hasted encouraged the boy by faking effects to convince him that his powers were working when they were not. A second cause for alarm became apparent when Humphrey's assistant bent a spoon when the boy was not looking and placed it on a table. The child's father noticed the bent spoon and pointed it out. The boy looked surprisedand said, 'These kinds of things often happen. Things just bend around me.'

Later, when Humphrey talked to the boy and asked how he had discovered his powers, the story was revealed. The child was a clever boy with an interest in conjuring, who enjoyed showing off to his parents. One day he saw Uri Geller performing on television, thought to himself, 'I can do that,' and after a bit of practice found he was able to fool his family. Immediately, his parents knew that they had a child-wonder on their hands, but his powers seemed very limited. Then one morning, his father showed him a drawerful of bent cutlery. Although he had no idea how he had done it, he clearly did have some sort of power and he began to believe in himself.

Now the pressure was on. He could not control the strange effects that were beginning to appear and had to become more sophisticated in the techniques he used to fool his family. While he knew that he was using magicians' tricks, there were things happening around him that he could not explain, voices emerging from walls, things moving without being touched.

Humphrey talked to the father as well, whose story neatly dovetailed with that of his son. He had realised that his son had marvellous powers, but they were limited. To encourage them and to help the child develop greater confidence, the father had bent cutlery and so on physically in order to reveal it as a mysterious phenomenon later. Over the years a *folie à deux* had developed with father and son fooling each other and at the same time believing that genuine phenomena were occurring. The whole tissue of deception had grown to such an extent that exposure of what really had been going on would have destroyed the very close relationship between father and son. Whatever happens, clearly the relationship can never be a normal, healthy one.

Sometimes the effects of childhood mischief can be long-lasting. Modern spiritualism owes much to the Fox sisters of Hydesville, New York State, who discovered that by cracking their joints they could convince adults that they were in communication with spirits. The raps started in the Fox household in March 1848 with three of the seven children involved: Margaretta, Catherine and Leah. They soon became a hit among the sophisticated city-dwellers of New York, who were, of course, far too clever to be fooled by such uneducated, unsophisticated country girls.

Three years later a relative, Mrs Norma Colver, said that the noises produced by the girls were fraudulent, but it seems that the sisters were bomb-proof. They continued their trickery until 1888, when Margaretta confessed to fraud and gave a demonstration at the New York Academy of Music of how the sounds were made. Her confession was backed up by that of Catherine. More than a year later Margaretta and Catherine, broke and alcoholic, tried to retract their confessions but failed to re-establish their previous eminence. Catherine died in 1892 and Margaretta in 1893.

The manipulator was Leah, a married sister who saw the commercial possibilities of the joint-cracking and helped set them up in business in Rochester. The Fox sisters still have their supporters who point out that Margaretta was paid for her confession and that she herself claimed that it was made under the influence of a senior authority in the Catholic Church.

When the phenomena began, Margaretta and Catherine were in, or approaching, their teens, depending on which version one reads. Their age was a significant factor in the acceptance of their validity as anything else.

Are children being similarly underestimated today? Professor John Hasted believes not. He prefers to work with children. 'To me, children are more genuine than adults and with adults there may be a chance that the chap is hoaxing you or defrauding you, as seems to happen sometimes.'

Hasted is confident that his experimental protocols and his understanding of children have led to secure experiments. 'They fraud in different ways [to adults],' he says. 'And it's usually a very simple, easy way, and slightly mischievous, which is very easy to detect.... In metal-bending I believe that the subject should never touch the metal, this makes it very difficult for him to fraud it.' According to Hasted he keeps the metal on his person and only transfers it to the laboratory apparatus when the subject is not there. The apparatus is switched on and the subject brought in.

> Of course, he could do sophisticated electronic things to foul-up my apparatus, but children are not really like this. The sort of thing they would do, or might do, is to wait until my back is turned and make a grab. And this has happened on occasion, but, of course, I am well protected against such a thing.

Many of Hasted's earlier experiments involved leaving children alone with the pieces of metal. In one series children produced 'scrunches' of paperclips inside glass globes. The globes had small holes in them. Hasted gave one of these to a magician who wanted to see whether fraud was possible. I was present when he returned it to him with just such a scrunch of paperclips inside. Hasted ignored it.

One of the five children filmed by Collins had not bent any cutlery a thirteen-year-old girl whom Hasted later tested in his own laboratory under his 'no-touch' conditions. He eschews the use of video-recording, believing that his system of observers, in which they themselves are also observed, is very nearly as good. The apparatus generally consists of samples of metal to which strain sensors are attached, feeding information into a chart recorder. Usually a second chart recorder is running, a 'dummy', to give background noise. This set-up raises an interesting question. Attaching strain sensors to the samples is obviously invasive, yet results are achieved. So this system can show that something has happened but not how it happened. Yet a non-invasive, passive recording device like a camera, which not only shows that something has happened but whether or not fraud has taken place, is said to prevent phenomena like metal-bending from occurring, even when the camera itself is recording secretly. Unless, of course, the camera is being operated by a television crew and the 'psychic' is getting an appearance fee.

The majority of bends, according to Hasted, are 'elastic' – the metal's own springiness overcoming the deformation – and are very small. On occasions, however, gross bending has occurred under 'no-touch' conditions with the influence of the girl. Unfortunately, such bends almost invariably occur when the experimenter is not looking, as Hasted has admitted. Professor John Taylor of King's College, London was once a firm believer in child psychics and wrote a book, *Superminds*, about his experiences with them. Later he was to change his view radically:

Initially I was very taken with them and thought there were some interesting phenomena occurring. We recognised that some of them were cheating and others, when we put them under perfect conditions, didn't cheat but did not achieve anything....I was a little surprised that some of them would cheat too easily and could be caught rather easily. I didn't work with them any further. They are still being worked with by various people – I am a bit surprised by that.

Taylor, unlike Hasted, did use video-cameras. He adds: 'I was surprised at their ingenuity, their wish to achieve these phenomena. It may well be that this was a way that they had of achieving fame, and in certain cases it was clear that this was their only claim to fame, otherwise they were unnoticeable.'

Pseudo-psychic phenomena can also help children control their elders, as may have occurred in the Colombus, Ohio, poltergeist case.

Joan and John Resch, parents of four children, have fostered some 250 children, one of whom, Tina, they adopted. A local newspaper, the *Colombus Dispatch*, published a story about the family and their fostering activities and sent along journalist Mike Harden to write it up.

March 1984 was a tough time for Tina. A hyperactive, emotionally-disturbed girl, she had been taken away from school for private tutoring, had just broken up with her first boyfriend and also with her best friend. She was also becoming increasingly concerned about finding her natural mother, who had abandoned her at the age of ten months. It was then that room-lights began to switch themselves on, showers to run when nobody was near them, stereo-players to operate while unplugged, drinking glasses to jump off shelves and furniture to move. Nothing happened when Tina was absent, although she insisted that she was not doing it. Joan Resch called Mike Harden, who visited the house and asked photographer Fred Shannon along. The Resches also called in a Lutheran minister to perform an exorcism.

One of Shannon's photographs, showing Tina squealing as a telephone flew in front of her, went around the world. Other pictures, which showed Tina with telephones in her hands immediately before they flew, were not so widely distributed and the *Colombus Dispatch* has forbidden access to, and publication of, the incriminating photographs. A good illustration of 'forbidden knowledge'.[4]

With the distribution of the *Dispatch* photographs came an influx of news media personnel, complete with cameras. At the end of one press visit a cameraman from WTVN-TV, Cincinnati left his camera running, unknown to Tina. The result was a tape of Tina reaching up to a table lamp, trying to tip it over and jumping back. The first try was a failure and she had another go. Much of the tape was edited for broadcasting and the segment in which Tina was seen looking around to make sure no-one was looking was omitted from the final version. Tina said that she had only been trying to get rid of the reporters, although, since the crew were packing up their equipment at the time, this excuse makes little sense. She was also seen moving a table with her foot. The movement of the table was later heralded as a paranormal event.

William Roll, a director of the Psychical Research Foundation, and an assistant spent a week living in the Resch household. They checked for wires and trick devices and found none. There is no evidence that any of the events actually required this level of sophistication. Roll reported a bar of soap falling in a bathtub, a picture dropping from a wall, pliers flying across a room, a tape-recorder moving. When he took Tina to the Psychical Research Foundation a door flew open and a telephone reportedly hit Tina. However, Roll never actually witnessed anything starting to move and only photographer Fred Shannon, out of all the witnesses, claims to have seen anything at the start of the motion.

Roll's report has, however, been heavily criticised. For instance, a picture fell from a bedroom wall and Roll started to replace it by hammering in a nail with a pair of pliers. As he did this, he was watching Tina out of the corner of his eye, or so he says, yet Roll is very short-sighted and it takes a brave man to hammer in a nail and attend to very poor peripheral vision at the same time. While he was doing this, Roll's tape-recorder was moved from a dresser that was immediately behind him. He turned to pick up the machine, which had come to rest between 7ft and 9ft behind him. As he did this his pliers were moved to a far wall. It is difficult to accept that Tina was sufficiently closely observed to preclude her moving the tape-recorder and pliers.

Then Tina broke her leg in an accident with a borrowed motorcycle and the phenomena came to an end.

Why didn't Shannon catch her cheating while he was taking photographs? Because Tina had told him to look away and to snap the shutter when she gave a verbal signal. Mike Harden didn't watch Tina either because he too was told that nothing would happen if she was watched. Tina got the attention she wanted. Indeed, she asked the press, 'Will you help me find my true parents.' She also suffered from the taunts of other children when she insisted on showing off her press cuttings. James Randi, who was barred from the Resch house, says: 'She created a monster that she will have to live with for the rest of her life.'

There have been many such poltergeist cases down the years, perhaps the most impressive being the Rosenheim case involving a nineteen-year-old secretary, Anna Marie Schneider. At the moment, it appears to be the strongest contender for being the genuine article. Certainly no attempts to demolish it have proven successful. Indeed, a book, [5] in which a magician claimed to have found evidence of threads being used to produce apparently paranormal effects, was withdrawn by a court order.[6]

Unfortunately, a full report on the case has yet to be published by its main investigator, Professor Hans Bender, although a 'preliminary' report was published in 1968.[7] When the full report finally becomes available it may be that the parapsychological community will be presented with an incontrovertible case of poltergeist activity, but a delay of some twenty years will inevitably cause tremendous problems in double-checking the data. It was, after all, seventeen years before Bender revealed that Anna Marie had been caught trying to cheat.[8] The hard evidence, it seems, always belongs to the past, never to today.

The question, however, is not whether children and young people are producing anything truly paranormal, but whether the attitudes of the investigators are sufficiently objective for a judgement to be made. Is the ratio of meaningful signals to spurious noise such as to preclude a firm conclusion?

Families afflicted by these phenomena are often deeply unhappy and this can put tremendous pressure on investigators, as John Hasted admitted when discussing one of Britain's classic cases, the Enfield poltergeist. 'When you go to such a disturbed family, and you are not a professional psychiatric social worker, you feel ashamed of yourself. You feel that you shouldn't be investigating them, you should be helping them.'

The main investigators were Guy Lyon Playfair and Maurice Grosse. Playfair, a devoted believer in Uri Geller, is the author of an assortment of credulous books on paranormal subjects. His book about the case, *This House is Haunted* became a best-seller.[9]

It is germane to the issue to note that data essential to any discussion of whether Geller's success at the Stanford Research Institute was owing to fraud or genuine ESP is regarded by Playfair as mere 'minor details', as he expressed it in a strongly-worded letter to *Radio Times* about the 'Forbidden Knowledge' programme 'To Geller and back'.[10] Included in such unimportant details are opportunities for fraud and the assistance of a confederate. He was, at the time of this spirited criticism, collaborating on a book with Geller, a minor detail missing from his letter. One may justifiably wonder what 'minor details' may have been expunged from his account of the Enfield case.

Maurice Grosse is an electrical engineer and inventor. A devout Jew, he had a daughter who died in an accident about a year before the Enfield case and he had just completed the eleven-month period of mourning. Maurice, who is a sincere and honest man, had only just joined the Society for Psychical Research. That organisation was, and still is, short of experienced investigators, so they appointed him to the case. One senior member of the SPR told me that they had done so because they did not think the case particularly important at the time and Grosse had been more than merely keen to do an investigation. He was not, therefore, an experienced investigator. 'It was my first major investigation,' he says, 'and fortunately turned out to be one of the best. Although I say it myself, one of the best investigations of all time.'

The case revolved around the Hodgson family of Green Street, Enfield. Margaret Hodgson, a divorcee, lived there with her two lively, athletic daughters, Janet and Margaret, and a mentally-handicapped son. Mrs Hodgson was frightened that her son would be taken away by the local authorities and her daughters objected to the visits of their father. Janet, the elder daughter, wanted to move away from home.

Thus was the stage set when, in 1977, noises began to be heard, furniture started to move and apparitions were seen. Janet began to levitate and objects transported themselves through walls – the whole gamut of the poltergeist phenomena. There were numerous witnesses, from Grosse, Playfair and neighbours to police officers, journalists and photographers. A particular characteristic of the case was a deep, gruff voice representing a number of 'spirits', including that of an old man who had died in the house.

The case remains very controversial. Grosse, Playfair, Hasted and others believe it was genuine, Anita Gregory and other members of the SPR were unconvinced. Magicians and ventriloquists came to the conclusion that Janet was cheating, which is what one would expect. Grosse admits that the girls 'played around'. He caught Janet banging on a ceiling with a broomhandle, and she also hid his tape-recorder, claiming that the ghost had taken it, not realising that it was still running. He believes that Janet was imitating the phenomena. In his view, if the phenomena were not genuine on those occasions when faking was not detected, Janet must have been 'one of the world's number-one conjurers. She was also one of the finest actresses I've ever seen...she could put on an emotional show that was actually unbelievable, if it wasn't genuine.'

No-one listening to the tape-recordings has, according to Grosse, come to the conclusion that faking was involved. He made some of the recordings available to me and, having listened to them very carefully, I came to the conclusion that there was nothing in what I had heard that was beyond the capabilities of an imaginative teenager.

Among the notable physical events was the dropping of marbles to the floor without bouncing. When picked up, the marbles were hot. It became clear when talking to Maurice that the marbles were rarely seen in motion and never at the start of the motion or, more importantly, at the finish. Reconstructing what happened, the investigators heard a noise behind them, turned and saw the marbles. If the marbles had been held in a warm hand by someone waiting for a suitable moment, then placed on the floor and the sound of them falling been made by some other means, the result would be the same.

Opinion is divided as to whether the girls would have been able to produce the voice, which was exhibited by the rest of the family too. This latter is an important point because the characteristics of the voice would make it difficult to locate the source; indeed, it was some time before Maurice determined that it originated from Janet. In her case the voice was being produced by the false vocal cords above the larynx, whether consciously or unconsciously, so it had a physical source.[11] According to Professor Hasted, Janet was unaware that she was producing the voice for some seconds after it started. However, in a video-tape of a BBC Scotland television programme featuring the case it was clear that Janet was attracting attention to herself by waving and getting in between the camera and her sister immediately before the voice was heard. And when the voice appeared she held her hand in front of her mouth.

The question for the psychic researchers is whether the motivating intelligence was that of the girl or girls or of some other entity. It had the general vocabulary of a child of the Hodgson girls' ages and of their particular social context. It also used the phraseology of a child:

> I'm 72 years old and I come from Durants Park graveyard and I'm right near the church where Rena lives. All my friends come from there as well and we all make a gang and go to the park and we picked your house because I used to live here. And I will tell you some more, that's if you don't tell anyone else except Mr Grosse and Mr Playfair.

Durants Park is a stretch of ground in Enfield, close to Green Street, where local children play. It leads directly into a graveyard. Maurice admits that the voice did speak childishly. 'But after all, it is manifesting through a child,' he says.

Grosse's son, Richard, a solicitor, spoke to the voice, with the girls' uncle, John Burcombe, acting as go-between. It told him that it had gone blind and had a haemorrhage and died in a chair in a downstairs room. While Maurice is impressed by Janet's use of the word haemorrhage in the correct context, and she apparently did not know what it was, it is conceivable that she was given the information about the manner of death by a friend or heard it from a neighbour. Eighteen months later Janet's mother was told while in hospital that the previous tenant had indeed died as described. Janet need not have known what a haemorrhage was to say that someone had died of one.

To see whether the voice knew something the others present did not, Maurice

Grosse wanted to carry out a test and John Burcombe suggested asking it where 30p, which had been lost by Burcombe's daughter, Denise, had gone. It told them the money was downstairs under a radio. When Grosse looked, the money was there. In the Playfair version Denise and her father decided what the question should be. But perhaps this is a mere minor detail. All the same, might it not have been that Janet had pinched Denise's 30p, as children often will?

When Maurice asked the voice where it was in the room, it said, 'On top of Janet.' Then he asks the voice, 'Why can't Janet feel you?' It replies, 'I'm invisible.' Here it has made a child's mistake. Being invisible doesn't necessarily make one weightless. She or it is using the word quite wrongly.

To those who remain sceptical Maurice Grosse says: 'What you're saying is that sophisticated people are being taken in day after day, night after night, week after week, month after month by two school-girls and we never once spotted them playing the fool.'

But what about the broomstick and vanishing tape-recorder?

In a BBC Scotland television interview which many sceptics regard as highly evidential, the interviewer asked, 'How does it feel to be haunted by a poltergeist?' Janet replied 'It's not haunting,' and Margaret quickly interrupted, 'Shut up.' Maurice Grosse says that the girls were always saying things like this and they were uncomfortable at the idea of a ghost at home.

Today, almost a decade after the events at Enfield began, it is all but impossible for an independent investigator to retrace the steps of Grosse and Playfair. Janet has married and left home, and her husband is sceptical about the story. Margaret still lives with her mother, still bitter about the harsh treatment meted out by the *Daily Mirror* reporters who, it is claimed, brow-beat her into a false confession. The Burcombes and neighbours involved in the case, the Nottinghams, are reluctant to discuss the case, perhaps not surprisingly in view of the circus it became.

Did the investigators underestimate the ingenuity of the Hodgson family? Did they overestimate the accuracy of their observations? Did they pay too little attention to the quirks of childhood fantasy, psychiatric problems, human greed and ambition? Was there someone outside the Hodgson household giving events a helping hand as did the father in Nick Humphrey's case? The whole truth may never be revealed. It was, after all, some sixty years before Frances Griffiths and Elsie Wright confessed to fraud. The Society for Psychical Research has been forced to suppress one extremely critical report on the Enfield case by the late Anita Gregory for fear of a libel action. She says: 'The Enfield case...unfortunately withers away on closer inspection.'[12]

Was that unexceptional council house in Green Street really the home of disembodied, violent spirits for a year and a half? Or was the real ghost the hopes, fears and ambitions of adults and the assumption, made constantly throughout the history of psychic research, that adult investigators are far too clever to be taken in by mere children? A ghost that continues to haunt psychical research with children.

8 — Starlight and Moonshine

Astrology falls in between the 'hard' skill of dowsing and the 'soft' talent of the psychic. The astrologer begins with a certain set of hypotheses about the influence of planets, carries out painstaking calculations on the relative positions of the planets in the sky and their placing in the various constellations, based on timings as exact as he can make them, and draws up a chart. Then the astrologer will try, through a mixture of intuition, experience, psychic awareness and preferably some knowledge of the person whose chart he is erecting, to weigh each influence against the others. Conclusions are drawn largely from the long tradition of astrology and many people have claimed remarkable accuracy for the system.

In fact, there are a number of different techniques used in astrology, some of them mutually incompatible, and astrologers themselves disagree on many points about how a chart should be erected and read, despite astrology's very long history. The one thing that all astrologers do agree upon is that horoscope columns in newspapers bear little relationship to the art, or science, which they practise. All the same, an overwhelming majority of newspapers carry daily horoscopes or regular features on astrology, from local newspapers and freesheets (where the television astrologer, Russell Grant, seems to dominate with syndication to about a hundred weekly and daily publications) to the *Sunday Times*'s Marjorie Orr. In the USA two out of three newspapers feature astrology columns.

These 'Lucky Star' forecasts began in the USA in 1928 and came to Britain in 1930, when N.R. Naylor was hired by the *Sunday Express* to cast the horoscope of newly-born Princess Margaret.[1] In those days newspapers tended to shy away from fortune-telling because, like Sunday newspapers, it was illegal at that time. Strictly speaking fortune-telling is still illegal, so for many years newspapers kept clear of horoscopes, but the *Sunday Express* ran further articles by Naylor, who hit astrological pay-dirt when he predicted danger in British aeronautics and the hydrogen-filled R101 crashed in France, killing forty-six people.

Other newspapers followed the *Sunday Express*'s example. Gypsy Petulengro appeared in the *Sunday Chronicle*, W.J. Tucker joined the *Sunday Dispatch* and Edward Lyndoe went to *The People*. Lyndoe died in the mid-1980s, a few days after ordering more copy paper for his column. Then, in 1936, a court decided that to be illegal a horoscope would have to apply to a specific individual, and that led to the modern newspaper horoscope column.

The Committee for the Scientific Investigation of Claims of the Paranormal issued a press release in 1984 to 1200 US newspapers suggesting that they carry a disclaimer on astrology columns and pointing out that astrology had no factual basis.[2] US newspapers are far more used to questioning their own ethics than is the British press, hence several American newspapers openly began to question whether or not astrology columns should be published at all. Jack Foster, editor of the *West Palm Beach Evening Times*, however, noted that, 'Killing an astrology column is an invitation to get your building burned down.'

But how accurate are newspaper horoscopes?

In 1982 a Canadian television programme called 'Live It Up' decided to test astrology. A dozen people were asked to keep a diary for a week. They were then given readings for each of the days by four anonymous astrologers for comparison, and rated them on a 0 to 4 scale. A perfect score would have been 336 (4 x 7 x 12). The famous Jean Dixon scored a mere 101 points, while Bearnice Osol made 91 and Sidney Omarr got 88. 'Live It Up's own astrologer topped the list with 112 – but there was no such astrologer; the horoscopes were faked entirely. Although in this case the horoscopes were faked for the test, some newspapers do save themselves the cost of hiring an astrologer by getting a junior reporter to put their columns together. And it is not unknown for astrologers to recycle their columns without anyone noticing – except for an astute sub-editor. I have tried out newspaper horoscopes on various people throughout the past ten years and it is a rare day when someone can pick out their own.

The accuracy of newspaper and magazine horoscope columns is something you can check for yourself. Indeed, you could make a positive contribution to the study of astrology by doing so, because you do not need an intimate knowledge of the 'science'. Ideally, choose a weekly horoscope column and separate each reading so that you have twelve slips. Make sure that you remove any mention of sun-sign, planetary rulerships or reference to symbols, i.e. 'being a bullish person' for Taurus. Mix up the slips, then number them on the back, ensuring, of course, that you know which slip refers to which sun-sign. At the end of the week to which the horoscopes refer, give the slips to friends or acquaintances and ask them to pick out the one which seems to refer most exactly to their week. Better still, get someone else, who does not know which slip corresponds to which sign, to ask their friends which slips correspond best. To do it properly, of course, the person who shows the slips should not know either the sun-sign of the person to whom he gives the slips or the signs to which each individual slip refers, and you should not know the identity of the people involved – perhaps they can be coded by a letter of the alphabet.

In effect, the person carrying out the experiment has no information to go on regarding who should be able to recognise which slip. The results are then given to you for analysis. Check which numbered slips have been identified by which letter-identified person or people. Then compare those results with the signs of the people involved. You should, of course, make sure that the subjects involved have not read the same horoscopes before! This sort of experiment is called a double-blind trial.

I have been trying out this sort of thing for several years without finding anything better than chance (one-twelfth of the people successfully identifying their own reading). If you get better results, let me know.

Astrology in the media generally seems to be less than very successful. I tried out

Russell Grant's sun-sign descriptions from a 1984 *TV Times* Special ('What your sun-sign is really like' said the front cover) without getting better than chance results. Grant was invited several times to take part in a study involving twelve people who would be asked to assess twelve horoscopes without being told which was theirs. Grant, who claims to see fairies, refused.

Psychics and astrologers do not seem to score too well on their published prophecies generally, in addition to horoscopes. Since there is wide agreement that astrology uses a psychic component, it is, perhaps, fair to look at both together. An American publication, *People* magazine, checked fifty-two predictions made by ten psychics for 1984. They included claims that Jackie Onassis would marry Prince Rainier of Monaco, singer John Denver would be buried in an avalanche, Sean Connery, the original James Bond, would be attacked by a mad gunman and Burt Reynolds would make a public admission that he was in love with a sixteen-year-old girl.

For 1983, psychics and astrologers had predicted, among other things, that President Reagan would have a heart attack, that investors should stay away from stocks (the stock market actually recorded an average 20 per cent increase), there would be a major earthquake at the beginning of the year in California, Reagan would resign from the presidency, the Queen would abdicate and Ayatollah Khomeini would be assassinated.

Things went no better in 1980 when ten psychics and astrologers came up with the election of Howard Baker to the presidency, Jimmy Carter's refusal to run, that Italy would send the Pope into exile, evidence would be found of a long-dead civilisation on another planet and contact would be made with an alien life-form.

Roger Elliot's scores for the *News of the World*'s 'Sun Day' colour supplement for 29 December 1985 were just as poor. He assured readers that Prince Andrew would not get married, which he did six months later. Labour leader Neil Kinnock did not write the book that Elliot said he would and Bob Geldof neither won the Nobel Peace Prize as predicted by Elliot nor persuaded the Russians to join in – indeed he refused to support a Russian charity event because of their refusal to be involved in his appeals for Ethiopia.[3] In fact, one could have had much more success than Elliot simply by predicting the opposite.

The response by newspapermen to questions about whether or not they should publish horoscopes is normally along the lines of 'the readers want them'. An NOP survey carried out for the *Daily Mail* in 1970 showed that only seventeen in a hundred people thought newspaper horoscopes were accurate, while 79 per cent thought they were not. 80 per cent of the people originally questioned read their horoscopes regularly. That, of course, is not a measure of how many actually believed or acted upon what the column said. Other surveys have put that figure as low as 1 per cent.

Of course, it is unfair to judge astrology by what appears in newspapers. As the Press Council intimated when it censured the *News of the World* in 1984 for its misreporting of a major survey on jobs and the stars, for the media horoscopes are merely an entertaining diversion. All the same, it is interesting to note that 80 per cent or more of the people that I have questioned over the years know, or think they know, their sun-signs. Only about one in four know their blood group.

'Real' astrology, the kind in which a single chart may take several days to erect and interpret and for which seekers after the future pay anything from twenty-five to several hundred pounds, is taken rather more seriously. And its history is a long one.

9 ⊷ History, Science and the Stars

The Chaldeans were the first to record astrological findings and the practice was part of most western civilisations by the first century AD. Up to the Renaissance, a knowledge of astrology was part of every educated person's store of learning. It appears to have started as a religion in Mesopotamia, and in southern Babylonia priests erected watch-towers which enabled them to note the movement of the Sun along Anu's Way, the path the Sun takes through the sky. The stars of the constellations became the fixed stars, a ground upon which the planets, wandering stars, moved and sent their influence down to the flat Earth, at the centre of the cosmos. At first, the stars only foretold the futures of rulers and nations, but in about 500 BC the Greeks developed personal horoscopes, which were introduced into Rome 400 years later.

So astrology flourished until the sixteenth century. A central premise was that the stars and the planets, which included the Sun and Moon, revolved around the Earth. With the development of astronomy, it was discovered that many of the basic assumptions of astrology were wrong – the solar system moved around the Sun, not the Earth, and the stars were at different distances from the earth and not all at the same distance as required by astrology. Astrology rather languished until the early 1900s when Alan Leo modernised it.[1] Many of its basic tenets, however, are still as they were when Ptolemy wrote the *Tetrabiblios*.

To understand some of the objections to astrology it is necessary to go back to basics. The Babylonian Anu's Way is today known as the ecliptic, the route that the Sun apparently takes through the sky during the year. The Sun moves against a background of stars which are traditionally grouped into constellations. A horoscope chart is a sort of 'bird's eye view' of a slice of the solar system through the plane of the ecliptic, showing the positions of the celestial 'lights' and the planets relative to the longitude of the place to which the chart refers. By knowing how fast planets move around the ecliptic, one can calculate their relative positions at any particular moment and work out how the influences of the various planets, stars, etc. should operate at that time.

The calculated angles between the planets are known as aspects. Certain of the angles have been given special meanings: if two planets are at 180 degrees from each other with respect to the Earth, at precisely opposite sides of the Earth, then their influences fight each other and the aspect is normally regarded as malefic. If the angle is 0 degrees on the chart, the planets coincide in the chart and their influences are added. The aspect is then commonly thought to be beneficial. This is a very much simplified description, of course, and there is some disagreement over the relative effects of the aspects, lights (Sun and Moon) and planets.

The chart itself is divided into sectors, derived from the constellations, and houses. The way that the division is done depends on the particular system used by the astrologer concerned. The divisions based on the constellations form the zodiac, consisting of twelve signs. Traditionally these begin with Aries and finish at Pisces, following the pre-Gregorian calendar year. Although twelve signs are used, this was not always the case, as there have been various numbers between eight and fourteen. (Oriental astrology tends to use up to twenty-eight divisions, based on the Moon's movement.) One or two of the constellations along the ecliptic recognised by astronomers are not used. In tropical astrology the sky is divided into equal 30-degree sectors named after each sign. Sidereal astrology uses divisions based on the actual width of the constellation in the sky, so the divisions are unequal.

As the Sun 'moves' along the ecliptic through the year it passes through each sector in turn. The sector through which the Sun is passing at the moment of your birth is your 'sun-sign' and this is what is used in newspapers and magazines. The sign coming up on the horizon is the ascendant and the one going, down the descendant. The zenith is called the mid-heaven. The zodiac moves around the chart as the day progresses. The chart itself is divided into twelve sectors known as houses which remain fixed with respect to the chart, and the zodiac signs move through each sector in turn throughout the day. Again, the divisions can be simple 30-degree sectors or uneven sectors and are numbered from one to twelve. Each house affects a certain aspect of life; the first house, for instance, into which the ascendant is moving (some astrologers use other starting points) covers home life. Briefly, then, this is the battleground for the sceptics and the believers.

Astronomers have a number of objections to the view of the universe used by astrologers. Although these do not prove that astrology does not work they are relevant to any theories about how it might work. An important point is that there is no real relationship between the stars in a constellation. They are many millions of miles apart. From our viewpoint they look close together, but they are at different distances from us. Indeed, the constellations themselves make sense only in the sort of flat, two-dimensional heaven imagined by the ancients. More damaging, however, is the fact that the zodiac we know was frozen about 2000 years ago. Owing to an effect called precession, the relationship between the Earth, Sun and stars has changed, so that today, when astrologically speaking the 'Sun' is in Aquarius, the real Sun is in Capricorn.

The vast distances involved produced a number of effects. First, the stars are no longer where you see them. Aldebaran, for example, the brightest star in the constellation of Taurus, is thirty light years away from the Sun. In other words, it takes the light that forms the image of that star some thirty years to reach Earth. Indeed, assuming that they have not disappeared by the time you read this book, the stars you are seeing now may no longer actually exist. Even the nearest star, other than the Sun, is 4½ light years away. All the stars are at different distances, so their effect on Earth will vary widely.

And how much effect could there be? The Sun is our nearest star and it is fairly ordinary, much the same as those stars that are said to influence our actions, so it should have similar influences. It seems reasonable to assume that these influences are not focused purely on Earth, that they radiate uniformly in all directions from the body producing them, like light, and that they move through space at a constant speed. If so, then these influences will follow the inverse square law, and there have been few, if any, arguments to suggest otherwise. The inverse square law states that the strength of radiation varies inversely with the distance. If you shine a torch at a wall the light falling on it will be four times weaker if you move twice as far away, and nine times less from three times the distance. To see how this would affect the strength of stellar influences, it might be useful to use the example of Aldebaran. At thirty light years' distance it is 1.9 billion times further away from Earth than is the Sun. This means that its influence will be diluted by more than 3 million billion times. Sceptics believe that any such influence would be too dilute to effect life on Earth. Certainly one would expect the Sun's own influence to drown out that of the stars.

Similar problems arise with the planets, too. When an astrologer draws up, say, an aspect between Jupiter and Saturn, his drawing bears no relationship to where the planets actually were at the time. With the two in conjunction, for instance, and with the Sun in opposition, Jupiter is being drawn where it was 35 minutes before and Saturn where it was 1 hour 11 minutes before. At the other extreme, a conjunction between the Sun, Jupiter and Saturn shows the positions of these as they were 8.3 seconds, 51 minutes 42 seconds and 1 hour 30 minutes in the past, respectively. This time problem rarely troubles astrologers, although it clearly should affect their calculations.

As far as influence from the planets is concerned, comparison with the Moon is a useful exercise. The Earth, Moon and Mars are very similar, so we have an opportunity of comparing like with like. Mars is at about 204 times the distance between the Earth and the Moon and roughly twice the diameter of the Earth. Its influence will be diluted by almost 42,000 times. Taking into account its size, the influence of Mars on Earth with the Sun in opposition will be about 10,000 times less than that of the Moon, while in conjunction with the Sun the influence will be almost 1 billion times less than that of the Moon.

The variation in distance between the Earth and the planets does not figure in astrological computation – a Sun/Mars conjunction is treated as the same whether it happens on the far side or the near side of the Sun. But there may be some superadditive or catalytic effect involved. And if whatever causes the astrological phenomena travels at the speed of light, then it would reach Earth at the same moment as the image of the star or planet, and the time objection disappears.

Cosmic influences certainly do affect Earth – the relationship between the Sun and the Moon affects the tides in particular. The human body is composed of 80 per cent water, so it seems logical to suspect that it will be influenced by the Moon's gravity which causes tides. But any combined gravitational effects from the Moon, Sun and planets can be countered by sitting down, and holding this book probably has more effect on your body than does the Moon. So, for that matter, does a quarter pound of licorice allsorts at arm's length. Thousands of times more. Why, then, can the Moon apparently lift millions of tons of water several feet? The answer, one that by-passes every astrologer, is that there is an awful lot of water. Gravity is a mutual attraction of masses, and the less the mass of one member of what might be called the gravity couple, the smaller the effect the other member has upon it. After all, a glass of water on the table doesn't leap towards the ceiling every time the Moon passes overhead.

However, down the years a tradition has developed that the Moon, when full, produces a variety of effects: more births, an increase in violent crime, a greater level of mental instability in hospitals and the like. For instance, Ralph W. Morris, professor of pharmacology at the University of Illinois, claims that the notorious 'Son of Sam' mass-murderer, David Berkowitz, had murdered under the influence of the Moon, saying that of the eight nights when he went out on the murderous rampage, five had a full Moon. In fact, none of the nights on which he killed had a full moon.[2]

Is tradition right? Nick Sanduleak, an astronomer at Case Western University, studied 3370 homicidal assaults in Cuyahoga County, Cleveland, reported over ten years between 1971 and 1981.[3] The dates are important because psychiatrist Arnold Lieber came to the conclusion that the Moon was able to cause psychological disruption in his 1978 book, *The Lunar Effect*.[4] Lieber used statistics from between 1958 and 1970, so Sanduleak's work concerned the decade immediately following. Three other studies, A.D. Pokorny's 'Moon phases, suicide and homicide' in 1964, Pokorny and J. Jachimezyk in 'The questionable relationship between homicides and the lunar cycle' in 1974 and D. Lester's 'Temporal variation in suicide and homicide' had failed to support Lieber's conclusions.[5] What Sanduleak did was to take data from the same area Lieber had done, with the result that no relationship showed between lunar cycles and homicidal assaults in that area. The only relationship found was, as might be expected, between the weekend and violent assaults. Many nation-wide studies in the USA have looked for relationships between homicide, mental health, suicides and the Moon. None have been found.

And what about the babies? George O. Abell, professor of astronomy at the University of California, and Bennett Greenspan, a doctor working in the department of radiology at the same university, studied that question.[6] They were not the first. E.J. Andrews concluded [7] that the full Moon led to more births in 1960. W.D. and A. Menaker, a year earlier, found that about 1 per cent more births occurred in the two weeks after a full Moon, while W.D. Menaker found, eight years later, a 1 per cent increase in the two weeks centred on the full Moon after a study of half a million births in New York between 1961 and 1963.[8] Another report, by M. Osley, D. Summerville and L.B. Borst, concerning half a million births over a three-year period found a 1 per cent increase in the two weeks before a full Moon.[9] All very confusing, since in 1957 E. Rippmann published a study of 9551 natural births over a ten-year period which found no correlation at all.[10] Greenspan and Abell studied all births, dead and live, between March 1974 and 30 April 1978. Of the 12,000 births between those dates, natural and induced, there was no correlation with phases of the Moon. While the results of these Moon and childbirth studies seem ambiguous, Abell and Greenspan admit that their results are at odds with other workers. However, the Moon certainly appears to have no influence on homicides or suicides.

Bearing all that in mind, it seems unlikely that astrological influences can be explained by any known physical or electromagnetic effect inherent in planetary or stellar bodies. If neither the Sun's nor the Moon's invisible influence can be detected adequately, as opposed to the provable effects of gravity, light and heat, then one must look towards some principle that is not only unknown but possibly unknowable. But that will not matter if astrology can be verified as an empirical system. It may be, for instance, that Jung's synchronicity has a hand in it – two events occurring together and somehow linked in time and meaning but without a known connecting causal principle.

It all comes down to whether or not astrology actually works. If it does, then it is an enormously important system.

10 ✦ Does Astrology Work?

There are actually two questions involved: does astrology work? and are astrologers accurate?

To look at the second question first, astrologers are always 100 per cent correct in retrospect, because it is always possible to fit facts post hoc to any given case. The Houdini confusion is a good example. For many years, Ehrich Weiss, better known as Harry Houdini, was thought to have been born in Appleton, Wisconsin on 6 April 1874. This makes him a Gemini, which explains his ambiguous feelings towards mediums, his expertise at self-publicity, his enthusiasm for collecting, writing and reading books, his muscular arms, his interest in breath control, and so on. But Houdini was, in fact, born on 24 March 1874 in Budapest.[1] This makes him an Aries, thus explaining his emphasis on physical activity, his sense of adventure, his piercing eyes, his forcefulness, his mechanical talents and his pioneering spirit.

I made up that reading myself basing it on standard astrological works, admittedly, but in the September 1982 issue of *Prediction* Chris Somerville describes how the stars affected Houdini's character, without explaining why previous astrological readings were apparently just as accurate, although based on a date which Somerville admits 'makes an appreciable difference'. He chooses a birth time of 8.30pm, still an unknown quantity, because 'it not only agrees with what is known of the magician's character but also provides appropriate directions to the major events in his life, which are well documented'. This process of working backwards from personality and biographical data is called rectification. if it is possible to identify a specific time of day for a birth based on historical biographical data, it should also be possible to ascertain a birth date. Prior to the discovery of Houdini's real birth date no astrologers appear to have questioned his false birth date or noticed the discrepancy there must be. Similarly, attempts by astrologers to rectify birth times for Churchill,[2] Queen Elizabeth II [3], and others have been unsuccessful.

Wrong data have never stopped an astrologer being 'right'. The June 1971 issue of *Dell Horoscope Magazine* featured singer Dean Martin's life as analysed from a birth date that was ten days away from the correct one. Another exmaple is K. Henderson's reading of Lenin in *Astrology* in 1971 which quoted the correct birth date but used a chart that corresponded to a date nearly two weeks out. An extensive astrological biography of Winston Churchill by A.G.S. Norris was based on a birth time two and a half hours adrift. Indeed, such evidence as there is strongly implies that time, place and date of birth have little influence on the result of astrolo gical influences as seen in the lives and characters of individuals, which makes nonsense of astrology.

Astrologer John McCall placed an advertisement in a Washington newspaper in the autumn of 1982, chiding scientists for not taking astrology seriously and saying that, given four different birth times, of which one was the true birth time, he could identify which was correct after interviewing the subject. Following a small-scale, unsuccessful test by the indefatigable James Randi,[4] Philip A. Ianna and Charles R. Tolbert of the department of astronomy at Leander McCormick Observatory, University of Virginia, examined his claim. They brought together twenty-eight students whose time of birth was known and who had been born naturally, that is, without caesarian section or induction. McCall drew up horoscopes for the times of day given for each student, then interviewed each of them. He scored seven correct, as would be expected by chance.[5] Philip Ianna was also involved in another study which took more than 3000 predictions by professional astrologers and astrological organisations. Only 10 per cent were correct.

Rectification may be an over-optimistic exercise but if astrology is even partially valid it should be at least possible to link charts to individuals. Tests carried out in 1970 by American psychologist Vernon Clark [6] suggested that astrologers could score above average when working with charts. One test, for instance, took ten spurious charts and ten real charts, five males and five females. The astrologers taking part were asked to match charts with job descriptions. Another test involved matching ten brief pieces of biographical data to ten charts, and in a third trial thirty astrologers were given ten pairs of charts, one chart being that of a gifted person with an IQ of more than 140 and the other of someone with cerebral palsy.

A number of similar tests were also run and although, overall, the astrologers did score better than control groups and above chance, the level of correctness was fairly low. The tests were replicated by others and astrologers still seemed to be able to spot spurious charts. However, they appeared unable to distinguish between charts for suicides and charts for others born on the same day, or to differentiate between gifted and retarded subjects.

The tests themselves are featured in *Recent Advances in Natal Astrology*, one of the most honest reviews of evidence ever published.[7] However, of 2756 judgements made by 198 astrologers, 1618 were correct, or about 59 per cent against an expected 50 per cent. That could indicate some ability among astrologers, although small. On the other hand, there are known seasonal variations that could account for the figure. There is some evidence that birth season affects intelligence, for instance, and that there is a link between social strata and birth seasons, but there appears to have been no weighting for these factors. Tests to see how well astrologers can distinguish personality characteristics, however, proved too ambiguous for any definite conclusion. Personality-testing itself is far from an exact science.

If astrologers score well, then tests of astrological hypotheses might reveal how much is owing to calculation and how much to the astrologers themselves, and a lot of work has been carried out to determine how true the tenets of astrology actually are. An obvious question, perhaps, is 'Why do people's own horoscope character-readings seem so accurate?'

Michel Gauquelin, a French psychologist, was fascinated by this problem. He had been taught how to draw up and interpret a chart by his dentist father, an amateur astrologer. Even though Gauquelin failed to replicate previous scientific work on astrology – in his view most of it suffered from bad experimental methodology and faulty data – the subjects of his charts still found them to be accurate. As an experiment, Gauquelin placed an advertisement in a French paper, *Ici-Paris*, offering a free ten-page 'ultra- personal' horoscope, and got some 500 replies. He sent all the respondents the same reading, that of a real individual, which had been calculated by Ordinastral, an IBM computer program by a French astrologer, André Barbault. With it went a questionnaire. Gauquelin then analysed the first 150 replies. Remember, all had received the same horoscope reading, but, all the same, 94 per cent thought that the fake horoscope was accurate and 90 per cent found that their friends and family also thought the reading accurate.

Well, the reading was not all that bad. It described someone who was sensitive, adaptable, devoted to others, a right-minded middle-class citizen. Sadly, the person to whom it did apply was Dr Pétiot, a notorious French mass murderer.[8]

Gauquelin's findings were confirmed by C.R. Snyder, a psychologist at the University of Texas. He and some colleagues drew up a character-reading which incorporated characteristics that they had found most people believed they possessed. This description was shown to three groups of people who were asked to rate it for accuracy on a scale of 1 to 5. Those told that this was a universal character-sketch gave it an average score of 3.2. A second group were told that it was a reading for their particular signs and they rated it at 3.6 on average, while a final group were told that it was a personal horoscope and rated it at 4.38. So the more the group believed that the reading was specifically for them, the more accurate they believed it to be.[9]

In both of these cases, however, the subjects had nothing with which to compare the false horoscopes. But at the City University of New York, Douglas P. Lackey, associate professor of philosophy at Baruch College, got the horoscope readings of thirty-eight students. Each student was given his or her own horoscope plus one chosen at random from one of the other students, but were not told which was which. In terms of overall scoring for accuracy, the 'wrong' horoscope scored higher than the right one. While nineteen students thought the real horoscopes were more accurate, the rest thought them less accurate, a split that could be expected from chance.[10]

All the same, astrology should be able to explain personality traits. Indeed, one of its values, if it can be validated, would be its aid in giving us insight into how and why we are what we are. However, Ralph Bastedo, professor of political science at the Laboratory of Behavioral Research at the State University of New York at Stony Brook, tested 1000 people from the San Francisco Bay area with regard to sun-sign and personality. The data used had not been specifically collected for such a test although it included matters about which astrologers make certain claims. He found no correlation between sun-sign and leadership qualities, political stance, subjective assessment of intelligence, observed intelligence, belief in astrology, or twenty-eight other possibilities.[11]

Gauquelin, too, made a study of sun-sign and personality. He took about 50,000 character traits from the biographies of 2000 people and compared them with traits given in definitions of sun-signs in eight standard textbooks. There was no correlation between them.[12]

How does this correlate with the apparent accuracy of personality delineations in horoscopes? This may partly be owing to the fact that all signs inevitably contain aspects of each of the others, thanks to polarity, triplicity and quadruplicity. For instance, each sign around the zodiac has, alternately, positive and negative polarity, so each sign will have the same polarity and with it certain similar characteristics to the other five signs in the same group. The twelve signs are divided into triplicities of fire, earth, air and water, with three signs in each. The three signs share certain characteristics – Aries, Leo and Sagittarius are fire signs and therefore energetic, positive, enthusiastic. At the other end of the scale, Cancer, Scorpio and Pisces are water signs – emotional, changeable, impressionable. In each triplicity two signs share the same polarity, with one being of the opposite polarity. Quadruplicities are groups of four signs categorised as to whether they are regarded as cardinal, which are active, fixed, which are cautious, and mutable, which are changeable. This means that Capricorn, a cardinal Earth sign, is both static and active.

Therefore, according to traditional astrology, all signs inevitably include traces of the others, even when sun-signs alone are considered. But a normal astrological reading includes consideration of rising signs and so forth. Clearly, this makes it difficult for the subject of a horoscope, or even those who know the subject, to make an objective assessment of a reading. What is needed is some measurement not dependent upon self-validation by the subject or fact-fitting by the astrologer.

The polarity of the signs should lead to each sign being alternately extrovert and introvert, a theory tested by psychologist Hans Eysenck and astrologer Jeff Mayo using a personality test, the Eysenck Personality Inventory. The study of 2324 adults, men and women, did, indeed, demonstrate an extroversion – introversion effect according to sign, as predicted by astrology.[13] True, it was only a very small effect, just 1 per cent or so, but it was an effect. Other scientists managed to replicate the effect, while others did not. And some who replicated the effect with one personality test could not do so with a different test. A study of 241 New Zealand students, for instance, carried out in 1981, failed to show the extroversion – introversion effect.[14] All of which was a puzzle until Eysenck[15] and others tested the possibility that the subjects' answers to the questionnaires were affected by their belief in astrology and found the key – when that factor was eliminated the effect disappeared. People had been seeing themselves not as they really believed themselves to be but as astrology told them they should be.

This is rather ominous. It suggests that instead of clarifying the human psyche, astrology could actually have an adverse effect upon it. Certainly, astrological predictions do affect people's actions. Possibly the worst example of this sort of thing occurred in the mid-1960s when Japanese astrologers were predicting that any girl children born in one particular year would make bad wives. As a result half a million Japanese women had abortions. In terms of loss of potential life that is approximately five times the death toll of the Hiroshima bomb and three times that of Hiroshima and Nagasaki combined.[16]

Since a workable personal relationship depends upon personality, one would expect to find a link between marriage, divorce and the signs. A Californian attorney, J.A. Hadaller, claimed to have found a link between divorce and the position of the Sun in the astrological charts of 1000 of his clients. No-one else seems to have replicated this, however.[17] Bernard Silverman, a Michigan State University pychologist, got the records of nearly 3000 couples who had married and 478 couples who had divorced in Michigan between 1967 and 1968. There was no correlation with anything astrological: 'compatible' signs married and divorced just as often as 'incompatible' ones.[18] In all, studies have been made of nearly 3500 divorces, with no established link between divorce and astrological signs or factors appearing.

Apart from personality-assessment, astrology also claims to be able to define the sort of talents available to an individual. That, in turn, should affect the sort of jobs people take up and whether they do them well or not. A degree of celebrity is some guide to how well people do their jobs. Gauquelin tested the birth dates of more than 25,000 celebrities and found that distribution among the signs was attributable to chance, taking into account the Sun, Moon and ascendant. He also tried assessing aspects, that is, the significant angles between planets in the charts, for 8000 people and failed to find any correlation.[19]

John McGervey, a physicist at Case Western Reserve University, checked out the birth dates of more than 16,000 scientists and more than 6000 politicians and found that the distribution of these among the signs was the same as for the public at large.[20] The largest single investigation of a link between astrology and jobs was carried out by Professor Alan Smithers for *The Guardian* in 1984, covering one in ten of the working population of Britain, 2.5 million people.[21] When adjusted for class differences in birth seasons and for the uneven level of births throughout the year, there was no definite correlation between sun-sign and job. Fifteen astrologers, however, did predict that certain jobs would fall under particular signs and had some success, in the case of trade-union leaders and nurses for instance, but the survey failed to validate astrological connections.

If astrology shows up anywhere, it should show up in the case of twins. Not only should twins look similar, which is a function of biology, but, when heredity factors are compensated for, there should be an unusually high level of similarity in life-style and events in their lives. But how similar are unrelated people of the same age, sex and background? Joseph Wyatt, assistant professor of psychology at Marshall University, Huntingdon, West Virginia, and three students, Anne Posey, William Welker and Carla Seamonds, set out to answer that question.[22] They tested twenty-eight unrelated people against thirteen sets of twins. People who were unrelated but of the same cultural and ethnic background proved to be just as similar in the events of their lives as were twins. Studies of time-twins, those born at the same time and the same place, have also proved ambiguous.

One man whose name crops up frequently as a critic of astrology is Michel Gauquelin. He says: 'Astrology is doomed, since its attempts to understand people and their fate are based on nothing but superstition; its roots lie in magic and the model of the world out of which it grew is long out of date....Those who oppose astrology have good reasons for being wary.'[23]

Yet Gauquelin's later findings gave rise to the most bitter controversy ever to hit the world of astrology, one which not only polarised believers in astrology and the sceptics, but severely split the ranks of sceptics, too. Briefly, Gauquelin had found sun-sign astrology to be wanting. But when he looked at which planets were in the sky at the time of birth he noticed something curious. He divided the sky into twelve sectors, much like the houses of a horoscope, and looked at the distribution of the planets throughout the sectors in relation to leading figures in various professions in France. He found that in the case of writers and politicians the Moon was in the sector just above the horizon and at the zenith more often than chance would suggest.[24] One of the biggest effects showed with sports champions, with about 22 per cent born with Mars in the two sectors instead of an expected 17.6 per cent – an effect replicated by the Belgian Comité Para using Gauquelin's data. Many of the planets also seemed to fit the relationship of planets to occupation defined by traditional astrology. The effect itself was quite small and could have been due to a number of causes: either there was some relationship between the position of Mars in the sky at the time of birth, or there was some geographical or cultural effect, or the sample of births was inadequately representative.

Some of the strongest criticism came from Dennis Rawlins, an astronomer then living in San Diego and a member of the Committee for the Scientific Investigation of Claims of the Paranormal. He points out that, after twenty years' research Gauquelin has not managed to improve on his original 5 per cent spread, that he misdrew the graph of the Comife Para results, that statistics demonstrated effects that might be expected by bias and that some sets of Mars Effect data showed below-average scores.[25] Gauquelin replied that the Comife Para tests had, in fact, confirmed his findings, although Rawlins still maintained that the test did not demonstrate the Mars Effect hypothesis.[26] He also became increasingly unhappy with the CSICOP's approach to the Gauquelin findings.

A test, however, known as the Zelen Test did show the Mars Effect. This used data from France and Belgium gathered by Gauquelin. This test Rawlins described as 'ill-conceived'.[27] Paul Kurtz, Marvin Zelen and George Abell had tested Gauquelin's hypothesis on US sporting champions and, they said, found it wanting. Gauquelin claimed, however, that this was owing to their sampling technique: major champions were being diluted by 'minor' champions. Claim and counterclaim bounced back and forth between the Gauquelins and the Zelen Test experimenters. Then, in October 1981, a bomb burst above CSICOP when Dennis Rawlins published an article in *Fate* magazine under the title 'starbaby'. In effect, war had broken out between Rawlins and CSICOP. Rawlins had criticised the Zelen Test because it was certain to produce a pro-Mars Effect if anything was wrong with the original Gauquelin data, and accused CSICOP of censorship and cover-up. He also accused them of various malpractices and incompetence.

Rawlins had, he claimed, been unceremoniously thrown out of CSICOP, having, it seems, made his presence less than pleasant – Rawlins does not seem to have much time for great diplomacy. The whole issue was a mangled mess. One member of CSICOP resigned and another told me that he had considered resigning but wanted to remain part of the information network, and remained unhappy about CSICOP's treatment of the whole affair. What tends to get lost in the general melee, however, is the fact that Rawlins was not complaining of a cover-up of proof of Gauquelin's findings but of an apparent cover-up of incompetence. Rawlins still maintained that Gauquelin was wrong.[28]

For myself, I feel that CSICOP grossly mishandled the whole affair. Certainly the taint, true or not, of having tried to cover up an embarassment will haunt CSICOP for years to come. And probably quite rightly. Ironically, the whole argument may be irrelevant. Gauquelin may well have uncovered a curiosity, one of those situations in which scientists have no option but to say: 'It happens because that is the way it is.' There is at least one precedent. Every US president to be elected at intervals of twenty years since 1840 has died in office (only one has died in office outside the twenty-year period) and all the assassinated presidents were elected at these periods (Lincoln elected in 1860, Garfield in 1880, McKinley in 1900, Kennedy in 1960; killed in 1865, 1881, 1901 and 1963 respectively). An artifact, perhaps, but the data is only applicable to the US and has not been replicated in other countries. All the same, it has so far shown 87.5 per cent accuracy. Which is why there were so many predictions of the death of Ronald Reagan.

It will take much more work to determine whether the Gauquelin effects are an artifact, a product of faulty sampling, or the first indication of a true link between mankind and the planets.

11 — Things Unseen

It was only a short trip between the factory doors and the warehouse, perhaps twenty feet of concrete, in a rough square, with a drain in the centre. There I discovered the fascination of dowsing.

One sunny day I walked across that yard to find about half-a-dozen white-coated men pacing the ground with pieces of bent welding rod in each hand. Every now and then the rods would cross. A programme about water diviners had been broadcast on televison the previous night and they were trying it out for themselves. After I had watched them for a few minutes one of them handed me a pair of rods: 'Here, have a go.' The rods were about two feet long, with a six-inch leg bent down at 90 degrees. A few tries gave me the right position – the hand held in a loose fist twisted outwards, the bottom end of the short leg against the fleshy part of the palm, the top end, just below the bend, against the index finger, so that the rod swings freely. With a rod in each hand, parallel to each other and to the ground, I walked gingerly towards the drain – and as I got closer the rods gradually crossed, even though, as far as I knew, my hands had remained still. I tried it again, and again it worked. One of the experimenters then suggested that I try doing the same thing about ten feet from the drain, where others had also got results. Sure enough, the rods crossed over the solid concrete – but a couple of feet beneath, and invisible, was a drainpipe. A while later we tracked down an underground waterpipe, too.

What was going on? I didn't know. All that I could concede was that, somehow, dowsing worked. I had become convinced by practical demonstration, as have many hundreds of believers in, and practitioners of, dowsing down the years. Of course, sceptics, inevitably, did not believe in it, so, in 1977 I set up a number of informal experiments to provide some sort of hard data as support. In essence, I developed a 'party piece' around dowsing, making it an extension of some mind-reading stunts. That sort of relaxed atmosphere should, I thought, be one in which dowsing could operate. There was no sense of challenge or competition, just some fun over a few glasses of wine.

The conventional wisdom is that everyone has the ability to dowse, and that was what I set out to examine. The procedure was for me to make up a pair of dowsing rods on the spot, usually out of coat-hanger wire. Then I would ask for a glass of water to be placed on the floor and would show that the rods would cross over it. The next step was to get other guests to try it out. Some people held the rods too tightly for them to move, others got no response at all. In all, about eight out of ten people got a response, often to their own surprise – just as I had been surprised ten years earlier.

For them, that was the most convincing part of the experience. They knew that they had not deliberately moved the rods and even sceptics were getting results and being converted. The next step was for me to show that the rods would cross over white wine, too, which caused a few laughs – and quite a bit of amazement when the rods did cross, and did so for others, too. And things did not stop there. I next showed that the rods would open out over red wine and, sure enough, when other guests tried, they got the same response. To reinforce what they had done, the two wine samples (I also used gin and Scotch at times) were placed in a line and the guests walked forward along it and saw that the rods would cross over one sample and open out over the other.

How much was due to suggestion? On some occasions I showed the rods crossing over the red wine and on others they would open out, and the direction of movement when the rods were in the hands of others almost always matched the direction that I had shown them. I say almost always because some people still had the rods crossing whatever I said, but not many.

The next stage was to use coins. The rods would cross over silver , or 'water-colour', coins, which seemed logical, and open out over copper or bronze coins. Again, I would demonstrate it first, then get the others to do it. So far, everything had been aimed at conditioning the guests to accept dowsing and enabling them to do it themselves. Then the real experiment started. Now they were conditioned to accept dowsing, would they be able to demonstrate the real thing? I placed one of the coins under a card, either a silver or a bronze coin, or nothing. As a 'randomiser' a six-sided dice was used and 'conditions' allocated to opposite faces. A silver coin would be chosen by my throwing 1 or 6, a bronze coin by 2 or 5, and nothing by 3 or 4. These allocations were rotated for each of three experimental runs to counteract any imbalance in the dice, and the identity of the number thrown was kept secret. The experimenters had a one in three chance of getting the correct response by chance.

The dowsing tests were carried out over a period of two years, in France, Britain and the Philippines, and involved 126 people, each of which was given three tries to discover whether there was a silver coin, a bronze coin or nothing under the card which was placed on the floor. There was not a totally equitable spread of samples throughout the runs. On 130 of the 378 runs there was nothing under the card, 124 had a silver coin and 124 had a bronze coin. With bronze coins, 110 calls resulted in 38 correct, or 34.5 per cent. Silver coins were called 139 times, with correct calls on 46 occasions, 33 per cent correct. There were no coins called on 129 runs, 40 of the calls were correct, or 31 per cent. For the total number of runs, correct calls were given 32.05 per cent of the time (10.58 for no coins, 12.17 for silver coins, 10.05 for bronze).

There were coins, irrespective of colour, under the card on 248 occasions, or 65.6 per cent of the runs, and they were called 249 times, or 65.9 per cent of the time. Correct calls were given on 84 ocassions, 67.74 per cent of all correct calls. All of which is so close to what would be expected by chance that there is no need to invoke a dowsing ability. Of the 126 people only two scored correctly on all three trials and subsequent tests on them showed a drop to chance expectation.[1]

The pro-paranormalists might describe this as the 'fall-off effect', which has been noted in many experiments involving paranormal skills. The idea is that some sort of psychic fatigue occurs and the psi-ability ceases to operate. Of course, one would see precisely the same phenomenon if probability had a hand in it. The obvious explanation is that the subjects were responding to visual stimuli and the rods crossed where they expected them to cross.

So, conditioning and expectancy appeared to explain much about dowsing. But I was reluctant to dismiss dowsing entirely, and something I discovered during a dinner party at the Kingston-on-Thames home of psychologist Glen Smith suggested that dowsing really worked. We had been talking about dowsing, although no experiments had been done, and I had demonstrated the crossing of the rods. One of the guests suggested that I should be blind-folded, something I had never tried before. He placed a bottle of beer on the floor. When I felt the rods cross, my wife, who had been silently following me to make sure that I didn't stick the rods through the panes of a glass cabinet along one wall, took off the blindfold and there, at my feet, was the bottle of beer. Yes, I could have cheated – you don't learn much about mind-reading conjuring effects without finding out how to defeat a simple blindfold – but I didn't, my eyes were closed under the blindfold.

Later, I took that experiment further. I asked someone to stand behind me, to preclude any cueing by eye movement, and just to imagine a bowl of water somewhere on the floor. And, perhaps six out of ten times, I hit the right spot. What on earth was going on? My own experience of finding hidden or even imaginary targets simply could not be explained in terms of visual stimuli.

Most dowsing experiments produce negative results, certainly those designed to avoid any cue or clue to the dowser. In Rome in 1979 James Randi tested four Italian dowsers, each convinced of his own ability and claiming a 100 per cent success rate.[2] Three 3cm pipes were buried in a 10-metre square and water pumped through them, the pipe used being chosen at random. Each dowser was given three tries at finding the pipes with water running through them, and each failed, even though they had agreed beforehand that the conditions of the test were suitable.

In 1981 a Boston University student, Perry Flint, tested Paul Sevigny, the president of the American Society of Dowsers. Four pipes were run under a carpet across a room, with a plastic bin at either end to act as reservoirs. The water-pump and its operator were hidden behind a screen and water was pumped through one of the pipes at random. In forty trials Sevigny was successful nine times, about chance expectation which would be ten successes in forty trials.

When twenty-five Australian diviners were tested in Perth for radio station 6WF the success rate was 18 per cent, against an expected 20 per cent. All the same, the most successful, Cecil Holmes, was then tested by David Smith, an Australian sceptic, and James Randi. The claim was that Holmes could detect which of several boxes contained a piece of metal – actually a gold ingot. Holmes failed on eleven tests.[3]

In 1913 a scientific committee, including believers, tested seven dowsers, who failed to find sewers, a reservoir and a fast-flowing spring. Two years earlier a dowser was blindfolded and let loose on an estate. He found eleven spots where there was water. Unfortunately, when the blindfold was removed and he tried again, his second eleven, so to speak, did not match up to his first.[4]

Another series of tests, reported in the *Journal of the Royal Society of Arts*, found that two dowsers were unable to find a well inside a room, even with three tries each, and only one of the total of six guesses was within ten feet. Another dowser was tested to see if he could tell whether water was flowing in a pipe or not – he actually did worse than he could have done by tossing a coin.[5]

Nature reported in 1927 that the US Geological Survey had found that dowsers did worse than chance.[5]

In 1970 the Ministry of Defence set up an experiment in mine-detection in which 160 dummy mines were buried in bulldozered heathland. The twenty-two dowsers involved failed to impress the experimenters.[6] In another test involving 400 acres and twenty defused mines dowsers managed to produce no better than chance results. The Royal School of Military Engineering, which includes dowsing in the subjects covered in its courses, also failed to produce good results. Which explains why, when I asked a US Army colonel, a veteran of the Vietnam conflict, what they called the men who dowsed for landmines there, he replied: 'Dead.'

On the other hand, dowsing seems to be accepted by waterboards in Britain and there have been some apparently remarkable hits – the water supply for the Mönchen Gladbach British Army base was dowsed by Colonel Harry Grattan and in India a Major Charles Pogson is reputed to have been highly successful.[7]

One thing that the dowsing community cannot claim is that it has been ignored by science. For twenty-five years, from 1918, water authorities in central New South Wales kept records of the performance of dowsers and geologists. And the geologists won, hands down, with half as many absolute failures as the dowsers and more successful bores.

But let's accept, for the sake of argument, that dowsers are successful with sufficient frequency to suggest that there is more to it than merely chance. Would it then be necessary to accept it as a paranormal skill, requiring senses other than those of sight, sound, taste, smell and touch? Before trying to answer that question, let us make sure that we know what we are talking about. Dowsing means different things to different people.

12 ← A Twitch in Time

No-one knows the origins of dowsing. Perhaps it grew out of the techniques of fortune-telling or true divining which used sticks rather as others use crystal balls or tarot cards. Such 'psychic dowsing' is still with us today in alternative medicine and in locating missing persons and objects. In their classic work, *The Divining Rod*, published in 1926, Theodore Besterman and Sir William Barrett say that dowsing was probably unknown in classical times.[1] Pliny wrote about water and its discovery, but mentions nothing about dowsing, and the fourth-century writer Cassiodorus does not mention it in his writings about water-finders. The *De Re Rustica* of Palladius fails to mention it, as does Vitruvius in *De Architectura*. In the eleventh century a monk called Notker in St Gallen, in Switzerland, mentions rods, but these may be *Wunschelrisz*, or wishing rods; in other words, rhabdomancy.

Most references, such as Moses striking a rock with his rod to produce water, are likely to involve 'psychic' rods rather than dowsing rods as we know them today. However, in about 1430 a Viennese manuscript referred to a mining rod which detected metallic 'exhalations', used in the Harz Mountains, and Martin Luther banned them in his *Decem Praecepta* of 1518. Whatever was going on, the use of divining rods was accepted practice in mining when the sixteenth-century writer Agricola first mentioned them. In 1556 Agricola returned to the subject of dowsing rods in *De Re Metallica*, wondering whether the nature of the response was more to do with the dowser than the rods themselves. Paracelsus mentioned them in 1531 and the next year wrote 'Vera atque brevis descriptio Virgulae Mercurialis', using the term 'mercurial rod' and describing the location of buried treasure by a Father Bernhardus.

The first reference by an English writer is in Robert Fludd's *Philosophia Moysaica* of 1638, written in Latin and published in the Netherlands. He says that they were used by Welsh silver-miners of his day. Dowsing for water appears to have started sometime in the sixteenth or seventeenth century. The use of dowsing rods seems to have been imported into England with German mine-workers. Intriguingly, it was these same miners who told tales of dog-sized ants who brought gold to the surface and protected it against would-be thieves. So the very people who brought dowsing rods to Britain were known to tell very tall stories.

The term 'divining ' is best limited to those occasions when it is used for clearly paranormal purposes and 'dowsing' should be used for to the detection of hidden objects or substances which have a physical reality, but excluding map-dowsing and long-distance dowsing. The term 'dowsing' is of dubious origin. John Locke referred to Deusing-rods in 1692, suggesting a derivation from the Latin *Deus*, meaning God. Sir William Barrett mentions other possible sources. In Middle English *duschen* means 'to strike', later becoming 'douse'. In Dutch the same meaning is given to *doesen*. Since the method was used for Cornish tin-mines it is probably also worth including *The dowses*, *dewsys* and *deuyse*, all meaning divinity in Cornish.

Over the years a considerable weight of literature has accrued about dowsing and many who do not accept psychic claims do give houseroom to dowsing. One of the things that tends to separate dowsing from other methods of divination is that it is an essentially practical skill, no specific world-view is required, and the normal rural practitioner rarely seems to become involved in the wilder regions of belief. Its supporters say that it can be demonstrated under rigid conditions in the field, even if controlled tests do not work. Interestingly, many hydrologists believe that dowsers do have some special skill, an ability to detect something that, to use the phrase of one, 'on occasion coincides with the presence of water'. Tony Debney, who was head of the groundwater section of the Institute of Hydrology, admits to keeping a pair of dowsing rods in his car boot but does not use them in his professional work of finding sites for bore holes. 'I can find no test that I can conduct to convince myself that there is a link [between the crossing of the rods and the presence of water].'[2] He points out that both water and minerals exist in the same sort of geological features in rocks. If dowsing does work, then this link could be important.

Duane Chadwick of Utah State University tested 150 people over a course in North Logan City Park, noted where the dowsing rods crossed, then went over the course with a magnetometer. There appeared to be a link with the dowsing reactions and the readings of the magnetometer.[3] In the absence of any other clues this might suggest a link between the effects of underlying geological formations on the earth's magnetic field and the dowsing response.

In 1913, however, hydrologists in Guildford tested seven dowsers over three types of test area: a field under which ran a stream, a lawn concealing a reservoir and another piece of land under which ran a sewerpipe. No dowser found the reservoir, one found the sewerpipe and one found the stream. And the dowsers disagreed with each other. Not an impressive score. The conclusions were that while there existed sufficient histori cal evidence for the existence of some form of dowsing ability, it was too uncertain a talent to be of practical value.

If dowsing does work it could be of incalculable value on archaeological sites. Often it is impossible to open a dig on a site of potential value, because the site is either still in use or has been built over, and the very process of digging can destroy valuable evidence. Dowsing would be totally non-destructive and non-invasive. A very tempting possibility. It is hardly surprising, therefore, that when Professor Richard Bailey of the University of Newcastle-upon-Tyne received a number of plans in 1981 from retired engineer Denis Briggs, he was intrigued. The plans of Northumberland churches dowsed by Briggs seemed to make sense. Together with Eric Cambridge of the University of Durham the men surveyed twenty-three churches, concentrating on those which were thought to date from early times and including a variety of different types of church.

Three of the churches studied were featured in a paper published in *Archaeologia*

Aeliana in November 1983[4] and in an article in *Popular Archaeology* in February of the same year.[5] Bailey's conclusion is that 'the results are sufficiently encouraging to suggest that dowsing offers a valid means of recovering evidence'. The *Popular Archaeology* article produced considerable controversy and Bailey was accused of being 'a purveyor of superstition'.[6] An intemperate response, one would have thought, to a paper which simply reported that there may be a link between a dowser's response and archeological features, having set out not to validate dowsing as such but to examine its validity as a working tool.

Really, the Bailey – Briggs – Cambridge paper reports half an experiment. One ought also to test predictions made by guesswork by non-dowsers at the same site, on a day when Briggs was not present, and in the company of a different set of people. Even if the dowsing trials did demonstrate an apparent link with actual archaeological features, the findings are meaningless without such control data. Unless one knows what is achievable without dowsing there is no way of judging whether or not dowsing is any more successful than a combination of guesswork and chance.

The first church in the paper is Woodhorn Church, owned by Wansbeck District Council and used as a museum and cultural centre. Briggs's dowsing survey found a number of foundations not visible on the surface, including that of an unsuspected apse. Permission was granted for two trenches to be dug. In the first was found a foundation of mortared stone precisely where Briggs had predicted one to be. Was it an apse? Nobody knows. Adjoining the foundations, however, was a flat mortared area, possibly the remains of another floor, which was missed in the dowsing survey, as was a large stone above the foundations. Other dowsers also traced the same foundation line but missed these features. In the second trench nothing was found to correlate with the dowsing survey. Bailey does not believe that this was because nothing was to be found and that the survey was invalid, but suggests that the survey may have traced something that was irretrievable by normal archaeological techniques. Later in the paper he discusses the possibility of imprinting, that the survey was marking the lines of details long since vanished. The Woodhorn survey by Briggs produced one empty trench, several large missed items, and a foundation, undated, where he had said there would be one.

The next church was St Mary's, Ponteland. Quite a number of foundations turned up in the survey, including, it seems the location of an altar plinth and a wooden platform removed in 1972. These were, apparently, confirmed by local dowsers, including two children found by Denis Briggs, according to a letter to me from Bailey.[7] Excavations showed a change in the foundations where predicted by the dowser and another foundation on a line also predicted by dowsing. My first impression is that the marks from the altar plinth and wooden platform are precisely where I would expect to find traces of something in a church, any church. My second is that the dowsing survey shows foundations roughly every ten feet, at widths of between two and three feet. As an experiment I tried jabbing blindfold at the plan of the church with a pin and got within 20cm or so of a foundation each time. Not very scientific, but if, for example, the trench being dug is 1.5 metres by 2.5 metres, then the margin for finding something is very wide.

The third survey was done at the Anglo-Saxon cathedral at Durham. Eric Cambridge has done considerable documentary research on the possible background to the cathedral and its location, which he believes is different from that generally accepted in archaeological circles. For instance, one writer places the limits of the original cathedral to the north of those found in the dowsing survey, the survey tending to agree with the conclusions drawn by Cambridge, of which Briggs, it is claimed, was ignorant. On the other hand, several features do not seem to match the survey which Cambridge admits contains 'internal discrepancies'. Obviously, the only way to really find out how accurate the dowsing surveys have been is to completely excavate the sites concerned, which is impracticable

Bailey is certainly well aware of some of the problems associated with dowsing and archaeology – that much of the evidence for and against is based on hearsay and that publications on archaeological dowsing seem ignorant of modern techiques of excavation and archaeological knowledge. And he quotes M.J. Aitken: 'Where success is not due to coincidence (on many archaeological sites it is difficult to dig and find nothing), it represents a high degree of archaeological intuition on the part of the dowser.' One should remember that Briggs has surveyed twenty-three sites, so certainly has some idea of what ancient churches look like. In addition, of course, there is the matter of subconscious cueing, which I will look at a little later.

The Bailey report, then, is ambiguous, and no account seems to have been taken of known theories regarding the possible psychological source dowsing response. The paper itself is a useful source of information on current dowsing techniques. Briggs uses L-shaped rods and walks across the site. When an interface or boundary between some feature in the ground and its surroundings is struck, the rods cross. Briggs outlines five possible sources of error for dowsers: fatigue, faulty interpretation of features on top of one another, reflection or diffraction of electromagnetic radiation, setting a false 'norm', and too many undefined interfaces.

The first thing about which there is no argument is that the dowsing response actually does exist. The rods do cross, the pendulum does swing, the stick does rotate. In most methods of dowsing, the equipment used acts in some way as an amplifier of muscle movements. The L-shaped rods, for instance, are held in such a way that their position is unstable and the slightest muscular movement will cause them to move. The hold used for the traditional Y-shaped hazel twig involves twisting it and holding it under tension, a process which puts a store of energy into the twig and keeps it in an uncertain equilibrium, so that any small change of muscle tone causes it to spring and release its store of energy, often very violently. Similarly, a pendulum also exaggerates minute movements of the hands and arms. If, for instance, you make up a pendulum – a ring hanging on a piece of thread will do – and hold it over a photograph, the pendulum will certainly move. If you now tie a pencil in the middle of the thread and support the pencil with, say, a book under each end, the pendulum will not move. So the secret of the response must lie with the person holding the rods, an assumption which today is hardly questioned by anyone who has seriously studied the subject.

Arnold Aspinall of the School of Archaeological Science at the University of Bradford is a wary critic of dowsing. In a telephone conversation in 1985 he told me that he had often seen a now-retired colleague, Arthur Bailey, an electrical engineer, perform well. 'I have seen him in action finding evidence that was confirmed by other means.' His criticism of the Bailey, Briggs and Cambridge findings, however, is that a valid technique would surely detect not just the walls but the associated rubble, too, which Briggs failed to do. Observing Briggs on one survey, Arnold noticed that he seemed to be detecting something along lines extrapolated from baulks between archaeological trenches. These baulks serve to separate one trench from another and do not indicate any underlying features. Arnold also mentioned to me that after a while one 'gets a feel' for what might lie beneath the ground at a site. But he also tells me that Arthur Bailey has found features which were not expected by the archaeologists present.

What is it, then, that makes the dowser twitch? Using a small mirror taped to his wrist which reflected a light beam, Briggs has established that the movement of the rods is caused by unconscious muscle movements. A number of mechanisms have been suggested to explain the dowsing resonse, from psychic sensitivity and ancient memories to the detection of some disturbance in the magnetic field. The detection of magnetism is certainly one method by which some living creatures gather data about their environment. Certain kinds of bacteria follow an internal biological compass which guides them north or south, depending on which hemisphere they live in,[8] and magnetic materials have been found in dolphins, bees and pigeons.[9] Although no-one has firmly demonstrated that any creatures other than bacteria respond to magnetic fields, it is certainly a possibility, and magnetism seems to be used by some animals such as pigeons.

In 1980 R.R. Baker reported some experiments suggestive of a magnetic sense in humans, and experiments showing a link with magnetometer readings were mentioned earlier in this chapter, but Baker's results seem unrepeatable. A machine developed by a Hampshire-based company, the DMO2 gradiometer, uses magnetic anomalies to map archaeological features. Although it is tempting to explain the apparent success of archaeological dowsing by invoking magnetism, humans seem to be insensitive to magnetic fields many hundreds of times more powerful than those detected by this sort of machine. But as we shall see. Chapter 16, human beings are often aware of stimuli which would normally be regarded as below the perceptual threshold. Other animals, such as sharks, are sensitive to electrical fields and there have been claims that humans are affected by the presence of high-tension electrical cables.

Engineer Tony Hopwood believes that because the brain itself operates electrically, 'it doesn't seem unreasonable to think that perhaps we might have an electrical field awareness, because the earth has got an electric field which extends up to the ionosphere and out into space to the sun'. Hopwood's early experiments involved running a voltage through a wire suspended between two poles in his garden. He agrees that psychological cueing could have produced many of the effects he observed but he did find variations in readings that were subsequently correlated with the position of the sun and climatic conditions, an effect that has been observed by other workers, too.

But does it really matter how it works? Clive Thompson, president of the British Society of Dowsers, believes that how dowsing works is, in practical terms, relatively unimportant. 'It doesn't [matter] to me and I don't think to anyone who is actively using it. All he is concerned about is that he is accurate in what he is forecasting.' Like many professional dowsers, Thompson does have a good track record. But until dowsing can be shown to work, unequivocally, and some sort of scientific basis can be given to it, it is likely to remain a fringe activity.

According to Tony Debney:

Accepting that there is a dowsing response and then trying to find out whether you can prove scientifically a link between a dowsing response and a supply of water is very difficult... looking at the tests that have been made around the world I finish up being very doubtful that there is a proven link.

And he adds:

Until you start to think about the origin of the signal that the dowser receives, rather than think about the dowsing response and what he is finding, then you are not really beginning to do serious research in the subject.

Tony Hopwood also thinks that too little work has been done on the dowsing signal: 'There has been a very real lack of actual scientific attack on the physics of dowsing.' In many experiments in dowsing, however, there does seem to be a strong possibility of psychological cueing.

A typical experiment was carried out at a school in the Black Country. Alderman John Uxford, chairman of a county education committee, and Miss Coe, a school headmistress, decided to teach children how to dowse. The initial practice was carried out in the school hall over a bucket of water. Then they went outside to experiment under the gaze of a foreman from a construction site who was a dowser and knew where pipes were laid under the ground. The first child to try produced a crossing of the rods near a drain. Other children tried with similar results. What is important is that the site foreman was present and that other children, whose rods crossed at similar places, saw where the rods crossed.[10]

As my own experiments demonstrated, a dowsing response will occur where people expect one and it will be of the type for which they are already prepared. But, of course, it seems that there are rarely such cues as to where something should happen, though this does not mean that there are no cues. What it might mean is that if a dowser is 'confirming' information gathered by other means, the responses are far more likely to be due to existing preconceptions rather than to anything else. As Arnold's observations of Briggs suggest, dowsers certainly do react to marks seen consciously or otherwise. Of course, in water divining, it often does not matter where the rods cross – in most parts of Britain you'll find water almost anywhere you dig. Despite the widespread belief to the contrary, most water drawn up through wells comes not from underground streams running through fissures in the rock but from seepage into the well from porous, water-bearing strata.

There are certainly plenty of stories of dowsers finding water where others could not. But then, with each well that is dug there is a progressively better chance of finding water, so the more attempts there are to find water before calling in a dowser, the higher are the chances of his finding it.

All the same, the phenomenon of finding water, minerals and archaeological artifacts by some strange talent does in my view need to be taken seriously. So let's take a closer look at each of these in turn. Would it be surprising if dowsers did find water more often than chance seems to dictate? Probably not. After all, humans can live for weeks without food but for mere days without water. Our ancestors may well have developed an in-built ability which increased their chances of finding water, an ability that we might still have. There is, however, no need to suppose that it is in any way a paranormal or psychic skill. After all, the presence of water brings with it differences in the landscape, plants grow differently, different types of plant may be present, the ground itself may be of a different colour and texture, it may even smell different. Certain types of geological formation lead to a higher likelihood of water being present. These are the sort of clues that hydrologists consciously look for.

In the past, what may have happened is that the repeated finding of water under particular circumstances led to the situation in which seeking out that type of environment became conducive to survival. We already have certain behavioural traits and reactions which may at some time, have been a learned response to environmental stress. If that is so, then all a dowser is doing is reacting to physical characteristics of the landscape. There is no need at all for magnetic anomalies, electromagnetic radiation or any of the other postulates. Indeed, Tony Debney points out that most of the dowsers he has talked to have 'an incredibly well-built sense of geomorphology, geology, the likely occurrences of groundwater' and they follow the sort of clues that I often follow. They back it up by being able to give them[selves] the confidence at a point to say, 'Here's where you drill.'

Given the sensitivity of the dowsing response to the various psychological quirks of the mind, if a dowser gets an accurate response in the presence of certain cues, the chances are higher of his getting a similar response under similar Apart from any in-built appreciation of changes in geography and landscape features there would also be an almost Pavlovian learning process. If this is true, then one might expect to find the dowsing response becoming inaccurate when cues are not available, which is what tends to happen. The excuse made by and on behalf of dowsers for their failure to their skills successfully under test conditions is that the stress of the experimental method somehow robs them of their skill, perhaps by making them nervous. Under those conditions, however, the environmental cues would not normally be present.

Dowsers are claimed to get better with practice; this could be caused by the reinforcement of the subconscious response in the presence of such cues. The response to visual, tactile, audible and olfactory cues may also help explain the claim that dowsers are able to find waterpipes, because, in contrast to the test conditions in Randi's experiment in Italy, mentioned in Chapter 11, pipes may be buried but they are rarely deliberately hidden. The operation of chance plus the conditions under which water tends to exist in the ground plus the learned or inherited ablity to react to subconscious cues provides an adequate explanation for the apparent success of dowsing. But, and this is an enormous but, the existing evidence for the success of dowsers is largely hearsay, anecdote and dowsers' own opinions. Failures are rarely reported. In *Site and Survey Dowsing* D.M. Lewis coments: 'There is noth ing that makes dowsing more suspect to the scientific world than the almost total absence of carefully described experimental or survey work, and results expressed in any quantitative form.'[11]

There may also be a psychological force at work on the dowser's clients. Digging a well takes a great deal of time, money and effort and I suspect that few people would want to go to that sort of outlay on a finger-in-the-wind bit of guesswork. Professional water-finders are expensive to hire and are often strangers to the locality. Far better not to rely on your own guesswork but to call in a well-respected local dowser. (A local man would, of course, have a better chance of finding water whether or not dowsing works as advertised.) The responsibility, therefore, is lifted from the shoulders of the person wanting the well.

And there is yet another twist to the story. In some US states, at least, when a successful well is dug it is necessary to lodge documents with the local authorities regarding how the water was found. As this is rather time-consuming, it is known that some well-diggers locate a likely spot, make their own tests and then call in a dowser. If water is found then the success is put down to him.[12] Dowsers being used by oil companies may actually make it easier for those companies to keep their own genuine geophysical methods secret. In some third world countries the registration of an oil-strike must include information on how the oil was found, information that might be of use to competitors.

Moving on to the finding of minerals, geologists searching for them will often look at plant-life, the colour of the ground, rock formations and so forth before making chemical tests to determine the presence or absence of the wanted mineral. As mentioned earlier, dowsing was brought to Britain by miners who used the sticks for locating veins of gold or tin. We already know that these folk were given to tall stories in order to protect their mines. An excellent way to get a good, surreptitious look at the ground, plant-life and rock formation is to wander around with a hazel twig. After all, if a would-be gold-miner sees you looking at a particular sort of plant and later sees you digging gold out of the ground nearby, then somebody is going to catch on to the fact that the presence of certain types of plant is associated with the presence of certain minerals. If you are carrying a rod and apparently concentrating on it entirely an observer will be looking at the rod, not at the ground. Your secret will be safe.

With archaeological dowsing one may well be dealing with similar subconscious cueing. Alan Arnold believes that some sites are too complex for this to be the case. He admits that working on sites does give a feel for what might be found and I suspect that the expectation of an archaeologist might show itself to the dowser in a way that neither is aware of.

Almost everyone must have marvelled at the aeriel photographs showing the outlines in a farmer's field of buildings that stood there many hundreds of years ago, but have long since gone. The sort of features that make these traces visible to the camera could well be detectable at ground-level, even though theoretically below the perceptual threshold. Despite Alan Arnold's objections, I think it is easy to underestimate the amount of subtle information that humans receive through their senses. Much of it is filtered out of our consciousness, so perhaps it can be retrieved by using dowsing-type methods.

The hard evidence for dowsing remains ambiguous. Ignoring the 'psychic arts' of map-dowsing and dowsing for 'health', which in my view properly fall under the heading of clairvoyance, there appears to be a good body of historical evidence to support the success of dowsers, which has far greater weight than that for any other 'paranormal' skill. Indeed, experts whom one would expect to be violently opposed to it certainly give it houseroom. However, if such a skill exists, it is not operable even under relaxed test conditions (by which I mean that the atmosphere, not the controls, are relaxed), the very conditions under which subconscious cueing is unlikely to be available.

At present, even if dowsers were more successful than chance predicted in their traditional skills of finding water, there would still be some considerable way to go before one could assume a psychic or paranormal cause. Would an apparently mechanistic solution rob dowsing of its undoubted magic? I think not. Whether the answer is magnetism, electricity or a subtle supersensitivity, in my view it would strengthen our appreciation of the planet on which we live and our interaction with it in a way that nebulous psychic powers would not.

PART THREE

TOWARDS AN ANTHROPOLOGY OF THE PARANORMAL

———————————————◆———————————————

13—◆—The Scientist's Quadrille

Orthodox scientists refuse to accept the reality of psychic phenomena because they fear the damage such acceptance might do to their own belief-system. Brian Inglis probably summed up the opinion of those unwilling to concede that scientists might be right in his introduction to the *Daily Mirror*'s 'Unknown factor' series: 'They [the scientists] cannot accept it because it conflicts with old, and now discredited, dogmas which lay down the laws of nature.'[1] In other words, if asked to define orthodox scientists, these same proponents will describe them as too hidebound by their own view of the way the world works to accept the greater reality of the psychic universe. This is a sterile, circular argument. It often seems that scientists who know their subject sufficiently well to be able to judge whether some psychic input is necessary to produce a given phenomenon are regarded as 'orthodox' and those working outside their own field are 'unorthodox'.

However, the whole matter of science and the paranormal raises important points about how we perceive science and scientists and how scientists perceive themselves. The common image of a scientist is of a cold, calculating, materialistic, logical, unemotional individual searching for the natural laws through purely materialistic, mechanistic avenues, with little time for the artistic, the poetic or the mystical. This is a pity, because it is an almost entirely false analysis. Albert Einstein wrote, 'There is no logical way to the discovery of these elemental laws....Here is only the way of intuition, which is helped by a feeling for the order lying behind the appearance.'[2] When his theories were first published, Einstein was criticised by churchmen, accused of being a charlatan, stealing ideas from Edgar Allan Poe, Mary Baker Eddy and even Thomas Aquinas, but not, by and large, by scientists. It was already known that Newtonian physics was inadequate and the aether theory, the assumption that the Earth moved through a static and invisible medium, was already redundant. Einstein doubted the reality of telepathy because it did not seem to obey the inverse square law, but within a decade and a half of the publication of his *General Theory of Relativity* he was beginning to feel like a reactionary. Like many great scientists before him, Einstein found that he could not keep up with developments in physics which owed their birth to his theories, and he never accepted quantum physics.[3]

As a personality, he hated fuss and had an almost pathological modesty. He was intimidated by butlers, hated hurting people's feelings and showed a contempt for money: he used a $1500 cheque from the Rockefeller Foundation as a bookmark and lost the book, he accepted only half his fee for a magazine article, saying, 'Do they think I am a prizefighter?' and turned down the gift of a Guarnerius violin valued at $33,000 because, although a competent violin player, he did not think he could do justice to such a fine instrument. He was kind, humanitarian, pacifistic. At least, most of the time. When sailing he became tough, autocratic and egotistical. When a painting which he had ordered to be removed was replaced he threw a tantrum. Einstein was also a militant Zionist who suggested, in the early 1930s, that conscientious objectors should be given a special dispensation allowing them to fight in any war against Hitler. For this he was eventually spurned by the pacifists. He was not quite the simple man often painted. He was not atypical of the scientific community. Above all, he was human.

So whatever happened to the cold, super-logical, unemotional, materialistic searcher after truth? Psychologist Nick Humphrey comments: 'There may be scientists who are cool, calculating, unemotional people, but they are not good scientists. If one looks at the life of any of the great scientists, from Charles Darwin to Einstein, one would find a poet behind it.'[4] The sort of imagination that makes a great scientist requires the same faculties common to artists, writers and others whose work is to look behind superficial appearances. 'Most science consists of making guesses about what might be there long before we have the evidence,' says Humphrey. This tremendous creative drive is ignored or denied by anti-science writers who see scientists in purely reductionist, even destructive terms. Yet there is an inherent mystical element in science which plays an important part in the formulation and acceptance of natural laws.

One of the measurements applied to scientific work is 'elegance'. You cannot get it out of a bottle and it is doubtful whether there really is an all-embracing definition. Elegance is a mixture of simplicity, 'rightness' and even beauty. Many scientific laws bear all the trademarks of mystical thought. A Buddhist may contemplate the sound of one hand clapping; a scientist can meditate on the rule that 'every action has an equal and opposite reaction'.

Intuition is an important element in science and scientists will come to a particular conclusion even when the experimental evidence is not there. Sometimes this leads them to 'improve' on their results, to introduce the 'fudge factor'. The fudge factor is more common than scientific papers would have one believe. It is the doctoring of data in order to preserve a prior judgement. A similar use is made of the phrase 'within the limits of experimental error' which can cover all eventualities, from a bottle-washer with a hangover to the laboratory roof falling in. We now know, for instance, that Mendel fiddled with his results in his research into heredity. He is forgiven for this because his theory actually worked and can be verified.

While the scientific literature may not admit the existence of anything outside the laboratory, scientists actually gather a far wider range of data than their experiments reveal. Archimedes did not discover the principle of displacement in his equivalent of a laboratory; he discovered it in a bath. This influx of information means that scientists may reach conclusions without being entirely sure why. But the traditions of science preclude a scientist from saying, 'I feel this may be the case. The evidence is not clear, but I have done a lot of work in this field.' Humphrey cites the case of Darwin, who had some inkling of what evolution involved and was prepared to overlook evidence against it. He came to an answer not merely without evidence, but actually against the evidence that existed at he time. Darwin actually came up with a largely correct theory as to how coral reefs were made even without ever having seen one. When he did see one, there was still no evidence that he was right, but he defied anyone to come up with a better story.

As is clear, the imaginary world of the science journal, in which facts are collected without preconceptions and conclusions drawn simply from the facts, does not really exist. Or, at least, it is not the way that great scientists work. Humphrey says:

> I think it is typical of great scientists that they puzzle away at surface phenomena until they have found a story which works. They then become wedded to that story because it makes such sense of the world to themselves and other people and then they are confronted by the problem that their story is not yet confirmed by the facts. In certain cases, sometimes positive ones like Mendel, sometimes in dangerous ones like Cyril Burt, they begin to distort the evidence and make it up.

This cheating is not necessarily a problem. No matter how good one scientist's experimental results are, unless they can be replicated by other workers in other laboratories they are not accepted into the main body of science.

So, while there has, in the past, been a degree of fraud in parapsychology, in this it is no different from any other field of study and experimentation. What makes parapsychology different is that experiments that do get positive results are often ambiguous and almost always irreproducible. This does not mean that those getting positive results are fiddling their figures. Reproducibility is an essential check on scientific work and leads to great problems, especially in dealing with scientists of the past.

While physical mediumship is still around today, it is a mere flicker of what it was when Oliver Lodge and others investigated it. We can no longer check on Lodge's work with mediums and no-one today is producing the regular, remarkable results obtained by him. Similarly, J.B. Rhine's remarkable results in ESP research seem to have been something that happened for a short while and then died away.[5] The numerous psychokinetic children who emerged during the mid-1970s with the growth of interest in metal-bending have now become a mere trickle.

It is rare for any genuine scientific discovery to be so time-dependent. Newton's first law of motion operates today just as well as it did a century or two centuries ago. Is it conceivable that such phenomena exist in any strength only at particular moments? After all, until about 1911 musk-flowers had a very sweet smell. In that year, for no apparent reason, musk-flowers in Britain lost their smell and within twelve months every one in the world had lost its smell. The flowers had lost the tiny hairs that produced the scent and there is no botanical or biochemical explanation for it. While some sort of mechanism can be postulated for such a change, perhaps an infection of some sort, there may be some link between this curiosity and the odd fact that once a substance has been crystallised in one laboratory it somehow becomes easier to do it in other laboratories.

These examples led Rupert Sheldrake to postulate the existence of a morphogenetic field in his theory of 'causative formation'. It is this field which makes a rabbit grow up to look like a rabbit and one salt crystal look like another.[6] According to this theory, the morphogenetic field not only lies behind the similarity in shape of things of the same class but also affects language and thinking skills. It is a sort of blueprint.

The most intriguing results of experiments to examine Sheldrake's hypothesis have been gleaned from tests using puzzle-pictures. At first, the pictures look like random blobs of black and white. Within the pattern, however, is a picture, say a cowboy on a horse. Once given that information it is almost impossible not to see the cowboy in the pattern. If Sheldrake's theory is correct it should be easier for one person or group to learn something once another person or group has learned it, even though there is no connection between them. To confirm this, one should be able to take two puzzle-pictures, let's call them A and B, and two groups of people. Both groups are exposed to the pictures and a poll is taken of the percentage of each group able to decode each picture. One of the pictures is now chosen as a target and its hidden subject revealed to one of the groups. The other picture remains a puzzle. The other group is then exposed to the two pictures and the percentage of those able to decode them is measured. The target picture should now be easier to decode because one group, which has no connection with the other, knows the answer. And that is what happens, almost. A number of experiments of this sort have been carried out and the effect predicted by Sheldrake actually occurs. But it seems limited to Europe.

There are many objections to Sheldrake's theory. Why doesn't everybody speak Chinese? How come Jews are not born circumcised? On the other hand, Sheldrake's hypothesis would provide a framework in which the paranormal could operate, and despite a number of problems that present themselves, it would appear that he is on to something. One should, however, be very cautious in assuming that remarkable results follow remarkable causes. There is much to be said for the philosophy which assumes that if, after examining all the evidence, one is left with a strange, weird, unlikely conclusion, the chances are that one does not have all the necessary evidence. There is always the possibility of a fly in the ointment. Anomalous results can prove very important indeed, although it takes a prepared mind to realise their importance, perhaps a touch of the scientist-as-artist.

A Russian endocrinologist, Andrew Nalbandov, was working on the problems associated with removing the pituitary gland from chickens, hypophysectomy, in the 1940s. Again and again his experimental birds died within a few weeks. Others working in the field had the same problem. Then, for no apparent reason, Nalbandov's chickens began to live longer, as many as 98 per cent survived for three weeks and many lived for six months. He assumed that the cause was an improvement in his surgical techniques and prepared for some long-term experiments. Then, once again, the chickens started dying, including those which had already survived for several months. His assumption had obviously been wrong. Disease and other factors were eliminated. Then came another period of long survival, again for no good reason.

The answer came when Nalbandov was driving home from a party at 2am, saw the laboratory lights were on and stopped to turn them off, assuming that a careless student had left them burning. A few nights later the lights were left on again. Nalbandov made enquiries and discovered that a substitute caretaker had left the lights on. It was his duty to ensure that all windows and doors were secured at night. The laboratory light-switches were at the opposite end to the door and he had left the lights burning so that he could find his way out. And the periods when the chickens survived coincided with the periods when the substitute caretaker was on duty. The explanation was that chickens kept in the dark did not eat and developed hypoglycaemia, from which they could not recover owing to their lack of pituitary glands. Those kept in the light did eat and thus did not develop the condition, so they survived.[7]

Fleming's discovery of penicillin is another example, even odder than is appreciated by some of those aware of the story. The account of a spore of Penicillium floating through an open window onto a dish of Staphylococcus culture is well known and almost certainly wrong. Fleming's window was hardly ever open and unlikely to have been so in the summer of 1928. Penicillium cannot act on mature bacteria, only on growing colonies. The only likely source of the contamination was another laboratory on the floor below, and only one of the strains of Penicillium being studied on that floor could have done the job. Attempts to replicate the precise conditions under which the initial discovery was made have failed to produce the same effect. That original contamination really was one-off.

When it comes to statistically-based work, odd results, even fantastically successful results, are virtually sure to occur. To give a simple example, let us say that 512 scientists carry out exactly the same guessing experiment. It might be a coin-guessing experiment where the odds are 50:50. One would expect half the experimenters to get above-average results. Those who got above-average scores, 256 of them, go on to carry out more tests to confirm their results. Half of them get below-average results, as predicted by probability, and give up the programme. Now there are 128 experimenters who have twice got better- than-average results. Again they repeat their experiments. Some sixty-four again get above-average results and these go on to further experimentation. Probability predicts that thirty-two experimenters will continue to get above-average results (the rest experiencing 'psi-missing') and we will assume that further experiments by this group show no psychic activity at work. Now there are sixteen experimenters, of whom half will get positive scores, the other eight getting confirmation of the psi-missing effect.

Eight experimenters set to work and this time four get positive results and go on to further experimentation. Finally there are two experimenters, one gets negative results, the other positive results.

This is the sort of result one would expect to get by chance alone, starting with 512 original experimenters. Now let's look at how it would have appeared to the experimenters themselves. Some 256 experimenters got no results and probably lost interest. A further 128 found that their initially promising results were due to chance and lost interest. At first, sixty-four experimenters got good results until psi-missing started to occur and their findings became ambiguous. A further thirty- two experimenters, after four trials, got confirmation of the fall-off effect frequently noted down the years. So did a further sixteen. Eight of the original experimenters now had glimmerings of hard statistical evidence and a further four confirmed their results with a slightly better score. Two experimenters achieved 80 per cent success, one experimenter had almost 100 per cent success and one had consistently good results all the way through.

The chances are that those who got negative results on the first trial and those who failed to replicate on the second trial will not report their findings. Even in mainstream scientific journals it can be difficult to publish negative findings and, in any case, they will probably have lost interest. So that excludes some 384 experimenters from the literature. Indeed, it is likely that those who carried out two successful trials before probability asserted itself will also not report, raising the figure to 448 unreported experiments. That leaves sixty-four experimenters with moderate to good reportable, even replicable, results. Those 'positive' results will be meaningless in any real sense but they will become part of the parapsychological literature as 'hard statistical evidence'. No-one will ever hear about the 448 experimenters who got nothing. When one realises that these experiments need not be connected in any way, other than having the same probabilities of positive and negative results, it is clear that statistical evidence needs to be treated very carefully indeed.

That example is deliberately simple, to illustrate the point. In practice, tests of significance are applied to determine just how important the observed statistical effects are. But if something like this is actually happening one would expect the literature to show a small number of experimenters reporting exceptionally good results and a larger number who experience the fading of psychic skills on the part of their subjects. And that is precisely what does appear to happen. If one looks at the responsible, rather than popular, literature, it is apparent that a tiny number of experimenters appear to be getting very evidential results and a greater number show just small positive results.

The problem with drawing conclusions from statistical data may simply be that no-one knows how many negative results there have been. So one would expect to find strong evidence for the paranormal in the literature even without the human factor.

Scientists are indubitably human, with all the quirks that this implies. Nick Humphrey cites the case of Charles Richet's work with Eva C.:

> [He] became so involved in his commitment to the work....It mattered to him so much, from the scientific-reputation point of view, and [he] wanted to believe in these events, he would help her to cheat, at the same time she was genuinely cheating him. A kind of mad involvement of two people was generated, neither knowing what was really true but both desperately anxious to believe that something might be true.

Potentially, the most important appointment in British parapsychology of recent years is that of Dr Robert Morris to the Koestler chair of parapsychology at Edinburgh, set up with the help of a £500,000 bequest in the will of writer Arthur Koestler. Dr Morris was formerly senior research assistant at the School of Computer and Information Science at Syracuse, where he worked on the interaction between humans and machines in which people seem to have odd good or bad runs of luck with mechanical equipment such as computers and telephones. He explains:

> We have been attempting to see whether or not there may be some so-called psychic component involved. We are well aware, from our knowledge of human factors in general, that sometimes people who seem to have bad luck with equipment are people who just don't read the instructions properly or who may scuff their feet when they cross the floor and build up a weak static charge which can set some equipment off.

What Morris and his co-workers have done is to introduce 'glitches', or sources of 'noise', into machines, which will occasionally cause the equipment to work well or poorly, and get subjects to concentrate on them. 'At present our research is still quite inconclusive,' he says.

Another area of research is popular literature: on examines old books and manuscripts on how to develop psychic talents in order to find the common thread which runs through the advice on offer, then tries to find out if it can be used to improve psychic abilities. 'It is an area that we are not ready yet to conclude anything from,' says Morris. 'We have some studies which have been completed and we have yet to find any set of procedures which, in our opinion, really accomplish this particular goal. We're still looking.' The sort of advice offered involves relaxation, vivid visual imagery, concentration and providing feed-back.

We find that when people participate in this kind of research, oftentimes they are not prepared for what it's like to participate in a study where we are really ruling out all of the alternative means of communications with your environment. We think that one of the things that may happen is that when people participate in such training courses they may, at least in part, be learning procedures for fooling themselves into thinking that they are more psychic. The more you start paying attention to your internal world the more chance you have of noticing a coincidence between your own impressions and what goes on around you. The more you start to look for coincidences, the more you start paying attention to things in the environment and attributing meaning to any correspondences you see between those events and what is going on inside your head, the more likely you are to say 'Well, I must be improving.

Morris believes that it is unwise for scientists publicly to commit themselves to an extreme opinion on as little evidence as there is available.

It seems to me likely that there is something new going on. I'm not inclined to favour one interpretation over another. I think it is a problem area involving lots of different disciplines that really deserves much more serious attention than it has received so far, and it's fine with me however the outcome of that research is.

If it turns out that there is nothing much new going on I think we'll still learn a lot of things about how people perceive the world around them.

If there is something new going on, then we'll learn whatever we learn from the research that we do.

To the outsider it often seems that the arguments within parapsychology resemble a conflict of faith rather than science.

I think it is important that people understand that parapsychology as such is not a belief system itself, it is an interdisciplinary problem area.

The philosophy I intend to have at Edinburgh is to be pursuing this area with vigour in what I hope are creative new ways, profiting from research that has been done in the past but avoiding such of the mistakes and pitfalls that have been made in the past. I'm not looking at the field as a source of data to fit into some sort of metaphysical viewpoint I already hold.

Morris hopes that his position at Edinburgh will enable him to encourage more international co-operation on the problem of the paranormal with the Para-psychological Association, which has members as far apart as the USA, Russia, China, Australia and Europe. He also feels that the very high standing of Edinburgh will enable the intellectual power of a large number of highly-expert researchers to be applied to parapsychology: 'Oftentimes this problem, or any other problem in science, can be pursued very intensely within one particular limited discipline and everybody who is involved with it is thinking like those folks think. It is better to have an interdisciplinary approach.'

Many believers in the paranormal, accustomed to a media diet of gee-whizz tales are surprised at just how little firm scientific evidence for the paranormal exists. Professor John Beloff, a trustee of the Koestler bequest and a parapsychologist, believes that while, progress is being made, there is still a long way to go:

> The trouble is that many people consider that before any scientific claims can be recognised and fully accepted by the scientific community one has got to be able to produce phenomena more or less on demand. That is a very stringent kind of requirement and not one that, with the very elusive phenomena with which we deal, can easily be met.

He compares parapsychology with psychology, rather than with the physical sciences. 'Very often it is not easy to replicate experiments in psychology,' he points out.

The psychic phenomena studied by Beloff and others can be broadly classified under two headings – ESP, the perception and transmission of information by non-physical means, and psychokinesis or telekinesis, influencing physical events by non-physical means.

> It would be hard to say whether the evidence for the one is any better than the other. Most people find it, perhaps, somewhat easier to accept ESP, they think that's something mental, something we could understand in terms of how the brain operates. They find it much harder, usually, to accept PK, which to many people looks much more like magic.
>
> But if you look at the experimental evidence, you will find there is not much to choose between them.

Beloff is particularly encouraged by research being carried out at Princeton University using an electronic random-number generator which the subject attempts to influence. He says: 'Over thousands and thousands of trials one can see a very definite build-up in a deviation from chance which would seem to indicate that a genuine effect is operating there, although it is a very, very slight one in any sort of absolute terms.'

On the ESP front, the most promising results, believes Beloff, come from the 'ganzfeld technique' in which receivers are blindfolded and white noise fed into their ears to prevent sensory leakage, while a sender tries to transmit a picture chosen at random. The receiver records his impressions and these are then compared with the pool of target pictures. 'This technique has very often proved effective in getting above- chance results,' says Beloff. Ganzfeld experiments seem to have provided the most convincing evidence so far for telepathy. Eysenck and Sargent comment: 'GZ [ganzfeld] works in that it does fairly consistently generate positive and strong ESP well above the chance level.'[8]

Charles Honorton of Princeton, who has been involved in ganzfeld work since the early 1970s, co-operated with Ray Hyman, a psychologist at the University of Oregon, in an appraisal of forty-two studies of such experiments carried out between 1974 and 1981. At face value 55 per cent of them showed evidence of psychic functioning. Hyman found that short run experiments tended to have a higher level of significance, which, he says, 'suggests a tendency to report studies with a small sample only if they have significant results'. He found also that when a pilot or exploratory series of trials produced noteworthy results they were sometimes treated as a trial proper, producing a retrospective bias. He claims that the chances of getting a significant result are four times as high as the experimenters had assumed and that there is a better-than-even chance of getting a positive result by chance alone. Other criticisms include inadequate randomising procedures, the possibility of feed-back to the experimental subject, inadequate documentation, poor security and bad statistical procedures. And there seems to be a correlation between the flaws and the levels of significance found in the experiments.[9] Honorton disputes much of Hyman's analysis but it does suggest that the ganzfeld experiments are less watertight than at first appears.

Another technique is to send one member of the team out to a randomly-chosen location while a receiver has to get impressions of the location. Someone else then compares the description with the site itself or with a photograph.
One significant problem for the experimenters with remote-viewing is making sure that the judges who compare the impressions with the locations can get no hint of which impressions belong to which locations. If this is not done, as David Marks and Richard Kamman showed, it can be all too easy for the correct pairings to be made.[10] Judges, of course, will insist that they ignore any such hints. Unfortunately, this is quite impossible for any human being to do.

Try the following yourself:
With hocked gems financing him
Our hero bravely defied all scornful laughter
That tried to prevent his scheme
Your eyes deceive he said
An egg not a table correctly typifies
This unexplored domain
Now three sturdy sisters sought proof
Forging along sometimes through calm vastness
Yet more often over turbulent peaks and valleys
Days became weeks
As many doubters spread fearful rumours
About the edge
At last from nowhere winged creatures appeared
Signifying momentous success

Now read this pusedo-poem, quoted by Marks and Kamman from Dooling and Lachman, again, but don't think about Christopher Columbus' discovery of America while you do so.

Like many other parapsychologists, Beloff has to accept on trust the evidence for the paranormal. He admits that his own experience has been:

Very frustrating. In the twenty years or so that I have been active in this field I have never got what I would consider to be sustainable results.

Every now and again we will get results from someone carrying out some tests which are significant by any normal statistical criteria, but until it is sufficiently sustainable [so] that we can actually demonstrate it to someone I never feel that we have achieved a satisfactory resolution.

Could it be, as some apologists for the lack of repeatable experiments insist, that he is a natural 'psi-depressor', someone whose presence dampens the operation of psychic faculties, the so-called 'experimenter affect'? According to Beloff:

This is something that parapsychologists in the last couple of decades have had to take seriously. It no longer looks, as it perhaps did in the earlier days, that everything depended on having the right subjects to test. Now it is the whole situation, including the experimenter, that is perhaps part of the situation on which a positive outcome depends. Just as replication is difficult, this factor enters into the equation and makes it that much more difficult.

However, Beloff leaves most of his experiments to his more enthusiastic students, who do not have the same experience of frustration, and they, too, have failed to find sustainable effects.

All the same, Beloff's faith in the existence of paranormal phenomena remains as strong as it was twenty years ago.

I've never let it depend on my own personal experience. I would be enormously happy if I could witness some very powerful phenomenon that would really impress me and be a sort of anchor that I could reply upon. I've had to make up my mind about the reality of the phenomena on extensive reading of the literature.

Having done this I am convinced that there are a great many well-documented cases in the literature, some of them going a long way back, which have never been satisfactorily explained.

I would say that I have not wavered in my conviction that there are genuine phenomena of which science should take cognisance.

Beloff does not believe that the risk of being deceived by experimental subjects is as great as James Randi's Alpha Project might lead one to suppose, provided that the experiment is properly designed. He says:

In the old days when mediums used to insist on working in the dark and under their conditions then obviously the situation was wide open to all kinds of jiggery-pokery. In the type of laboratory experiment which is now the staple of the parapsychological laboratory I don't think there is a great deal of danger from subject deception.

No-one knows what the level of subject deception actually is, but Beloff is correct, provided the conditions of the experiments are adequately controlled. Unfortunately, it is not always possible to determine whether a particular control is adequate or not, as Eldon Byrd's work with Uri Geller on Nitinol illustrates.

Probably the severest shock to scientific parapsychology came when, in 1983, two psychics, Steve Shaw and Michael Edwards, who had been making something of a splash in the now-defunct McDonnell Laboratory in the USA admitted that for the previous two years they had been cheating. They had, in fact, been planted by magician James Randi.[11] The two young men had operated under apparently scientifically-controlled conditions. Their success was based on three factors: by throwing the occasional tantrum they were able to have the conditions of the experiments loosened, so that the experiments were no longer under the control of the scientists; if conditions were too tight to carry out the experiment asked for, they produced a different effect which would be accepted as 'paranormal'; and the experimenters had such a deep-seated need to believe that even something as simple as the image distortion produced by spitting on a camera lens would be accepted as 'paranormal'.

In fact, no experiment is fraud-proof and given sufficient time and determination no protocol is secure against a deceptive subject or a fraudulent investigator. But there are obvious precautions that should be taken. Experimental materials, for instance, need to be kept under tight control. If a psychic is to bend a key, only that key should be available and all other material should be removed. What does happen from time to time is that a laboratory ends up with various bits and pieces strewn about and, consequently, effectively uncontrolled. This seems to have been the case during John Hasted's studies of Uri Geller, for example. Each item of experimental material should be individually marked and whatever is used for the marking should be safely locked away. It should also be unique to that laboratory; Shaw and Edwards were able to duplicate a wax seal by going down to the local stationery store and buying a duplicate stamp. In the case of ganzfeld experiments it is vital that the recipient subjects have no access to the original target-pictures when making comparisons of their impressions. One of the basic assumptions of forensic science is that of transference, that something is always brought to the scene of a crime and something is always taken away. When an object or a picture is handled there is bound to be some trace of the handling left behind.

One should also ensure that observation of the subject is adequate at all times. In one experiment reported by J.B. Rhine regarding his first high-scoring subject, Linzmayer, the experiment took place with the two men seated next to each other in a car. Rhine placed a notebook on the lap of Linzmayer, who was looking at the roof of the vehicle, and took a deck of ESP cards from his own pocket. The deck of cards was cut, although not shuffled or mixed, and Rhine took the cards off the top, one by one, placing them on the notebook on Linzmayer's lap. Linzmayer scored fifteen correct in the first fifteen guesses.[12] To accept this trial as evidential one has to accept that Rhine was able to look at the card, check that Linzmayer was looking towards the roof, and make notes, all at the same time. It is one of the few trials with Linzmayer in which any inkling of the test conditions is given.

It is important that experimenters carefully note the precise conditions under which a test takes place, and how those conditions were themselves tested. The Targ and Puthoff work with Geller referred to in Chapter 1 is one example of where this has not been done and it is impossible to reconstruct the precise conditions under which it took place.

It is also important when reporting an experiment to mention in the results only those effects that the experiment was designed to test. If an experiment is designed to test whether a psychic can receive impressions of cards from a sender, it is not good science to search through the results for some other effect, for example, correctly guessing the card before or the card after the one being transmitted, then, if a correlation is found, to report that as the result. In a hypothetical test, for instance, the sender and transmitter are in different rooms. The sender looks at a card chosen at random and the receiver writes down his impression. After the trial the experimenter notices that the immediate results are no better than chance. On looking further, however, he discovers that the receiver has guessed the card after the one the sender was looking at more often than chance would suggest. Can he then report this as evidence of precognition? No, he cannot. The scientist must now design another experiment specifically to test for that effect.

If a psychic is trying to bend a spoon in one room and a computer goes haywire in another, it is not justifiable to report the effect on the computer as evidence of psychic functioning. The literature of the paranormal is chock-full of examples where this basic safeguard has been ignored.

One should also be wary of introducing assumptions which the experiment cannot test. Hearne, for instance, says in a survey of premonitions: 'The results tend not to support the following explanations of premonitions: chance – coincidence, the 'death wish' or 'psychobolie', and telepathy.'[13] But the survey was of claims of premonitions which were accepted at face-value without checking their veracity, so it can only tell us about the sort of people who make claims; it cannot refute any explanation. What Hearne's survey does show is that anecdotes tend, rightly or wrongly, to be reported in such a way as to eliminate the hypotheses which he mentions.

Ideally, of course, a researcher should ensure that each of these safeguards is in place during the experiment and is mentioned in the report of the results, and in an ideal world that is precisely what would happen. But even the best of scientists is far from perfect and it is not wise to assume anything that is not stated in the experimental paper. Unless the author specifically says that a particular safeguard was present or that the conditions of, say, sensory isolation were tested and how they were tested, it is not good science to assume that these things were so.

Another fly in the ointment can be the experimenters themselves. 'Once in a while you might get fraudulent experimenters who cook their results and it can take a long time before they are found out,' says Beloff. 'I don't think that is common either, but it has and can occur.' Indeed it can. The British researcher, S.G. Soal, whose work is still highly regarded by the less intellectually honest, fiddled with his results by changing a figure 1 to a figure 4 on score-sheets to produce above-average scores. The original sheets were 'lost' but the fraud was uncovered by a statistician, Betty Markwick, who realised that if Soal had done this, there would be too many 4s and not enough 1s in the score, which is what she found. The original random-number sequence used by Soal was located and helped confirm this evidence.

Melvin Harris shows another example of fraud by Soal in the Gordon Davis case.[14] Here, a medium, Blanche Cooper, gave messages from a Gordon Davis, who had died in the First World War. Soal reported his sittings with Blanche Cooper in 1925, although these had finished in 1922. Davis was, in fact, alive. But the mysterious thing was that the description of Davis's house that Soal gave in his paper was accurate. Unfortunately, the truth was that Gordon Davis lived close to Soal and Soal had altered the records of the sittings after checking out the house, which was within fifteen or twenty minutes walking-distance of his own. Soal's co-workers had even seen him fiddling the results but were kept quiet with threats of libel suits.

Only when fraudulent researchers are dead is it legally possible to expose their sins, a point worth keeping in mind when sceptics are accused of attacking those who can no longer defend themselves.

The fact that some evidence is remarkable is no proof of the fraudulence of that evidence, but sometimes one wonders. Films made by the SORRAT group in the USA, for instance, show objects moving and sometimes linking while sealed inside adapted fish-tanks. Although stills taken from the films seem impressive, the movies are strongly suggestive of something 'not quite right'. Objects are rarely seen moving during the exposure of a frame and they are clearly motionless in each frame, except for cases like partially-obscured balloons inflating. Any movement would result in blurring of the image. This means either that the objects accelerate at tremendous velocity from rest and stop dead in the forty-fifth of a second between frames or that the objects somehow teleport from place to place within the tank. This would produce the animated appearance of the films. Far more telling is that the cameras move slightly between each frame, producing a jumpy picture which is characteristic of amateur stop-action films and comes from the camera being locked off between shots.

Earlier, reference was made to the forensic concept of transference, and this would appear to be another example. In making a stop-action or animated film, a frame is shot, the scene before the camera is changed, another frame is shot and so on. The camera itself is kept still, 'locked-off', during the process. But unless an expensive camera-mount is used, each time the camera-shutter is triggered the camera itself moves slightly. These movements are exaggerated in the projected film and cause the scene to jump about. One has to ignore the internal evidence in order to accept the film as genuine.

Scientists traditionally take what outsiders believe to be a naive attitude; they are reluctant to believe that one or other of their number is dishonest. Because replication is so difficult and rare, ultimately one is left with having to trust individual researchers. This is, perhaps, the only area of science in which trust is so predominant and so much patching-up is needed to make the results acceptable. One excuse for the lack of replication is that subjects 'freeze up' when under controlled conditions, possibly because of the presence of the measuring equipment, no matter how sympathetic the researchers or how relaxed the atmosphere. Professor John Taylor comments: 'If that is the case, I can only say that it is not possible to use the methods of science.' This would mean that the paranormal can never be incorporated in the body of science and one is left with purely subjective knowledge. As Taylor points out:

> If you look at the way science has progressed, it has become very successful in explaining the way the universe works, down to very small distances, right inside the nucleus, to very large distances, out to the quasars and the beginning of the universe. That body of knowledge coheres so magnificently together, to suddenly say that there is a phenomenon that might only occur once or twice but yet destroys all that coherence, all that carefully built, elegantly architectured body of understanding, to throw that away because of this single phenomenon, would seem to be very inefficient.

If one is going to dump science and knowledge as it is, then it has to be replaced by something that not only explains the new phenomena but the old as well. Taylor believed that the only gap for the paranormal within the accepted body of scientific knowledge was within electromagnetic phenomena. One of his reasons for now being sceptical is that he discovered no trace of any electromagnetic effect at work. 'I can only conclude, with my scientific colleagues, that we stick to our science and the non-reproducible phenomena in the paranormal are either a complete illusion or are achieved by fraudulent methods,' he says.

Critics of those scientists who do not accept the paranormal often suggest that it is because the paranormal challenges their belief-systems. Paul Kurtz, chairman of the Committee for the Scientific Investigation of Claims of the Paranormal and a philosopher at the State University of New York, believes this is wrong.

Science, of all the areas of enquiry, is most open to new hypotheses, new ideas. The whole history of science is that it is constantly being revised.

It is one thing having an idea based on pure speculation and another to have one based on evidence. So the scientist insists that if you are going to make a claim, however revolutionary it might be, then support it by proof, by evidence in the laboratory, by supporting reasons. The paranormal does not meet the test of any science, you need replicable experiments.'

In many ways the most serious objection to the acceptance of psychic functioning within science as a whole arises because of the concept of falsifiability.

In the simplest terms, this concept teaches that if an idea cannot be proven wrong it is not scientific. It might be, for instance, that every time you open this book a small green elf in gumboots and top hat appears behind your back. However, if you turn round to look at him, he will run away and hide. He is also camera-shy. There is no way that you can demonstrate that the elf does not exist, any more than you can prove that winged horses or Santa Claus do not exist. You can hypothesise that the elf is there, but you can never prove it is not, and you can, if you wish, believe in its existence.

The sad fact is that after a century of hard investigation, millions of man-hours and not a little – though never quite enough – money, science is as far from finding solutions as ever it was. Not one single factor has been determined under which a psychic effect came be produced reliably and in the absence of fraud.

There are, of course, many theories about the paranormal, but theories are two a penny. What matters is the ability to test them. It is rather like having an infinite number of sponge-cake recipes without having the flour, eggs, sugar or oven to try them out. Without the means of testing them theories are useless. One might suppose, for instance, that ESP is carried out by invisible fairies capable of passing through walls and other solid objects. These fairies look at the target before the sender concentrates on it and fly to the receiver and whisper in his ear. This process goes on all the time. However, these fairies have bad memories. Many of the fairies have forgotten what the target was by the time they reach the receiver and, too shy to admit they've forgotten, they whisper the first thing they think of, which is why in the vast majority of experiments the results are no better than chance. A few fairies do have good memories and when these are at work the ESP score is high. Some fairies fly quite slowly and by the time they deliver the message the sender has already moved on to the next target, giving the impression that the receiver's correct guesses lag behind the sender's choice. Other, impatient, fairies grab a quick glimpse at the next target and fly as fast as they can, reaching the receiver before the sender has moved on to a target, thus making it seem that the receiver has precognitive powers.

The 'Tinkerbell' hypothesis explains all known ESP effects, including that of the psi-depressor – there are some people that this elfin crew just don't like, whether they believe in ESP or not. Unfortunately, it cannot be falsified. It is not, therefore, a scientific hypothesis. Indeed, there may be a case for saying that no hypothesis is scientific. The initial thrust of a theory generally comes not from logical deduction from observed data, as it should in classical science, but from flights of creative dreaming, sometimes literally, as in the case of Kekule's benzene rings, when the rational mind loosens its stays and the creative mind can run its fantastic cross-referencing system between unrelated data.

The part science plays is in the verification of the theory. What made Einstein such a great scientist was not so much that he thought up the theory of relativity, but that he also knew means of testing the theory. Indeed, at the time some of the experiments he proposed were not technically possible. Since then, they have been carried out and his theory has generally been found to work.

Alfred Russell Wallace developed the theory of evolution through natural selection, but it was Darwin who put in the hard work of demonstrating it.

It is important to ensure that the tests actually do tackle the phenomenon being investigated. Henri Becquerel believed that X-rays were the product of fluorescence produced by some substances when exposed to sunlight. To prove his point he wrapped a photographic plate in black paper, on top of which he placed a piece of metal with holes in it and some uranium compound. This he exposed to sunlight and, he thought, produced X-rays. When he examined the plate, sure enough, X-rays had been produced – so proving his point. Later Becquerel put the uranium into a drawer with some wrapped photographic plates and eventually discovered that the plates were fogged even without sunlight, and that led to the work of the Curies. Which leads on to the concept of the controlled experiment which so frightens psychics and many believers in the paranormal.

The term 'control' has come to indicate the dehumanisation of an experiment, the total exclusion of the human element. For the anti-scientists this is an ideal situation, yet, in the scientific context the term 'control' merely means isolating the specific effect one wants to look at. In most parapsychology experiments some form of randomising is used to choose targets. The reason for doing this is to control for the inevitable human tendency to choose certain numbers or designs more frequently than others.

Most people use some form of controlled experimentation at some time in their lives. If, for instance, the electric light goes off, you know that the causes are limited. There may have been a power-cut, the main fuse might have blown, a wire may be loose or the bulb might have 'gone'. First you look out of the window and see that the lights are on across the road, so you know that it is not a power-cut. Next you switch on electrical equipment on the same circuit as the light. If it works you know that a main fuse has not blown. Next you try a bulb from elsewhere which you know to be working. It lights up and you know that the cause was probably a broken bulb. At each point you have performed a controlled experiment.

In fact, what those who suggest that psi cannot operate under controlled conditions are saying, is that it can operate only under conditions in which other explanations are possible. Also, by implication, the operation of psi is indistinguishable from the operation of probability.

The most outspoken critic of parapsychology in Britain is probably Mark Hansel, emeritus professor of psychology at Swansea University:

Most of the major experiments in this country are known to have been fraudulent because people have admitted it. One pair, Smith and Blackburn, provided the main evidence for ESP for some 30 years before one of them wrote an article admitting fraud. Then we had the Soal experiments, which were extraordinary things because so much was kept dark about them in the reports, but eventually there was convincing evidence that he had committed fraud. He did further experiments with the Jones boys and was caught in the act.

In the early days, some very high odds were produced in ESP experiments, but in recent years the odds have reduced dramatically and, says Hansel, 'one is not so much concerned with fraud at the present time'. He is critical of the ganzfeld experiments:

I've only seen one of the reports in this country. It is such a pitifully-designed experiment, it should never even have got into publication. It doesn't help parapsychologists when they produce this sort of data.

The results of these experiments are so slight that unless the experimenters produce something a bit more substantial and produce their reports more carefully written, and their experiments better designed, there is very little point in going on with it.

Even many sceptics feel that Hansel's view is extreme. He says:

There is no point in having to do with experiments with the slightest weakness in the experimental design, the thing to do is throw it away. You can't throw the whole of physics away because of new phenomena which are based on experiments of that sort.

He points out the difficulty of publishing papers with negative results:

Some journals have even refused to publish them. If you get 50 per cent one way and 50 per cent the other there is no point going on, looking at those experiments. To confirm an effect you have got to have a demonstration which will almost invariably produce the same result...such a demonstration has never been provided. Parapsychologists have sought it for very many years, and after 100 years of research they are hardly likely to do so. They've tested every possible variation and nothing seems to emerge.

However, Hansel's own books on the paranormal[15] have been roundly criticised by Stevenson, Truzzi and others.[16] Despite the evident inaccuracies Hansel does show just how difficult it can be to get a fraud-proof experiment.

One aim of James Randi's Alpha Project was to try and encourage parapsychologists to seal up the sort of loopholes to which Hansel refers. John Hasted believes that the Randi hoax may have done parapsychology some good, but also a lot of harm.

They have created a great deal of polarisation in the world of studying the paranormal. Nobody now trusts anyone else.

You can carry that to a certain stage, but you cannot do science if colleagues do not trust each other. This is precisely what David Bohm and I said in our first *Nature* article when Geller first came to this laboratory – if this subject gets into the state that nobody trusts each other, advance will be impossible. And that, I believe, now is the case. The advances are not impressive at all. There is great mistrust and demoralisation.

He still defends the scientific method – double-blind trials and the like. 'Science must proceed in that way to try and eliminate the effect of the individual....We are not without fault, we are always catching each other out.' On the conflict between the scientists who do believe and those who do not, Hasted comments: 'The whole idea of a sceptic or a believer is a very unsatisfactory thing. We should try to eliminate sceptics and eliminate believers and just become scientists.' Amen to that.

Of his own, very controversial work he says:

I have often used the words 'with the eye of faith you can see a little bump here' and I leave it to the people who read the paper to decide whether they have the eye of faith or not, although I would not give an opinion. I may have an opinion but I would not put it in print.

While John Hasted is apparently fortunate enough to achieve frequent positive results, others are not so lucky, like Dr Sue Blackmore of the Brain and Perception Laboratory at Bristol University. Her examinations have taken her from belief to open-minded scepticism. She originally believed that ESP might provide solutions to another mystery, that of how memory is stored in the brain. She tried various experiments and subjects, including young children, all to no avail.

I would say that twelve years ago, when I first got involved, I was convinced there was ESP, I was sure that psychologists were idiots for not looking at it and were just bigoted and biased against it, that it held the solution to all our problems.

Very gradually I began to understand why they did not believe in it and my views have become more sceptical.

Like many believers-turned-sceptics Dr Blackmore went through a phase of complete and utter disbelief, but this, too, changed. 'Now I'm not sure. Now I feel there is evidence for ESP; it's very dodgy, there are a lot of problems with it, and I'm not convinced by it. Nevertheless, there is evidence and we cannot just ignore it.'

Parapsychology does have one singular achievement which no other area of scientific enquiry can claim. After a hundred years there has yet to be a single breakthrough. Maybe parapsychology is not a science at all, but a pseudo-science. Dr Blackmore disagrees:

I don't like the idea that you can demarcate things into science and pseudo-science, or science and not-science.

Generally speaking, parapsychology is a science, it sets out to ask questions and to carry out experiments to answer them, and that I think is the hallmark of a science, that you actually pay attention to the results.

Contrary to the teachings of the pro-paranormal lobby, it is not just the sceptics who, apparently, refuse to face facts. 'You could ask what sort of results might convince believers that there wasn't any ESP, and I think it's possible there are some people working in the field who, whatever their results, would never be convinced that there wasn't ESP.'

Of the repeatability problem she says:

You can argue that it is possible to carry on science without repeatability, but the problem is we don't know why there is no repeatability. Is it because psi is fickle and peculiar and doesn't 'want' to be found out? Is it because God's sitting up there and trying to trick us? Is it because we haven't discovered the relevant factors? Maybe the temperature of the room is important or maybe the position of the stars or some odd thing we haven't thought of. And we don't know what to do about it. Of course, maybe we haven't got repeatability because there is no psi. But we can't be sure of that either.

So is it still worth continuing? The answer is, undoubtedly, yes. First, there may be something, somewhere, that no-one is yet taking notice of, but which contains the key. Before Kepler, astronomy was seen mainly in terms of geometry and, it was believed, planets moved in circles. Kepler worked out the orbit of Mars and noted, to his consternation, a difference of 8 minutes of arc between the predicted and the theoretical position of the planet. For centuries that 8 minutes had been regarded as relatively unimportant and certainly within the limits of experimental error. Ultimately it led to the correct delineation of planetary orbits.

Even without the existence of ESP, research should continue. Blackmore says:

It is vitally important that we carry on with parapsychology, whether or not there are psychic phenomena. There is no doubt at all that people experience odd things: they think they have communicated with other people, that they have an experience of seeming to go out of the body and see it from a distance, that they have experiences in which they see other worlds and are quite convinced they are real. We don't understand those experiences. If we did we would be much closer to understanding the nature of the human mind. Psi, ESP, PK may or may not be involved in those things but the important thing is to study them.

Oddly, the sort of experiment that one would expect to give definitive evidence without question has had no impact at all on parapsychology. If, as its adherents believe, ESP is a built-in extra sense, a means of experiencing the environment and of communication, then the best place to look for it should be among those whose other senses are restricted. In the case of the blind, for instance, the usual human dependence on sight is thrown onto the other senses, so hearing, touch, taste ans smell become more acute. It would seem reasonable to suppose that if ESP exists, its use by the blind, and possibly the deaf and dumb, should increase. While sensory deprivation has been applied in the ganzfeld experiments, the subjects themselves were only temporarily robbed of their senses. ESP should be developed to a higher degree in those who are permanently handicapped. A negative result from testing those who are sense-handicapped would show that they do not have ESP to any greater extent than the rest of the population. It would also suggest that whatever ESP is, it probably is not a sense or means of communication. A positive result would prove that the sense-handicapped do have ESP to a greater degree, and that ESP exists. Such an experiment would require one less condition, at least, to be controlled, and would test a falsifiable hypothesis. The fact is, that the few experiments that have been done have had no influence whatsoever on parapsychology. Indeed, between March 1970 and April 1986 not one single paper concerning psychic functioning of the sense-handicapped appeared in the *Journal of the Society Phsychical Research.*

If we assume for the moment that ESP, PK or some other paranormal skill does exist and that a significant breakthrough is made, it is possible to identify some of the conditions that are likely to be present. It is almost certain that the individual or group involved will be younger than forty years old (most of those whose discoveries or inventions have changed our world have been under forty); the breakthrough will involve more than one scientific discipline and probably one not yet involved in the investigation of the paranormal (most breakthroughs involve some cross-fertilisation from fields outside those immediately concerned with them); the individual or group involved will be largely ignorant of the main scientific discipline involved and unaware that rules are being broken; the breakthrough will involve a simple, elegant solution, leading everyone else to say, 'Now, why didn't I think of that?'; it will take two to five years for the breakthrough to make its mark; and within the decade the knowledge of those who made the breakthrough will be outstripped by other developments.

It is very possible that professional scientists will not make the breakthrough. Parapsychology is one of the few 'problem areas' of science where the amateur enthusiast could still make a contribution.

And if there is no breakthrough? Well, we may not learn anything about the psychic, but we will learn an awful lot about ourselves.

14 ⋅ Faith and Fantasy

When I look at the scientific evidence for the paranormal, the sensation is rather like that of driving in a car full of people along a road beside a wall. Every now and then a hole appears in the brickwork and one can see a glimpse of the countryside beyond. But the holes are never in the same place twice and the countryside always looks different. And no-one else in the car can agree where the holes are or what the landscape beyond looks like.

On evidence like this it is difficult to understand quite why so many believe implicitly in psychic powers. But then, the belief is never a result of logical analysis, whether it is belief that the psychic dimension exists or that it does not. After all, how can one rationally deny the existence of psychic forces when it is impossible to demonstrate that they do not exist?

Perhaps those who suggest that 'science' cannot solve the problem of the paranormal are, in one way, correct. Most of us see science in terms of the hard sciences: physics and chemistry in their various incarnations, test-tubes, nuclear accelerators and the tremendous, thrusting, 'masculine' force of the rocket. These same sciences have failed to keep the promise imposed upon them. They have led to tremendous improvements in material standards of living and, despite the faith of the 'holistic' school, have tackled the health dangers of the past: smallpox, bubonic plague, cholera and typhoid. But poverty, unemployment and the arms race are still with us. Science has lost the public confidence that it had in the 1940s and 1950s. It has become increasingly clear that the solutions to our social problems will not be born in a test-tube. We are in the uncomfortable position of knowing that we must solve them ourselves. And that has led to the anti-science movement, and where science is put to one side, superstition and pseudo-science take over. This does not of itself explain belief in the paranormal, but it is certainly part of what we shall see is a very complex mix factors.

Sceptics often cite the gullibility of the media in their coverage of the paranormal as a cause for the high level of belief in things 'psychic'. While radio, television, newspapers and books do, indeed, present an overwhelmingly 'pro' view of the paranormal, it is as good a way as any of building up circulation (at least, so it is believed). The media tend to reflect public concerns and beliefs. They do not so much form opinions as legitimise and give currency to existing ones. This is not to deny the fact that public access to data critical of the paranormal is limited; it is. In

1982 I met George Dearsley of the *Daily Star* tabloid and spent four hours in a photographic studio with him and one of the newspaper's top photographers, Ken Lennox, exposing various pseudo-psychic techniques. The story was 'spiked'; although had I exposed the techniques of magician Paul Daniels, it was intimated, it would have been used.

Again, in 1985 my daughter and I were invited to the *Sunday People* by journalist John Deighton for an equally long session of photography, during which my six-year-old daughter visibly bent a 6in nail. Again, the story was spiked. Spiking a story is not, in itself, unusual. What I found unusual was that in both cases the entire sets of photographs taken simply vanished and apparently ceased to exist within days of being taken. After I had set forks and spoons bending and watches ticking throughout Britain during a Radio 2 'Nightride' programme I was telephoned by a journalist from the *Sun* newspaper. When I explained that there was nothing psychic about it, and it took several minutes to convince the journalist that this was so, all interest vanished. But all this is more likely to reinforce existing prejudices, rather than to form them in the first place. It is a symptom of uncritical faith in the paranormal, rather than a cause. There is, however, a more indirect way in which the media affect and promote belief in the paranormal.

Belief in the psychic dimension increases with a decrease in control of the environment, just as magic is a response to living in uncontrolled situations. Modern newspaper astrology, for instance, was born during the depression in America and the increasing political tension in Europe. As information about what is going on elsewhere in the world becomes more available, the more it becomes clear, given the news values applied by the western media, that the world is an unpredictable, uncomfortable place to live in. With the spread of this idea, belief in the paranormal has increases.

When faced with harder evidence than public opinion, sceptics will often fall back on an ill-defined 'will to believe'. One researcher in the USA, at least, is a scientologist. This cult, invented by the mad science-fiction writer, L. Ron Hubbard, believes, among other things, that its adherents can reach such an advanced stage of development that they can re-grow lost limbs and teeth and have total control over their bodies and environment.[1] For the sceptics this is sufficient proof that their data must be disregarded because their 'will to believe' would ensure that they got only positive results. The assumption is that a commitment to belief robs the individual of any critical faculties. If the phenomenon of belief in the paranormal is regarded in the light of this theoryit appears a poor, feeble thing, an inadequate, unproven assumption of dubious veracity. Just as many, if not more, exposures of fake mediums have been made by those with a committed belief in spiritualism as by sceptics. Just as many, if not more, scientists who are committed to the paranormal have got negative results.

John Beloff and other parapsychologists draw parallels between the problems of experiments in parapsychology that are difficult to replicate and those in psychology. Indeed, the more one looks at the failure of the hard sciences to handle the paranormal, the more it begins to feel like a problem of psychology, sociology or even anthropology, rather than physics. After all, what westernised observers refer to as paranormal phenomena have been known in every culture and in every age. The present attitude, which interprets these phenomena in terms of anomalous science, is extremely ethnocentric. In other cultures they are interpreted as being due to the action of spirits, an hypothesis which is equally justified in those cultures.

There are advantages in treating the paranormal as a problem of sociology, psychology or anthropology. First, the issue of whether or not the phenomena are 'real' in the objective sense is irrelevant. Second, it raises the possibility of including sceptics in the equation in a way that is far more productive than the sterile assumptions of Gertrude Schmeidler's Sheep – Goat effect, in which sceptics are said to score lower in ESP tests than believers,[2] or the psi- depressor effect. Including the hard-line sceptics, those committed to an anti-paranormal belief-system, is vital. They are part of the social mix in which pro-paranormal beliefs exist and so must have some bearing on it. Curiously, Blackmore and others have shown that sceptics actually are more rational than believers. But groups of sceptics will often use the same terminology as the believers, referring, for instance, to their 'cause' and 'preaching'.[3] And many have as mad a gleam in their eyes as have the fervent supporters of the most outrageous and nonsensical belief-systems.

Obviously, one should avoid too much drawing of parallels between the aspects of various cultures, but there are identical pressures affecting all societies, although their causes may be different. The pressure on an Ethiopian, dependent upon growing sorghum in order to feed himself and his family, who has his crops destroyed by drought is not far removed from that on the steel-worker in the Midlands who gets a redundancy notice and wonders how he is going to feed his family.

So far in this book I have concentrated on specific individuals and specific types of claim, and left aside the personal experiences which form the impressive body of anecdotal evidence that so many people find convincing. As we shall see, there are very special problems in determining the accuracy and reality of personal experience and placing it in context. All the same, many, many people, possibly the majority of the population, do have experiences which they categorise as being of a paranormal nature. There are also many people who provide and explain such experiences, mediums or psychics, and others who seek very hard to explain the experiences as something other than psychic or paranormal, the sceptics. Actually, today's use of the term scepticism is misleading in that it has come to mean total rejection of the psychic-power hypothesis, instead of an analytical approach which is dependent upon the questioning of evidence and the study of alternative hypotheses. There is a world of difference, however, between the approach of Professor Hansel and, say, Dr Sue Blackmore and myself. Since we have the terms Sheep, for those who believe in the paranormal, and Goats' for those who do not, maybe the rest of us should be termed PsIM – Piggies In the Middle.

Between 60 per cent and 80 per cent of the population believe in some aspect of the paranormal[4] many because of their own experiences. While there appears to be less actual commitment in Britain than in the USA, there seems to be a firm belief that is not justified by the experiences, which seem to others infrequent or trivial. Whether or not the source of the experience is faulty perception, fraud, coincidence or a genuine psychic force, something else is going on deep in the individual or collective psyche that is extremely important to ourselves and our society and that we scarcely understand, something that has a vital bearing on our relations with each other and our environment. If this were not so, one could reasonably expect to find a society somewhere in which there were no superstitions, no religions and no experiences classified as 'psychic' or spiritual. No such society exists. Blackley[5] nominates the communist bloc as such a society, but belief in the paranormal and the spiritual is certainly still there, judging by reports that continue to surface about psychic research in the USSR and China.

The way in which belief in the paranormal is expressed may be culturally determined, but belief itself seems to be universal, despite the feebleness of the evidence for its reality. To me this suggests the working of some very basic drive, almost a biological imperative. It may be that there is a need to believe that we can control our environment. After all, one of man's special skills is to control the environment in a manner which promotes survival. All living creatures depend on food-supply for survival and seasonal variations in supply threaten existence. By developing storage methods and cultivation, by acquiring an omnivorous diet – humans probably have a wider choice of food than any other creatures on Earth – mankind has established two survival mechanisms: the control of the food-supply and the ability to take advantage of edibles that are available.

Weather conditions affect wildlife viability, too much heat or cold, or rain or sun can destroy whole populations. While a variety of animals have acquired a degree of environmental control, like bees which control hive temperature and air flow and birds and ant species which build nests of various kinds, only humans have developed techniques by which they can survive and function in almost any conditions, from the sea-bottom to the airless voids of space. This success is approached only by bacteria, but even they have to become specialised, whereas humans do not. This too is another survival mechanism. In the Midlands or Ethiopia not only must the predictable threats to survival, like seasonal rains, be compensated for, but also the unpredictable ones.

If intelligence has a survival value, a premise which has yet to be proven, the value is in the facilities that it provides for controlling the environment. One might expect that a faculty of such importance would become something more than a learned response. The need to control may be as much a biological fact of life as breathing, eating and drinking. The 'need to control' hypothesis allows us to make certain predictions. Unfortunately, these have to be 'retrospective predictions' which rather robs them of their scientific validity and takes them dangerously close to pseudo-science. All the same, there are fascinating ramifications. A 'need to control' should lead to a mechanism by which humans seek to find order in apparently random events. They would then use that order to control the environment and to find the mechanisms underlying the way the world works, again with the aim of controlling the environment. There are such mechanisms: science and technology.

These mechanisms themselves should also lead to a tendency among humans to find ways of categorising and stereotyping the world around them, and, of course, they do just this, whether in the form of a collecting hobby or a study of, say, geology. In fact, all intelligence tests are aimed at determining the ability of the subject to detect order in an arrangement of numbers, drawings or words. With greater speed at making the correlations necessary to detect hidden order, and greater ability to detect hidden and distant correlations, the quotient of intelligence rises. The nature of intelligence is still a very controversial issue, but if one looks at how terms like 'gifted intelligence' and 'brilliant intelligence' are used, one finds that, almost without exception, one is talking about the ability to find a hidden order.

If the ability to make hidden order really is a measure of intelligence, then it might be supposed that the more intelligent a person is, the more likely he is to detect spurious relationships in random data. Even if this is not so, one would expect those who are especially good at finding order in confused data to find relationships in random data as well. As yet, there is no evidence for this that I can find. It does, however, suggest the possibility that people who report psychic experiences such as premonitions or believe they have personal proof that astrology works – evidence that could be an artifact of random data – should perform well in intelligence-test tasks involving finding a hidden order. There is no evidence that any sort of mental threshold exists beyond which one decides that an order is non-random, and it would be difficult to examine the problem of discrimination between 'genuine' and 'spurious' order. This is not to say that they can be expected actually to be more intelligent – intelligence is certainly a far more complex matter – but they should perform well in such tests and would probably be perceived by others as being of higher-than-average intelligence. Another part of the mechanism should be a drive to find out what is going on in the world, and that is called curiosity.

One could go on to find further parallels in, for instance, the very formation of a society or culture. This can be seen as another step in controlling the environment, of which society is a part, and enables its members to help each other achieve control both individually and as a group. Indeed, one could see the 'need to control' reflected in dictatorial regimes and the undoubted popularity of 'strong' leaders who, by proxy, promise control of the environment, and even in the 'socialist struggle' which may reflect the desire of a population to gain control.

Science and politics are mechanisms which provide humans with the ability to control much of their environment. But not everything can be controlled. What happens about aspects of the environment that remain random? This leads to the paranormal. Since that which is uncontrolled represents a threat to survival one would expect human beings to formulate mechanisms that apparently do control the uncontrollable, or at least remove the sense of threat and hence the stress. Without such a displacement for situations in which control is not possible, the individual would be unable to survive. Thus, belief in the paranormal becomes a survival mechanism. Unless we believe we can somehow control our environment, or have it controlled, for us, we would cease even to try and find a way to control it. The paranormal provides a framework, in which control, whether illusory or real, can be exerted. In other words, even if no evidence existed at all for the paranormal, the chances are that it would have been invented.

For some people, however, the paranormal represents an area of the 'unknown', a potential threat, in which case they would tend totally to reject it and to assume that those areas of knowledge in which control has not yet been achieved either do not exist or will eventually become controllable through advances in scientific knowledge. There is some evidence that this sort of thinking does occur. Dr Sue Blackmore[6] and others have shown that those who believe in the paranormal tend to overrate their influence on random events, as one would expect from people with a 'need to control' drive. The other side of the coin, that sceptics would tend to underrate their influence, when a degree of control is available in complex and apparently random events, has yet to be demonstrated. Blackmore's experiments suggested that sceptics were fairly accurate in assessing their performance, but as with any test that aims at examining the characteristics of sceptics there is the underlying problem of determining just how sceptical the subject is. One might expect, however, that faced with a situation in which a choice does affect the outcome, although there is no visible way in which it could do so, the sceptics would underestimate their success.

One might, for instance, secretly wire up a stand that holds five ESP cards so that when a card is removed a signal is sent to a computer. The computer generates pictures of the cards at random until the subject picks one up to concentrate fter a time-delay to allow the subject to concentrate, on. the signal from the stand then induces the computer, to alter its random picture-generation to increase the chances of the chosen picture being displayed. One can then carry out the same experiment again but give the subject a button to press. If sceptics really are more accurate in their assessment of success, there should be little difference between their assessment of success in the two tests. This would suggest that sceptics do not require the illusion of control, which is, in fact, suggested by the Blackmore paper. I would suggest, however, that sceptics might tend to assess their performance in the first test at about chance level. Blackmore's experiments show that sceptics have a better grasp of probability than believers. An interesting outcome of her work is that believers actually underrate their success, and she has a fascinating theory to account for it. In assessing success one takes what one believes to be the chance level and adds a factor to it. Believers tend to believe that their chances of success are low, so the baseline they work from is erroneously low to begin with.

Seen in the light of 'the need to control' it is perhaps less surprising that some very knowledgeable scientists, like Oliver Lodge and William Crookes, became involved in occult and paranormal beliefs. They, more than anyone else, can see the disorder underlying the apparent order of the universe. This process seems to have speeded up with the development of quantum physics which shows that the universe is even weirder and more unpredictable than anyone could hope to have thought. The 'need to control' hypothesis also goes some way towards explaining the burgeoning interest in the occult and the paranormal in increasingly technologically-sophisticated societies in the west. In the low-technology state, with little environmental-control ability, the cost of turning to the paranormal to acquire the sensation of control is small. Once the level of technology rises, and a greater level of control becomes possible and an even greater level seems to be promised, occult belief levels should drop, as indeed they appear to do, because there is little benefit to be gained and the cost to survival is high. But the more one knows about the world, the more one is forced to face its unpredictability, and since technology will fail to satisfy the need to impose predictablity, there will, inevitably, be some return to the use of paranormal methods of control. In addition, technology and science become increasingly complex and less accessible to the non-specialist, and since most of us are scientifically illiterate there is little perceived benefit in turning to technologies that we do not understand.

So far, we have been dealing with the more obvious aspects of the environment, but there is still one which has yet to be mentioned – our own minds and personalities. There are few things more unsettling than one's own or someone else's insanity. It implies a lack of control and an unpredictability that are usually thought of as 'dangerous'. So necessary is it to us to think of ourselves as predictable, controlled human beings, that we have developed the concept of a fixed personality. The existence of such a personality is very questionable; in fact, we seem to be far too complex for our own comfort. When faced with actions or thoughts or responses that do not appear to be congruent with this fixed personality, the cause is often ascribed to an outside agency. Even if we do not recognise that we are making this attribution, we still use the language of possession – 'I don't know what got into me' – thus maintaining the comfortable illusion of control.

As we shall see in the next chapter, there are clear links between the traditional approaches to possession and modern attitudes towards psychics, poltergeist infestations and, more obviously, mediumship. Perhaps it is not entirely coincidental that in spiritualist circles a synonym for 'spirit guide' is 'spirit control'.

15 ⟶ Madness, Mystics and Shamans

If the man or woman sitting next to you on a bus, or in a pub, suddenly asked, 'Do you know anyone called John, or Fred, or Bill, or May, or Anna, or Tony? Because a voice has just told me that everything will be all right,' you would, not unreasonably, doubt that person's sanity. If the same statement were made in a seance or during a psychic demonstration, your analysis would be entirely different. You may not believe in mediumship, but you are not likely to diagnose insanity.

Most mediums display symptoms that, in any other context, would be regarded as evidence of severe mental disturbance: hearing voices, seeing visions, speaking in tongues and the like. In a few cases there are characteristic symptoms of personality disorders, which can be regarded as such even allowing for the context in which they are displayed. This is particularly so with displays of paranoia, in which the psychic claims to be the victim of some dark plot and has his 'spies' looking into the background of those who are 'out to get' him, at the same time promising retribution through secret psychic or governmental authority, or even a secret army of supporters in high places – the same places from which their persecution is coming. One may find the CIA or the KGB, the perennials of the persecution complex, being cited as the movers behind sceptics and exposures, sometimes both organisations at the same time being both supporters and persecutors. This should not be confused with the milder form of apparent persecution mania displayed by enthusiastic promoters of the paranormal, who like to suggest that their particular beliefs are somehow 'unorthodox', and are being suppressed by the forces of orthodoxy. Since belief in the paranormal is so widespread it is difficult to see how it can be regarded as unorthodox. Such people often try to suggest that information that validates their beliefs is being suppressed. In fact, the evidence shows that paranormal beliefs and hypotheses are given enormous media coverage of a very supportive nature. This paranoia is not a sign of madness but of the romanticism of the believers, and is really propaganda aimed at reinforcing their beliefs. The perception of what is insanity is at least partially dependent upon the context in which the strange behaviour is exhibited. If the responses and actions are appropriate to the situation, they cease to be signs of unpredictable, uncontrollable madness to the observer and the 'sufferer'. By treating what would otherwise be regarded as signs of insanity as evidence of the psychic, they are placed in a 'safe' context, which then enables integration of the unpredictable personality into society and culture.

This sort of idea is not new; Lévi-Strauss has suggested similar theories.[1] Nor, however,is it adequate to explain the whole existence of psychics, mediums or, in other cultures, shamans. One objection is that shamans, psychics, and mediums generally, do not display their 'paranormality', or insanity, in the mundane portions of their day-to-day lives. There are no reports, for instance, of mediums going into trance in the bath. It may be that becoming a 'wonder-worker' enables the sufferer to limit the display of his abnormalities to a context in which they cease to be 'abnormal' and, indeed, become 'normal'. Clearly this would be of benefit to both the sufferer and the surrounding community. All the same, this is far too simple to apply to all. There are links much more common than personality disorders and which seem to apply to mediums and psychics throughout the world. A first parallel is that between the possession of paranormal powers and traditional attitudes towards possession by spirits. In both cases the powers or spirits are capricious; anyone may be visited, whatever their moral standing. Their actions are unpredictable, and while possessed, the 'sufferer', or possessor of psychic faculties, is not morally responsible. Another parallel is revealed by anthropologist Ioan Lewis' who writes of the female shamans of the Hausa Bori cults: 'A high proportion of those who become shamans are in fact either women past the menopause, or their barren sisters...[they] find in the shaman's role an exciting new career.'[2] In a society dominated by men, these women are regarded as 'half-men'.

If one looks at the roll-call of female mediums in Britain and in other western cultures, one also finds a predominance of post-menopausal and childless women. Female mediums seem to come almost exclusively from one or other of these two categories. In a number of issues of *Psychic News* of 1986, taken at random, I found 61 photographs of people with various psychic claims. A crude count showed that of these, 21 were women clearly post-menopausal, 20 were men older than 40, 7 were women either under 40 or of indeterminate age and the remainder were males under 40. Hearne's survey of premonition claims produced a mean age of 46.[3] While it is true that many of these reported having had premonitions at a much earlier age, what is of concern here is the age at which claims to psychic functioning were made.

However, there are other psychics and male mediums, so one needs something further to complete the picture. This piece of the jigsaw becomes apparent when one looks at shamans in other cultures. Among the Somalis of north-east Africa there is a belief in possession by Zar spirits. The sufferers are both men and women. In this male-dominated society the sufferers are poor, hard-working wives and males with low social dominance.[4] In the Bori cults, men who become possessed are almost exclusively foreigners with little social standing.[5] Further afield geographically, in Trinidad, the Shango cults involve women, unemployed labourers and domestic servants.[6] One can go back in time to a similar situation in the Greek cult of Dionysus. There are many other examples in the literature of anthropology and there is little point in over-egging the cake. The fact is that a very high proportion of shamans and the possessed come from those sections of society which are low down on the scale of social dominance.

Does the same apply to the western situation? One should look towards a working-class, dispossessed or poor background, or one in which the psychic or possessed person would normally be regarded as lower down on the social scale, and one finds it. While Doris Stokes and Doris Collins both fit into the mould of the post-menopausal medium, the David Smith from Glasgow – who has moved into the middle classes from a working-class background, Daniel Home – dispossessed of his family, Uri Geller – who as a Jew and from his personal history is twice an outsider, and Eusapia Palladino – an ill-educated working-class servant, are much as we should expect.

Of course, this could mean that psychic powers or possession by spirits – the latter with or without trance – affect the same sort of people throughout the world. Equally, it could indicate that possession and psychic powers offer a means of manipulation and dominance to those usually without access to it. It would be difficult to find a better means of manipulation or dominance than pretence to psychic powers. Those who are more overtly possessed, in the traditional sense, are not held responsible for their actions because it is not the sufferer who is the culprit but the possessing spirit. This enables the sufferer to make demands which, under any other circumstances, would be forbidden to them and to use language, and even abuse, that in a day-to-day context would lead to punishment or social ostracism. ('Why don't you fuck off?' screamed the Enfield poltergeist.) This actually has quite important ramifications when dealing with fraud among psychics. If psychic powers and possession are true equivalents separated only by cultural interpretation, then the psychic who uses fraudulent methods is not himself responsible; it is the fault of the pseudo-invasive personality. Few sceptics have looked at this possibility, being locked into the simple genuine – fraud equation. In effect, it means that when somebody like Uri Geller is caught cheating and denies it, he is, for all practical purposes, telling the truth.

As we have seen in this and the previous chapter, there are a number of social, cultural and possibly biological imperatives and dynamics which affect mankind throughout the world and which may lead to the development of belief in the paranormal, 'psychic powers' and even mediums, psychics and the like. These form a framework in which apparently paranormal or psychic experiences can occur. This framework does not require paranormal events for its formation and there is no need to suppose that psychic belief-systems, from the Ethiopian Zar cults to modern spiritualism, developed out of experiences triggered by genuine events.

But neither this nor the previous chapter should be taken in any way as suggesting that the hypotheses put forward effectively discount any need to explore whether or not psychic powers exist. That is an entirely different problem. What I have attempted to do is to explain why such a feeble effect (and after a century of failure to find it, it must be feeble) remains so tremendously important in the lves of individuals and their society. Just as it has been by and large a failure of parapsychology that it has not examined the social context of the psychic and the psychic experience, so it would be also a failure if one looked at the social context without considering the individual's experiences and the nature of perception.

16 — The Evidence of Experience

PARIS
IN THE
THE SPRING

It is a salesman's truism that once the potential customer experiences the benefits of the product or service on offer the sale is more than halfway made. The same applies to the paranormal – in general it is personal experience that appears to convince the believer. I say 'appears to convince' because despite the many claims by those convinced of the reality of psychic powers that they were highly sceptical before the event, it is far more difficult to assess scepticism than belief. It is more than likely that experiences confirm rather than convince.

For the sceptical, as opposed to us PsIMs, Piggies In the Middle, it is easy to dismiss the experience as due to belief and retort, 'You only had the experience because you wanted to have it.' This, of course, is simply the old 'will to believe' in another guise. The experience of the paranormal simply cannot be dismissed in this glib fashion. People do have very strong, meaningful, tremendously important experiences which they regard as psychic. It is in the nature of these experiences that they must be either inexplicable in terms of known science or, in the present day, explicable by reference to little-understood scientific phenomena like quantum physics or electromagnetism. Quite often this assumption of inexplicability rests on a certain level of scientific illiteracy, out-of-date scientific theories and the often appalling inadequacy of science education.

Bernassi and Singer note: '[Science is taught] as a set of facts and concepts to be learned by the same rote methods as used in other academic subjects.'[1] It is perhaps significant that one of today's most vociferous evangelists and apologists for the psychic, Brian Inglis, says: 'I was brought up to regard science almost as a religion ....We should take it for granted, much as we took Jesus's divinity for granted.'[2] When science is taught as a sort of catechism it is hardly surprising that when experience seems not to accord with received scientific facts the effect on the pupil is to make him eventually reject science. Imagine what might happen if someone educated in traditional multiplication table recitation came across a situation in which 2 x 2 did not equal 4. He might then feel that mathematics as a whole could not be trusted and that mathematicians were foolish for insisting that 2 x 2 was equal to 4. How could that person then decide how many pints of milk to order for the weekend? But under certain conditions, using different number bases, 2 x 2 is not equal to 4, and the mistrust would be based on an inadequate knowledge of mathematics.

When science is seen merely as a belief-system in which Newton's First Law of Gravity and Einstein's General Theory of Relativity are perceived as articles of faith on the same level as the Immaculate Conception, transubstantiation, the holiness of the literal word of the Koran and the uncleanliness of pig meat and prawns, then it is not surprising that the psychic experience becomes almost a religious one and leads to a conversion from trust in physical sciences to belief in the paranormal. No doubt there are scientists for whom 'scientific facts' are articles of faith. But science is not a belief-system on equal footing with Christianity, Spiritualism, Buddhism or Islam. It is a rolling roadshow of discovery, a process, a means of discovery, not the discoveries themselves.

Included in the tiny body of knowledge that we have about the way people think, is the fact that converting people from one set of extreme beliefs to another is easier than converting a middle-of-the-road wonderer. All that is required is that the new set of beliefs either performs the same function as the old or that the new set is more socially acceptable.[3] Undoubtedly, it is even easier when the substitute beliefs actually seem to perform their function better than the old. In Chinese *hsi nao* the subject is first shown the 'falsehood' of his existing beliefs. This is backed up with further 'evidence' until the subject does not know what to believe, and the new set of beliefs is then inculcated. Those old enough to remember the newsreel shots of 'confessions' and 'conversions' of American military personnel captured by the North Vietnamese forces during the Vietnam conflict may have wondered what was going on. Similar effects were noted in the earlier Korean War. In this case what had happened was that American military personnel were indoctrinated by their own officers into the belief that if captured they would be subjected to the most appalling atrocities by the godless yellow devils. When they were captured, however, they were greeted in the prison camp with a smile, a handshake and a cigarette and congratulated on escaping from capitalist bondage.[4] From the moment the prisoners arrived they were forced by their own experience to face the fact that what they had been taught was false. Then, through exposure to what was, in effect, social pressure and propaganda, they were gradually converted.

The process of conversion to faith in psychic powers follows the same lines. An initial experience, which may in itself be quite minor, causes the person to question the veracity of views he has assumed to be true. He may mention the event to others, who respond with further tales of paranormal experiences. Next, the person takes a greater interest in books and media reports about paranormal events. Since little critical appraisal is publicly available, the experience is seen as being normal and socially desirable. The process may go further and the person may join a group orientated towards psychic activities and, finally, become a 'psychic' or clairvoyant himself. Believers can be converted to extreme scepticism in the same way. In this case, however, since extreme scepticism receives little support, there tends to be a back-sliding towards a neutral view. This is certainly what happened in my own case, and in conversation with other PsIMs I have found many who began with an almost extreme belief in the paranormal, were converted to extreme scepticism, then settled into an attitude of: 'It's a problem area, maybe it's there, maybe it isn't, all the same it's fascinating and potentially important, so let's go on finding out more about it.'

This has an important bearing on why psychic experiences seem so important to the person involved. David Marks, an apparent PsIM and by no means an extreme sceptic, has found that believers in the paranormal tend to find it difficult to change their views.[5] What we do not know, of course, is whether it is people who believe who have difficulty changing their views or whether it is people who have difficulty changing their views who tend to believe in the paranormal. Given the paucity of real, hard-line sceptics it is difficult to determine which is true, if either, but I would tentatively suggest that both believers and extreme sceptics find it difficult to examine alternatives.

The perceived importance of an event that calls into question strongly-held existing assumptions will probably be artificially boosted. After all, there is the tale of the caterpillar who, when asked how he managed to walk and keep his many legs co-ordinated, became paralysed. While perhaps explaining the apparent importance of the experience, the foregoing does not explain the experience itself.

Given the ease with which an experience can remove trust in science as understood by the person involved, it is not surprising that many people feel safer trusting in intuition. It may indeed be that intuition is more accurate than chance. That does not necessarily mean that it is paranormal. Our senses collect a massive amount of data every living moment, far more than we are consciously aware of, and that extra material is filed away in memory, only accessible through techniques like hypnotism and meditation. Only immediately important material is consciously accessible.

As you read the following statement, count the number of Fs aloud, count once and read once only.

FINISHED FILES ARE THE
RESULT OF YEARS OF SCIEN-
TIFIC STUDY COMBINED WITH
THE EXPERIENCE OF YEARS

How many did you find? Three? Four? In fact there are six. What happened to the ones you missed? They must be inside your memory somewhere, you just did not consciously perceive them.

Given the brain's immense powers of cross-referencing and ability to find order, it would not be surprising to find that every once in a while a complex network of links between the various data should produce an intuition. While the intuition may surface into an upper consciousness there is no reason to suppose that the process by which that intuition was reached should be accessible through normal consciousness.

If you concentrate for a moment or two on the following list of words, you may get that sensation of intuition:

DELICATESSEN
BOTULISM
KINGLET
FIRM
DICKEY
HEBREW
CUDDY
BEGGAR
OFFICIOUS
ORDINARY

Like the example of pseudo-random poetry in Chapter 13, this list really is random, or at least as random as a computer can manage. Yet it seems to have some sort of order – the sort you cannot quite put your finger on, rather like intuition.

In normal, day-to-day life, we should expect intuition to be more accurate than conscious guesswork or chance, because chance 'hits' are added to true, sub-consciously determined 'hits'. Intuition certainly has helped science progress down the years and the literature of science history is full of examples. One difference between real scientists and pseudo-scientists is that the true scientist seeks to validate his intuition while the pseudo-scientist uses it to build untestable theories. The danger is that intuition can lead to false assumptions and pushing the mind into a rut, as P.C. Wason showed. He asked students to discover the rule by which a series of numbers was generated and gave them an example: 2,4,8. Typically the students would start generating series by multiplying by two. When told that their series obeyed the rule they went on to test the hypothesis by generating more series by multiplying by two. There they would stop and give the rule as 'even numbers being multiplied by two'. But they were wrong. The results of their trials confirmed their hypothesis, but the real rule was 'any ascending series of whole numbers'. The initial assumption was intuitive; testing falsely confirmed the intuition.

In the mid-1950s a number of experiments were carried out in which subjects were presented with pictures that started as unrecognisable blurs and were gradually brought into focus. It was found that subjects who made an erroneous identification early on found it more difficult to change their identification than subjects who made their decisions later in the focusing process.[6]

Here we have findings that have a significant bearing on eyewitness accounts of paranormal events. Intuitively we tend to see order in random data; we tend to test hypotheses in a way that confirms rather than questions them once a false assumption has been made we tend to stick to it despite later evidence; and believers tend to stick to their assumptions more than others. What we really need to know is whether believers tend to make early identification, true or false, of random or ambiguous data. Again, I am not aware of any experimental evidence for it, but I would offer it as a testable hypothesis.

A particularly interesting experiment in conditioning was carried out by the American psychologist, B.F. Skinner, an especially tortuous version of Pavlov's experiments with dogs. Animals like pigeons can be trained to react to a particular stimulus when rewarded with food. They can, for instance, be trained to peck at a button when a light goes on, receiving food in exchange for the peck. What happened when the food was given at random? A reinforcement mechanism took over; the pigeon would be doing something when food pellets fell, perhaps stretching its neck or airing its wings or preening its feathers. When the food appeared the bird would start to repeat the action more often, making it more likely that it would be doing the same thing the next time the food pellets arrived. This reinforced the bird's perceived link between the food and its action, and so it went on.[7] Skinner was left with a laboratory full of stretching, preening, wing-airing pigeons, all conditioned into what in human terms would be a superstition.

Let's take the hypothetical example of a gambler. In this scenario he might have been given a tie for his birthday. That evening he goes to the casino wearing the new tie and has a lucky night. He now has a lucky tie, so he starts to wear it more often when he goes to the casino and each lucky night is credited to the lucky tie, reinforcing the link between luck and the tie. Something similar may happen to mediums. Visiting large numbers of mediums, one is often struck by the similarity of the information given at their sittings. Nearly always one comes across references to 'someone involved in music', 'someone with lots of books around them', a death involving chest-pains, young and tragic deaths. When a medium begins a career there may be a tendency to give relatively random information. With time, those statements that are met with affirmatives by the sitter are likely to be repeated more often to other sitters and to be reinforced. Does this explain why the older a medium is, the more accurate, in my experience, they are perceived to be? Maybe this happens simply because they get better at mediumship as they get older. This is testable. 'New' mediums should make a wider variety of statements than those with more experience, if the hypothesis is correct. If the apparent increase in accuracy is due to better-developed medium-ship, the experienced mediums should give a wider variety of correct information. The same applies to astrologers and other fortune-tellers.

Methods of 'psychic training', as mentioned by Robert Morris in Chapter 13, tend to rely on techniques of relaxation and concentration on internal mental processes. The more notice one takes of these processes, the more meaningful they appear to become and the more one notices correlations with what is going on in the outside world, thus reinforcing a spurious link between the two. Another effect to come into play is selective memory, in which details that make an event seem less mysterious are forgotten or distorted. Targ and Puthoff's supposed 'one-way' communications device, discussed in Chapter 2, may be of this nature.

I once watched a performance by Uri Geller on television and next day asked several people what had happened. They told me tht Geller had taken a key, shown that it was straight and immediately started to rub the key until it bent. What actually happened, I confirmed later, was that Geller had shown the key to be straight and then, in full vision, hidden the key behind the attached key wallet for several seconds. After the key came back into view it was kept well obscured and indeed, as one watched, it was possible to see exactly how he handled the key to give the illusion of movement. The television company concerned, TV – am, refused to allow the technique to be explained to its viewers and has failed to respond to letters regarding its master-tapes of the broadcast. Perhaps it suffers from justifiable embarrassment.

Sometimes the memory is of an event that never occurred. Hearne's paper on premonitions[8] mentions Dorothy, a sixty-three-year-old, who submitted the follow-ing premonition:

> I dreamt I was with three horses that were being groomed. One was called Fats Waller, the other Duke Ellington, and the third Count Basie. The next morning I looked in the paper and saw that they were to run in a race that afternoon. I backed all three. Fats Waller came in first, Duke Ellington second, and Count Basie third. You can imagine my amazement.

But this race never happened. Two horses called Count Basie and Duke Ellington did race during the 1970s, according to bookmaker William Hill, but they never raced each other. I was unable to trace a Fats Waller, which means that if it existed it certainly was not racing at the same time as the other two horses. I would suggest that Dorothy was remembering a dream; she certainly was not remembering reality.

Not all cases of supposed precognition fall apart so easily, but obviously one must treat all such claims with the utmost caution , no matter how convinced the originator is of the truth of the story. However, there is sometimes reliable supporting evidence and there are cases in which there has been good confirmation that the precognition did occur before the event.

One of the best cases of premonition, the Brennan premonition of the Flixborough disaster, may be explicable in terms of both intuition and selective memory. Hearne's 1982 paper[9] brought the case to light. During a television screening of the film *The Nevadan* on 1 June 1974 a Cleethorpes housewife, Leslie Brennan, saw a newsflash about a chemical-plant explosion at Flixborough, twenty miles away. She was irritated at the interruption but remembered the story because it was local.[10] She told her family about the newsflash. Later that evening they watched the early evening news and thought that the reports about the explosion occurring at teatime were wrong because of the earlier newsflash. In fact the disaster happened at 4.53pm, twenty-eight people were killed and thirty-six were injured. The factory, which made highly-explosive Caprolactam was 'virtually demolished by an explosion of warlike dimensions'.[11]

Mrs Brennan's mid-day newsflash appeared on no other television. This 'vision' is not in itself remarkable; such hypnogogic or hypnopompic imagery is not unusual and may even be encouraged by the flickering of a television screen. The content does appear remarkable. So much so that the whole thing has been largely ignored by sceptics. What we have to decide is whether the information in the vision was unobtainable. Was there any source of information that might have led to the vision?

The Flixborough explosion occurred at a time when concern was already growing about the safety of chemical plants. As there was such a plant relatively close to Cleethorpes it may be that Mrs Brennan had become aware of fears about it, perhaps from an overheard but unremembered conversation. As it happened, there was a leak at the Flixborough plant on 27 March and it was shut down and alterations were made to it. Between 1 April and 29 May it was shut down twice more while an investigation into a loss of high-pressure nitrogen was carried out. On Wednesday 29 May the plant was shut down again and restarted on 1 June. Between 4am and 7am that day another leak was discovered but was not dealt with by the shift at the time because the necessary spark-proof tools were locked in a shed. That shift finished at 7am.

What we have, then, is a chemical plant, manufacturing a highly dangerous substance – the resulting explosion was estimated to be the equivalent of 15 to 45 tons of TNT – with a history of leaks, restarting after three days. Hence it cannot be remarkable that if any of this information had been available, knowingly or otherwise, to Mrs Brennan, it should have led to some form of intuitive apprehension that surfaced as her vision. It is probably impossible to determine today what information resources might have existed of which Mrs Brennan has no conscious knowledge, short of hypnosis. Cryptamnesia, as this 'unremembered remembering' is termed, has been implicated in several cases of supposed 'regression to previous lives'. A classic instance was that of a young Finnish girl who sang in medieval English under hypnosis. She had seen, just once and without being aware of it at the time, the words of 'Sumer is i-cumen in' in a book by Benjamin Britten. Mrs Brennan's 'premonition' may have been sparked off by information gathered and remembered this way.

One has two choices: either Mrs Brennan's vision was the result of established psychological quirks of memory that apply to us all, or it was a genuine premonition. In support of the psychological explanation is the fact that whether or not she was consciously aware of it at the time, there was cause for apprehension about Flixborough on the very day she had her vision, and the information was available in time for her to be in receipt of it through any number of mechanisms. That, though, is not the end of the matter. Mrs Brennan had her vision at around mid-day. On page 12 of the official report of the Flixborough Inquiry, in its account of the events of that dreadful Saturday, when 2000 houses were damaged, is this note: 'At about 11.30am to 12.00 noon the shift superintendent was out on the plant and the Process Control Technician (PCT) noticed that pressure had risen to the point where corrective action was necessary.'

There is evidence that our perception of ambiguous events is coloured by what we have been exposed to beforehand. Bruner and Minturn have shown that if subjects are given an ambiguous figure, partly like a B and partly like a figure 13, those subjects who have previously been shown numbers see it as a number while those previously shown letters see it as a letter.[12] Research by psychologists has shown that observers can accurately report characteristics that they are specifically asked to note but other characteristics tend to be ignored. When Dallanbach presented subjects with various coloured shapes and letters in groups he found that when the numbers of shapes or letters were asked for 80 per cent were reported correctly. When numbers and names of letters were asked for some 60 to 80 per cent were reported correctly. With numbers and shapes only 50 per cent were correctly reported and with numbers, colours and shapes a mere 30 per cent were correct.[13]

This implies that the more detail an eyewitness has to contend with, even when he knows what he is supposed to be looking for, the less accurate he is likely to be. What appears to be happening is that the same amount of total information is recalled but it is distributed more thinly with each task. It also suggests that the more detail an eyewitness recalls, the less accurate each detail is likely   We know all too little about the way we perceive our world and even less about how we process the information we receive through our senses. Of only one thing can we be sure – we cannot trust our own interpretations of what we see, hear or feel when faced with ambiguous data or events seen fleetingly for the first time. And we cannot trust our memories either to fill in the gaps or not to recycle old information into something new.

The work of S.J. Davey shows how unreliable even well-briefed observers are and how even shared experiences may be suspect. (See Chapter 4.) Sherif has shown that the perception of autokinetic movement, the apparent movement of a stationary light in a dark room, by an individual can depend on whether the person is alone or in a group.[14] Many other experiments have shown that group pressure seems to alter perceptions.[15] In practical terms, this means that if the people around you expect to see, say, metal-bending and believe that they are observing such a phenomenon, there is a strong possibility that you will be encouraged to perceive it happening. Coupled with the conjuring used to produce the effects you'd be hard put not to see it happening. For many, this assertion may seem as unlikely as the paranormal hypothesis itself. It makes more sense when one realises that what we 'see' is merely an interpretation of electrical signals, nothing more.

The closer one looks at how we perceive the world, the more one realises just how faulty those perceptions are. You might be wondering why this chapter began with the phrase 'PARIS IN THE SPRING'. Read it again and you'll find an extra THE which most people miss. The phrase 'Paris in the Spring' is so well known that in fact we do not read the whole thing but snatch bits of it and fill in the gaps with previous assumptions. We tend to do this with visual and auditory perceptions, too. In the case of visual 'filling in', as in that of mental, a false perception, or optical illusion, is produced. The brain is fooled into seeing something that it does not – stationary concentric rings start to move, the moon appears to get smaller as it rises, wire-frame boxes flip inside out. When we are presented with an optical illusion we are amused or entertained and we accept that our senses are fooling us. In a real-life situation we feel threatened by the idea that our day-to-day, dependable senses are unreliable, which explains why those who have observed paranormal events find it so difficult to consider the possibility of faulty perception.

An effect I have noticed, both personally and in others, is what might be termed 'the shock of revelation'. If one is shown a figure, say one of those that looks at first like a beautiful young woman, and one accepts that interpretation, there is a physical sensation of shock when the hag is pointed out and becomes clearly visible – and then one begins to oscillate between the two. This sense of shock is absent in the case of spacial illusions, like the line with arrows at the end which seems longer when the arrows are pointing outwards than the same line with the arrows pointing inwards. I don't think any research has examined this shock of revelation and its correlation with mystical experience. The illusion of visible 'metal-bending' produces such a shock – could it be that in this case the brain is actually misinterpreting the shock and turning it into a mystical experience?

So far I have discussed false and faulty perceptions and memories, but by no means can all paranormal events be disposed of by such labelling. In Chapter 12 I pointed out that archaeological features apparently invisible on the ground were often visible from the air and suggested that one element in the supposed success of archaeological dowsing might be that these features could be detected at ground-level. This would require us to be able to 'see' what we cannot perceive with the senses, and not be aware of it.

There are two effects to be considered: hyperaesthesia and subliminal perception. Hyperaesthesia is the heightening of the senses so that information that would normally be below the perceptual threshold is actually available to the perceiver. As we grow older our senses dull, but at a different rate for each person, so each of us has a different sensitivity to visual, audible and tactile stimuli – but hyperaesthesia goes beyond this.

In the early 1900s Gilbert Murray, who died in 1957, carried out some experiments in ESP in which he was in one room and the sender in a hallway, often with an open door between them. These experiments were successful. Most of the time the target was spoken aloud. When it was not, there were negative results. This is suggestive of a hyperacuity of hearing, especially since on at least one occasion Murray complained about noise coming from a milk-cart in the street next to the one in which the experiments were being carried out.[16] Many years later E.R. Dodds[17] found records of experiments carried out between 1920 and 1946, the latter when Murray was eighty years old, and he still seemed to be successful in perceiving the nature of statements made by others at a distance. Unfortunately nothing is known about the conditions under which the tests were done or the security arrangements to ensure that Murray did not simply listen at keyholes. That Murray was very respected and respectable is undoubted, but this is no reason to assume lack of fraud, and such an *ad hominem* argument is unacceptable.

Hyperacuity is an established phenomenon. If someone can hear a watch tick from a distance of 31ft, as Dingwall mentions, then it is certainly possible for another person to hear words spoken a few feet away. But hyperaesthesia is not necessary, because we can consciously detect information way below the normally-accepted threshold. For instance, when a series of shapes was projected on a screen at an intensity below which they would normally be perceived subjects were able to guess the shape more accurately than they would have been able to do by chance.[18] In another experiment a visible square was projected onto a series of lines which were below threshold for 0.25 seconds and the square was seen to be distorted, just as it would have been had the lines been projected normally.[19] It has also been found that subliminally presented words were produced by subjects more often than they would have been by chance. It was not always the presented word, but sometimes one somehow connected with it.[20]

In addition, there is evidence that motivation, emotion and stress all affect our perceptions, increasing our sensitivity to stimuli, both in normal and subliminal perceptions. And since psychic events seem often to be related to crises there may be a case for linking the apparent psychic event with the increase in perceptual sensitivity. There are apparently psychic events, usually extremely trivial, which cannot be explained by physical perceptions of which we are not aware. For many people it is 'knowing' that a telephone is going to ring and 'knowing' who is going to speak, or experiences like that, which convinces them.

In the previous chapter reference was made to Susan Blackmore's experiments which showed that believers in psychic powers overestimated their influence on random and part-random events. Her finding that believers tended to underrate their success suggests that they were underestimating the probabilities involved. A good example of this is the question of how many people you would need to invite to a party to have a 50:50 chance of two having the same birth day and month. Given the choice of 22, 43, and 98, most people, and most believers in psi, will go for the higher numbers, but statistically the answer is a mere 22. This is a hypothetical exercise but it does have relevance to our perception of the 'accuracy' of mediums with regard to dates. When a psychic or medium asks an audience something like: '18 November means something to somebody here, who is it?' the odds are pretty good that in any audience of more than twenty-two somebody will respond affirmatively, possibly several, making the mentioning of the date seem even more remarkable.

If a coin is tossed five times and comes up heads each time, what are the odds of it coming up heads the next time? The answer is 50:50, as it was on each of the previous five throws. It feels wrong, of course, but it is true, and the reason it feels wrong is that we confuse the odds related to a single throw with the odds on a series.

Luis W. Alvarez, a Nobel Prize physicist, was once surprised to read in a newspaper a phrase which reminded him of a friend he had not thought about for some thirty years and then to come across the obituary of that same friend a page or two later. He calculated the odds of thinking of a particular acquaintance within a five-minute period before learning of that person's death and concluded that, given the population of the USA, some 3000 such events should occur every year, about ten times a day. In the UK this would be 600 times a year and twice a day.[21]

Over, say, a thirty-year period some 90,000 people in the USA and 18,000 in the UK will have experienced a strange coincidence. In a fifty-five year period, an average human life-span minus our the first ten years of childhood, the figures will be 165,000 apparently meaningful coincidences in the USA and 33,000 in the UK. We all have parents and grandparents and any 'funny coincidences' that happen to them are likely to be retailed to us. So, by the time we are thirty-five, there would have been, say, fifty-five years' worth of experiences of our grandparents, a further fifty-five years of our parents and twenty-five years of ourselves, 135 years in all, during which some 405,000 strange coincidences would have happened in the USA and 81,000 in the UK. So the odds of us hearing about coincidences or experiencing them from our immediate family are getting pretty high. And if we add to that the experiences of our friends and what we read in newspapers, see on television and hear on the radio, it is highly unlikely that there is anyone alive who has not been exposed to an apparently 'paranormal' coincidence.

Our personal assessment of the chances of an event occurring depends on what that event is. If it is the failure of a nuclear reactor, supposedly once in ten million years, we are intuitively aware that it could happen in the first year, the ten millionth, or anywhere in between, and we feel very uncomfortable. If the event is the meeting of a friend you haven't seen for many years, that intuitively feels very unlikely. We prefer to ascribe the event to some sort of psychic working.

Some writers, like the late Arthur Koestler, sought to show that coincidences must be meaningful because the are so common.[22] Indeed, once one starts collecting coincidences they do appear to be common because they *are* common, but then, if one is collecting them one gets an unrepresentatively large sample. If the laws of probability are working properly, I can take a deck of cards, give it to somebody, say 'you will pick the two of clubs' and be right once in every fifty-two tries. If I do it only once to each person I'll end up with one person saying, 'Amazing, how did he know it would be that card out of fifty-two?' and the rest will not remember the trick in the first place. The successful subject is not aware of the failures.

Saying of an unusual coincidence, 'Well, that's the way it goes, just chance,' is deeply unsatisfying. By imputing some deeper meaning we give ourselves the comforting illusion that the universe is nicely ordered and controlled. Sceptics may protest that the illusion that random events are coincidences promotes an unreal world-view, and Skinner's experiment with pigeons mentioned earlier graphically demonstrates the dangers. Maybe instead of Sheep and Goats the term should be Pigeons and Goats. But in taking this attitude the sceptics are overlooking the survival value of interpreting our experiences in this way. Experiments with dogs have shown that when given a means of escape, dogs will try to avoid an electric shock. If subject to shocks when denied escape the dogs will, subsequently, accept their fate, i.e. being shocked, even when given a means of escape. Children who tend to give up on difficult tasks usually fail to link effort with outcome. When shown that they can affect outcome they try harder for longer. Extrapolation is a dangerous pastime but the above seems to mirror the attitudes noted by social-workers among families and individuals who believe that they have lost control of their lives. Indeed, I suspect most of us know some individual who moans and groans about a situation but does nothing to solve it, yet we, the outsiders, can see that if only they got their backsides into gear they could actually do something about it.

But while an illusion of control may help us maintain our psychological and sociological integrity in the face of truly uncontrolled situations, there is the danger that we will seek to use 'paranormal' controls in situations where it is not appropriate and even harmful. There is, for instance, a fashion today to suggest that PK can be used to stop weapons of war by diverting them or destroying them. If we believed this to be possible then we might be encouraged to give up talks on disarmament, proceed as before and simply try to 'think' the missiles out of existence when the conflict begins. Clearly this attitude is counter-productive in terms of survival. Psychic powers have been applied in attempts to stop wars. In the heady, days of the 1960s there was an attempt by hundreds of hippies to stop the Vietnam War by levitating the Pentagon to a height of 300ft, where it would vibrate, turn orange and disappear. It didn't work.

As in previous chapters, I must emphasise that this chapter should not be taken as a discounting of all apparently paranormal experiences. It is a warning that before we assume an event to be paranormal we have to ensure that none of the psychological, sociological and physical effects referred to are at work. Once we have filtered out such effects, we are left with two options: fraud and genuine psychic powers. In the next chapter we uncover the real secrets of psychic fraud.

PART FOUR

HOW TO BE PSYCHIC

17—·—How to be Psychic

The intellectual fraud of many writers about the paranormal is fairly easy to spot. For instance, any book that claims to take a balanced, impartial look at mediumship but contains no reference to M. Lamar Keene's *The Psychic Mafia* or to cold-reading can be assumed to be hiding something. Books about psychokinesis which exclude reference to techniques of misdirection should similarly be treated with considerable circumspection. And any book that makes claims about psychic effects and assures the reader that certain phenomena cannot be produced by a magician, without referring to one of the many textbooks for magicians on methods of misdirection, is not only being economical but positively parsimonious with the truth.

More interesting is psychic fraud, its methods and psychology. For a magician this presents a problem, because so many of the basic methods used by psychics are ones which conjurors use to earn an honest living, that to expose all would not be fair to fellow magicians. On the other hand, to keep all methods secret means that the magician has to fall back on the excuse, 'Well, I can do it so the psychics must be doing it, too,' which is not a logical assumption. Instead I have chosen what I hope is a middle way. For those open-minded enough to want to know more there are sources of information available that they can track down by a trip to a magic dealer or retailer. A specialist dealer worth knowing is 'Magic Books by Post'.

The only way to judge how effective fraud can be is to learn the techniques and experiment with them yourself. That was how I learnt to see through a combination of a quarter inch of bread dough, an aluminium foil blindfold and an over-the-head blindfold.

But this chapter is called 'How to be Psychic' and its aim is to reveal a few of the more important hints and tips that the would-be pseudo-psychic can use to improve his or her lot. Since so much is merely practical advice that they can try out for themselves, there is little to be gained by including all the references, as one would for a purely scholarly exercise.

When psychics are accused of fraud one often hears the defence: 'If he is so clever that thousands can be fooled, he could make millions on the stage as a magician.' The American specialist in pseudo-psychic effects, Robert A. Nelson, says in his autobiography:

> If I were twenty or thirty years younger and decided to enter the [mentalist]

profession, I would definitely proclaim myself a genuine psychic. Who is there to say whether I possess a sixth sense or not? Who can prove otherwise? I could create an image of a true 'mystic'. I would play the part to the fullest extent. I would then analyse the possibilities and set a definite goal based on financial returns. In my haste to 'get under way', I would seek as much exposure to the public as possible. I would seek a national TV guest appearance, after perfecting a suitable program.

Sadly, making a living out of magic is damned hard work. It takes tremendous talent and application, hours of practice and lots of luck. And it doesn't pay well even if you are good at your job. Why go through all that when a thirty-minute psychic reading can earn more than a ninety-minute show? Besides, as a psychic you are allowed to make mistakes; screw up the trick and it will be regarded as a sign that you must be genuine. But if you were a magician you'd get it right all the time, wouldn't you? And not many in your audience will have read the suggestion in dozens of technical books on mentalism, pseudo-psychic magic, that you should get things wrong occasionally because it makes the audience believe in you all the more. Even if you are caught cheating it will not matter. Simply accuse those who catch you of lying, or seeing what they want to see, or trying to bask in your reflected glory. What about really hard evidence of fraud, like video-tapes? Don't worry, they will not be seen too often and in any case only prove that when you were not caught you must have been demonstrating the real thing. You'll find that all sorts of coincidences over which you could have no control will be credited to you and you can challenge critics to reproduce the effect, safe in the knowledge that they cannot. Neither can you, but who notices?

During my time as a guest magician on Radio 2's 'Nightride' two policemen happened to be in the studio. I was to perform some metal-bending under the watchful eye of presenter Bill Rennells. I was searched by the policemen prior to the performance and at 1.30am, after the officers had left the studio, I bent and broke a fork and set forks and spoons bending and watches ticking throughout the country. At about 2am one of the policemen telephoned the studio in some excitement. His watch had stopped at precisely 1.30am, the exact moment when I was extending my 'psychic influence', and he was not even in the building. Who could replicate that?

You need not worry about being exposed by magicians. There are very few specialists in pseudo-psychic magic, fewer still have worked as a 'psychic' and even those who have cannot expose you adequately without revealing their own methods. Just because a magician can do the same thing under the same conditions, it does not prove that you are using the same methods. Besides, there are so may ways of producing a given conjuring effect that there are bound to be differences that you can emphasise to prove your point. If you do get caught bang to rights, fear not. Go quiet for a few months and start up again.

Don't get into direct confrontation with critics – you're above that sort of thing and the more they yell, the more publicity you'll get. Money need not be the major, or even minor, benefit to you as a pseudo-psychic. There is a tremendous 'buzz' to be had from fooling other people and having them running around proclaiming your amazing powers and building up your reputation. Remember, as they talk about you their tale will get more and more mysterious as they 'edit' the story at each telling.

It is a tremendous ego-boost to get the respect of the rich, the high and the mighty, who can be fooled as easily as the man in the street, if not more easily, and who'd not give you a second glance otherwise. And people's belief in your powers will enable you to manipulate and dominate them to an extent not usually possible for ordinary folk. Not the least advantage is the enormous sexual attraction the psychic acquires, particularly the younger ones. It was Henry Kissinger who said that power was the ultimate aphrodisiac, and psychics are a powerful bunch.

I don't want you to go out and start pretending to be psychic, but I'd like to provide you with sufficient information so that next time you are faced with someone claiming psychic powers you will be in a better position to judge the truth of the claim. Every one of the methods outlined is being used today and has been used in the past. It is not a comprehensive selection, for reasons stated earlier. You will not see many of them described in the average magic book as most are limited to the private diaries and notebooks of practitioners of what I regard as one of the highest forms of the conjuror's art, Mentalism.

THE INNER EYE

To some extent all of us really do read minds. We get information about others in several non-verbal ways. Often we are non-verbal ways. Often we are not really aware of how we get the information. The moment we meet somebody we know something about their social and cultural background. Are they coloured or white? How are they dressed? Are their fingernails clean? What sort of clothes do they wear? With this information we can get an idea of somebody's social and financial standing, make guesses about their background, how they like to be seen by others and their ambitions. Even the way they move can tell us something about their physical and mental health. Is the hair short or long? Dirty or clean? Dyed or natural? Are they married, engaged or widowed? Is a woman wearing her mother's or grandmother's wedding ring? Is she wearing a man's signet ring, often the sign of a widow? Clothes are very revealing – are they new or old? Expensive or cheap? Worn out or looked after?

The moment a client, a 'punter' or 'mark' in the jargon, opens his or her mouth they are giving data about their education and social background and, by the way they alter these, you can make some estimate of their aspirations. Within seconds one already has a tremendous amount of data, enough to start making guesses about life-style, probable history and the like. Indeed, much of the sort of data that so impresses the clients of mediums. In Chapter 5 I mentioned the bruised thumb of David Smith's father. That sort of detail is very evidential. Tone of voice and intonation provide information, too. If a client says: 'Put me in touch with my father,' an aggressive tone suggests a sceptical challenge, a pleading tone can be a desperate cry for help. How is the person responding to what you say? Do they lean back with arms folded, a sign of scepticism – the arms become a barrier – or are they leaning forward, wanting to know more? In this silent conversation we are gathering a vast amount of information and the more we use these skills, the better we get at them.

A good way to start developing a skill at reading people is to study strangers in the street, on buses or trains, anywhere and everywhere. Note the way they dress, take special notice of shoes and jewellery like finger rings, the way they move and hold themselves, think about where they might be going and why, construct a background story for them. You may not always be right and you certainly will not be able to check every time, but the practice will help develop your 'mediumship'.

The next technique to master is 'pumping' or fishing for information, using questions that sound like statements. Few people realise just how many questions the average 'medium' asks under the guise of confirmation. The reading might go something like this:

Psychic: I'm getting something about a car crash?
Client: Yes...my brother.
Psychic: Because he keeps talking about his shoulder, he's saying 'It doesn't half hurt.'
Client: He had head injuries.
Psychic: That's right, dear, his head and his shoulder are hurting. It was your brother, wasn't it?
Client: Yes, that's right.
Psychic: He's saying, 'I was a fool for not doing up my seatbelt.' He didn't do up his seatbelt did he?
Client: No, he didn't, that's right.
Psychic: Now we haven't met before, have we? I couldn't know that your brother had a crash unless I was really in contact with him, could I?

And if asked afterwards what the psychic actually said, the client will say: 'He told me that my brother had died in a car crash from head injuries because he didn't do up his seatbelt. And I didn't say anything at all.'

The trick is to listen to the answer and build on it. Why the hurting shoulder in the above example? Because seatbelts are compulsory in the UK and the impact of an accident frequently leads to bruised shoulders. When the client mentioned head injuries it was clear that the belt was not done up. And if there had been no accident? Simply say: 'There was something wrong with a car that might have caused an accident,' and if there is still no response, try, 'He's saying be careful, because there might be an accident.' After all, there is no time in the hereafter and it is easy for a spirit to get confused between past, present and future, isn't it? You will also notice how the 'psychic' in the example fed back information that was supplied by the client, an essential technique, and, with proper timing, very convincing. If you tend to interrupt the clients as they speak, they'll often forget what they said anyway. It is vital to get constant confirmation that you are correct. It doesn't actually matter what the clients are saying 'yes' to, as long as they say it a lot. They, and others, will not remember what was said, but they will remember saying 'yes' a lot, so you must have been giving lots of accurate information.

You do have to be careful. My wife, a believer in the paranormal, once went to a tarot reader while I was making a programme on the paranormal. Only she, the tarot reader and the tape-recorder where present. Listening to the recording later I noticed that she hardly uttered a word. When I asked why, she told me that she just wanted to find out how good the reader was. If you get a client like that, cut your losses and move on.

Another technique is the use of what I call 'specific generalisation'. This comes in two forms: people's concerns and personal data. Most of us tend to think that our problems are unique to us, but we have all had much the same sorts of experiences throughout our lives at about the same time – loving and losing, being ill, losing and winning money, and so on. There are crib sheets available that provide lists of the major concerns of different age groups. For instance, up to the age of twenty or twenty-five the main concerns are sex and relationships of different sorts. From then to the mid-thirties the concerns are mainly about jobs, money and the home. For the next ten years there is a shift towards worries about children's futures, parental health, rethinking careers and so on. From about forty- five onwards there are worries about personal health, one's own marriage, a desperation about the direction of one's life, concern about grandchildren and so forth.

Try it out for yourself by choosing someone of roughly the same age, social background and education and propose to read their palms, cards or whatever. Give them a general run-down on your own life-story, angled as though it was theirs and you'll be astonished at how 'accurate' you appear to be. There are some stock ploys to throw in like 'there was a major change in your life about two years ago' or 'you had problems coming to terms with your sexuality' or even 'there is an elderly woman in dark or black clothes and she is complaining about her legs'. Be sure to take account of the time of year. For female subjects you can talk about shopping in January and July, because of the sales, and in the spring months mention household decoration and textiles like carpets, curtains and towels. For more personal details you should mention operations – 'not necessarily yours', a member of the family with a 'nervous condition', a male dying with a painful chest complaint. Some fishing can narrow it down a bit; people dying or recently dead, strokes, dead children, smallish animals and so forth. Most of these should strike a chord. If you are wrong, don't worry. Tell your subject to go and talk to relatives, family and friends and they will confirm what you say. Whatever can be experienced by a human being will have been experienced by some member of the family.

To get names, try throwing out several, not too rare, like Ann, Mary, Joan, John, Arthur, Joseph, remembering that the further north you go the more traditional the names are likely to be. If none of them connect, suggest that they belong to someone sitting close to your client or wearing similar clothes, or simply fall back on 'are you quite sure?'. If it is said with enough conviction, few people will stand their ground and say no, the names definitely mean nothing to them or their family. You can use the same technique for surnames, too. Keep away from Smith, but you could try Williams, Willcox, Robinson or Clark, all common but not too common. And if you've sold tickets by post you should have a few names to use anyway.

Remember that people see order in randomness, and the more obscure something sounds, the deeper its meaning will appear to be. If pushed for inspiration try utter nonsense, it really sounds deeply meaningful and most clients will dig out something. Don't believe it? Try this: 'The circle that was open is now closed by the knot of life. All things have a natural attribution and the colours melting like dew.' Dip into the *I Ching* for a few meaningless phrases. At worst, try falling back on something like: 'He is saying he's getting a feeling that...things are coming to a head and you must be careful. Then, with as much hidden meaning as you can muster: 'You know what I'm talking about, don't you?' You'll soon start to develop the methods unconsciously and just about every magician I know who has dabbled in it, including the most famous, has started to believe his own balderdash at some time or other. Yes, even me.

There are many mediums and psychics who are using these methods, consciously or otherwise, as the examination of accurate transcripts shows. Don't take my word for it, go along yourself and listen to them working.

Several things will work in your favour. First, people will actively seek to make links between your 'statements' and events in their own lives. Second, they will assume that you know more than you actually do. Third, they will forget the incorrect guesses and remember only the correct ones – after all, they were saying 'yes' a lot, weren't they? Plus they have no interest in wrong information so it gets ignored. Fourth, when you are wrong the assumption will be that they themselves are at fault rather than you. If it turns out that an event you describe hasn't happened yet, it is because it lies in the future. If it doesn't happen at all, it's because you gave advance warning. You will note that it is actually possible to learn the foregoing techniques without being aware of it and to use them instinctively, believing that you yourself are genuine. The next few techniques are pure fraud.

The most important is foyer reconnaissance. At a public demonstration you, or an assistant, mixes with the early arrivals. They'll be keen to meet you and feel flattered by your attention. As you chat to them you are collating data from what they tell you and what you overhear. You are also watching what people take out of their bags when they present their tickets. Later on, before the big rush, you go backstage, out of sight, so that the later arrivals are not fully aware of what you've been doing. On stage you regurgitate some of the 'conned' information. People who arrive early will often be regular, keen visitors to other such performances and may know each other enough to talk to. What are they going to be talking about? Not the weather, that's for sure. They'll be discussing the sort of information they've been getting from other mediums – just the sort of data you or your assistant needs to overhear. At the same time, you're noting the women wearing men's signet rings – usually widows – and those wearing extra wedding rings. If the ring looks old enough it probably belonged to a mother or grandmother. Every little bit helps. And if there is a cloakroom, provide your own cloakroom attendant. It's interesting what people leave in their pockets.

You cannot refer to written notes on stage or in the sitting, so you'll need a memory system. You might, for instance, hear a woman in a black dress refer to a relative called Jack. By linking Jack and Black in your mind you'll find it easier to remember later. The problem comes when there is someone else around wearing a black dress. Your spirit guide can get confused.

Doris Stokes used such letters to their full advantage. I'm indebted to writer Ian Wilson for the information that Stokes would reserve the first three rows in theatres where she was performing. She would then offer free tickets for her 'sold-out' shows to people who had written to her revealing personal information. She would also contact others who had written in for tickets, quiz them, get information about them, and send them tickets from her personal stock. For a fuller account read Wilson's book, *The Afterlife Experience*, published by Sidgwick and jackson, 1987.

If the 'donations' are big enough or the client well known enough it might be worth hiring a private detective. These are much safer than assistants – it was Archie Roy's assistant who first exposed him. As private detectives need to impress their clients with their confidentiality and discretion, they dare not expose you. And as you become famous you'll pick up all sorts of gossip about other celebrities and be able to give them information that even they are unaware of.

So much for mediums, clairvoyants, astrologers and assorted fortune-tellers, for whom various permutations of the foregoing can provide fame, fortune, and a better-than-average income.

What about mind-reading?

THE INNER MIND

Generally speaking, mind-reading consists of discovering information that has been chosen by some form of random process: a word, a design, or even a situation. It is often known by the term ESP, extra-sensory perception, itself a misnomer.

In the presentation the material may either be apparently determined by the psychic before the choice is made, transmitted by the psychic to another person, transmitted by someone else to the psychic, or it may be determined after a choice is made. Whatever the effect only four principles are used.

First, the choice may be limited by physical or psychological means. An example of the first is the 'one-way' deck occasionally used by magicians, consisting of fifty-two identical cards. Psychological forces are best explained by practical examples. Ask someone to think of two geometrical shapes – not squares or oblongs because they are too obvious – to place one shape inside the other and to concentrate on them. Suggest that they are thinking of a triangle and a circle and most of the time you will be right. If you've drawn a triangle inside a circle design beforehand you'll be credited with a hit. (Ah, yes, you're the artistic one, you thought of the hexagon, it was the person behind you who had the circle, you know what psychic powers are like.)

Next, suggest thinking of a two-figure number. Both numbers must be odd, so 16 or 32 would be wrong but 17 or 19 would be okay. They must both be different, so 33 or 11 is out but 15 or 31 is okay. And make the number between 1 and 50. While they are thinking, write down 35, cross it out but leave it visible, and write 37. The latter is the number most often thought of out of the eight possible options (13, 15, 17, 19, 31, 35, 37, 39). Why cross out the 35? You'll impress the people that picked 35 and kept to it, those who picknged their mind, and those who picked 37. Believe it or not, these puzzles have been used by fake psychics as proof of their 'powers'.

Psychological forces take various forms. If you try making a number of drawings and 'transmitting' them to your 'mark', but fail to get an initial hit, you'll still get some idea of how your victim's mind works. If you start thinking, 'What would I now draw if I were in his shoes?' and draw what you come up with, you'll often get an impressive hit.

The second principle is to find out what the choice was at the moment it was made, either by using an assistant who can tell you or by ensuring that some mark is left on the experimental material, which you can later use to identify the choice. For instance, if a number of photographs are used an assistant can watch to see which one is chosen or he can check them later for finger-prints on the glaze.

Principle three is to determine the choice while it is being drawn or written down. An assistant can be used, or you can keep an eye on reflecting surfaces like a convenient mirror, window, metal or polished surface, spectacles, a watch face or a tiny reflector – a dental mirror does nicely – hidden in the hand or attached to a watchstrap. Another method is to get an impression. A varnished desk-top will nicely take an impression of something written on a piece of paper resting on it and sheets of paper underneath will also take an impression successfully. If you can't see the drawing or writing, try pencil-reading – watching the end of the drawing-instrument, or elbow-reading – more difficult but still useful, or even sound-reading – working out from the sounds made by the drawing-instrument on the paper. All have been and are being used with success.

A sneaky technique is to pretend to make a drawing which you will try to 'transmit' to your mark. You retain the pencil and paper in your lap as the mark draws a 'received' design. All attention will be on what your mark is doing, so you can get an idea of what his drawing looks like – you've already made yours so there is no need for him to hide his – and quickly and quietly do your real drawing. It should take only a couple of seconds to get an idea of what his picture will be and that is all you need. It is startlingly bold and because it is bold it works.

The fourth principle is to gain access to the material after it has been chosen and noted. An envelope containing a drawing can be held up against a lightbulb to get an idea of the contents, or it can be switched for a similar envelope, opened in privacy and switched back later, or a solvent can be applied – even water will do – to make the envelope transparent. Many more methods can be used – whole libraries have been written on these four principles and variations of them. The best methods are ones that you invent or re-invent yourself.

A MOVING EXPERIENCE

While psychokinesis, the movement or affecting of physical objects, tends to be lumped together with physical mediumship, by spiritualists, at least, the latter tends to operate in darkened rooms while the former is normally observed in full light, although this is by no means a hard and fast rule.

Methods for producing seance-room wonders have been well covered elsewhere in the sceptical and conjuror's literature, so there is little point in rehashing table-tipping (try putting your fingertips on a table and pushing forwards or pulling backwards, and a foot under a leg helps), levitation (in the dark? Who can tell. A well-timed flash photograph helps, too), spirit raps, manifestations and assorted fraudulence; but fake psychokinesis and telekinesis had less coverage.

Again, there is a limited number of principles to apply. You either use a motive force that is 'invisible' or one that leaves no trace afterwards. Invisible force is normally applied by air-movement, magnetism or static electricity. Each has its own use. Light objects such as ping-pong balls, cigarettes, pencils, cigar-tubes and the like can be moved by a simple blow. Don't blow directly, unless the mark is a photographer who is looking through his viewfinder – they never will learn to use fisheye lenses. Instead, blow in a short burst from a small distance. By the time the breath hits the object you can be looking away or even talking. A limited stunt? Not at all. The objects can be moved away from you or towards you, by blowing behind or slightly in front, or even from side to side if you direct the airflow with your hands. Theoretically this can be countered by putting the object under a glass dome, but James Randi's fake-psychics were able to arrange for a small unnoticed gap which enabled them to set a paper arrow spinning under such a dome. Do not underestimate simple lung-power.

Magnets can be used in a number of ways and hidden anywhere. You can move compass needles, affect watches in certain ways, move light ferrous-metal objects, even fritz computer tapes and disks. With care, even the most careful search, by the most sensitive instruments, will not find the 'gimmick'. And if you are really in trouble you can get an assistant to pass it to you after the search, or simply dump it and pick it up again later. Suitable magnets are available from magic dealers, gift shops – those magnetic note-fixers used for sticking paper onto fridges and other metal surfaces do nicely, and can even be found in executive toys. You'll also find suitable magnets in earphones and loudspeakers. Only the merest touch or close approach by you or your assistant to a magnetic tape or floppy disk will stop a computer in its tracks with ease. Not that computers take much stopping. The more complex the computer, the more often it crashes.

Static electricity is unreliable, but if you are working on a plastic surface in a dryish atmosphere a quick rub will get bits of paper balanced on needles whizzing around and similar light objects moving. Suitably handled, static will also blast a computer memory like a bolt of lightning – and you can pick up the necessary static charge from the VDU.

Under the second principle comes threadwork: using thread, nylon or even hair to move objects. I have several types of thread that you'd be hard put to see at a distance of inches. Once movement has been achieved (and you only have to start the movement, inertia will do the rest), the thread can be dropped on the floor and you are left 'clean'. A piece of thread can be stretched between the hands and used to move objects across smooth tables. If, like the famous Russian psychic, Nina Kulagina, one works on a lighted table even a heavy thread will be lost in the glare, especially on film and photographs. A few turns of thread around a bottle or any other object only need a sharp tug to send it flying across the room, and the thread comes loose – no evidence. Even simpler is muscle-power, as many children with a friendly poltergeist have discovered. Throw an object when backs are turned and look surprised and innocent and you'll be amazed what you can get away with. Objects can be thrown against a wall or window and appear to come from a direction from which they could not have been thrown. By hooking a foot under a chair you can cause furniture to move or overturn. By easing the foot upwards until the furniture begins to topple slowly you can be several steps away by the time it hits the floor and everyone notices it. You were nowhere near it. Similar techniques can be used with table lamps, telephones and other objects.

METAL-BENDING

Whole books have been written on this single subject and there are as many methods as there are people to try it and opportunities to do it, for effective metal-bending is a triumph of timing, misdirection, psychology and opportunism. Which is probably why children do it so well – a five-year-old can learn the basic principles.

The two-handed bend is the surest and easiest to start with:

1. Take your spoon or fork, not too hefty, at about waist-level and held at the extreme ends with thumbs on top and your other fingers opposite the thumbs on the underside. Now, using wrist action only – don't let it spread up to your arms or shoulders – press inwards and downwards. This gives you your bend.

2. Swivel the handle forward and hold it so that it is parallel to the floor, the hand holding it being palm downwards and the prongs or bowl bent up behind your thumb towards the palm. Let go with the other hand.

3. Rub the handle just in front of the thumb quite rapidly, slowly pull back with the thumb holding the spoon or fork and start angling the bent end upwards. This is the 'visible bending'.

4. Give spoon or fork out for examination.

These are the simple, physical steps but you will need some misdirection. At step 1 make some excuse for either you or your victim to move. 'I need to be near metal' is a good one. Do the bend on the move and it is difficult to spot even if someone is looking directly at it. Step 2 can be done at the same time and it helps enormously if your victims are moving.

Another technique is to press the spoon or fork against a table or chair as you get up to 'find some metal'. Practise the timing and the illusion will be perfect. Similar methods are used for keys. Strong hands help but you shouldn't look like Charles Atlas. Bends can also be done one-handed using the thumb.

The most important thing is to maintain pace and flow and talk, talk, talk. Nobody can listen to what you are saying, watch what you are doing and move, all at the same time, and observe accurately. Following exposure of the first bend you'll have plenty of opportunity to add a few extra tweaks in the excited moments that follow. Choose your moment and place well, at least until you gain confidence. Radio and television stations are ideal. They are pretty chaotic places at the best of times and the misdirection is so great you could almost produce an elephant. Wait for commercial breaks when broadcasting – everybody relaxes a little for those few seconds and the director or producer is often talking to the presenter.

Here is merely an apparent bend, to make things look at though they are really bending or continuing to bend visibly. Take your bent implement and hold it up so that it looks either straight or just a little bent, and twist it. I know it sounds silly, but it works a dream, especially with nails, letter-openers and the like, even when seen from a couple of feet away. I remember my then six-year-old daughter using a special variation of the above technique during a photo session for John Deighton of the *Sunday Mirror*. The nail 'bent' to 45 degrees, having been examined moments earlier. At the end of it Deighton said, 'Ah...could you straighten it out again so we can take the photographs again?'

It is possible to buy special equipment for metal-bending from magic suppliers but these are recommended only *in extremis*. As with any other trickery, try to avoid anything advertised in the conjuring press but do use their techniques.

Believe me, all you need to start you off in your new career as a world-famous psychic is in the foregoing few pages. To be really rich and famous you'll need some rich and famous admirers. Many of these people tend to be fairly vulnerable anyway, particularly those in show-business. Once you start operating and get mentioned in the psychic press, put on a few stage shows; they will tend to seek you out. If you are concentrating on being a fake medium you have life easy – you can claim to be in contact with deceased celebrities like John Lennon, Elvis Presley or anyone who takes your fancy. If you are lucky, and have a good act, you might try getting a job aboard Virgin Atlantic airlines which sometimes has fortune-tellers as live entertainment. There you should meet a few show-business personalities, and keep dropping names.

So long as you have the gift of the gab – try telling people to distrust you and they'll take to you all the more – you'll be invited to various functions to add atmosphere. In no time at all you should have a very creditable list of people around you. Even the odd Member of Parliament, and MPs can be very odd. Celebrities can be fooled as easily as anyone else. One or two scientists in your entourage will help – these can be picked up fairly easily – and if any of them spot your faking just threaten libel; the very thought of it makes them go white. There will always be one professor or doctor willing to support you, but keep clear of Edinburgh. If you get controversial you'll find the scientific crooks will come out of the woodwork.

Now all you need is the media.

THE MEDIA

All the media want is entertainment. They really don't care whether you're genuine or not, or about parapsychology.

Pick one or two convincing items that you perform well and claim that nobody can explain them. You can even get away with the schoolboy's five-finger lift as an example of levitation – the *Daily Mirror* fell for it, so why shouldn't anybody else? Develop an interesting story about yourself and invent some remarkable experiences. These do not have to be true because the chances of anyone actually checking your claims are pretty small. Even if they do, the story will be so old that the information will be spiked. Besides, editors are just as defensive about their preconceptions as anyone else. I once bent a key secretly for one who had been taken in and later checked to discover that he'd straightened it out! Even if the truth comes out, blame it all on negative attitudes, a plot to get you, and make some really incredible claims – not about what you have done but about what you are going to do, like photographing the dark side of the moon with an Instamatic or turning the Voyager space probe round and sending it back. The claims will be reported, the non-event will not.

Never get into direct confrontation, although it is a good practice to suggest that your accusers haven't the courage to meet you face to face.

It helps to get a literate friend to submit freelance articles to the popular national newspapers and local press. The nationals will rarely check. Or write the articles yourself under a fictitious name. You'll be amazed at what you can get away with. Don't forget that in television studios you'll be able to tell the directors where to put the cameras, and threaten to walk out if they don't do as you want. Few will dare risk a walk-out and none will think of sneaking in a camera behind you to see how it is all really done. They want their jobs as much as you want yours and if you've made the right friends – and you should collect a few senior executives from the media – you'll be able to pull considerable weight.

Develop your public charm glands, seem open, innocent and vulnerable, and few will have the courage to expose you. In any case, it really doesn't matter what they say about you, as long as they spell your name right and pay the appearance fees on time. All publicity is good publicity and their public is your public.

It might be argued that this chapter is cynical, but then so are the frauds. Frauds exist in non-western tribal societies and they exist in the sophisticated corridors of late-twentieth-century cities. It is your right to be fooled if you want to be. Equally, it is your right to know what really is going on, and everything in this chapter has happened and is happening now. By all means argue, but argue after you've tried it out for yourself.

EPILOGUE
The Blue Jay

The blue jay isn't. This is an easily established fact – take one blue jay feather, put it under a microscope and *voila!* No blue pigment. But the damned bird looks blue, for much the same reason as the sky looks blue. The feathers bounce the wavelengths of blue light back to the eye while allowing other wavelengths to pass through.

What has this to do with psychic powers or psi? Psychic power, or psi, is much the same as the colour of the blue jay. Overall it seems to be there, but look closely and it lacks the promised depth of colour. As the means of monitoring and investigating psychic phenomena have become more and more accurate and capable of seeing finer and finer detail, so the phenomena being investigated have dwindled in size. A century ago it began with 40lb tables flying around rooms, incredible materialisations capable of being medically examined and impossible messages. Today it is seeking out a tiny effect that might or might not be significant if a thousand people and an uncle get one extra guess right.

Not only do blue jays' feathers lose their colour when you look closer, but mirages disappear, too. It is tempting to say that there is no psi, except that psi is defined by what it isn't, as Dr Sue Blackmore has emphasised in her excellent autobiographical '*Adventures of a Parapsychologist*, published by Prometheus Books, 1986. Psi is the getting of information by non-sensory means, which makes it possible to design an experiment to prove that it does exist, but not one to prove that it doesn't. The sad thing is that parapsychologists today are still by and large doing the same experiments that Myers, Gurney and others were carrying out a century ago. With even less success. No chemist in the world is trying to isolate phlogiston, astronomers no longer draw complex circular orbits for the planets, today's architects no longer insist that pillars of concrete should look like palm trees because they would be stronger, yet parapsychologists continue along tramlines, constructing ever more complex experiments on the assumption that psi is there and all they need is a trustworthy, reliable experimental methodology.

Psi is not repeatable. But experience is, and that experience is much the same, whether or not the trigger for it is the result of apparently psychic powers or conjuring tricks and quirks of perception. Parapsychology has resolutely failed to produce any real knowledge about that phenomenon and there is an increasing disillusionment because of its stagnation. What is needed is a radical new approach to parapsychology. An approach in which scepticism or belief is irrelevant, in which fraud and false perception and self-deception become a true part of experimental study. It is no longer enough to go on collecting data and testing hypotheses as though psi were a 'thing', an effect with a single cause, which can be discovered. What the new parapsychology should be doing is once again asking questions about what it is trying to achieve and what it should be studying.

The search for psi will go on, but it is unlikely to progress any further in the next century than it has in the past hundred years. We should forget about psi. Instead we should concentrate on the experience itself. Why is it so important? What is happening psychologically and physiologically when the mind seems to leave the body? How can we generate these experiences ourselves? And what do they really mean to us? And why? We need a parapsychology without psi, without the blinkered vision of the past ten decades. One that can make a genuine and unquestioned contribution to our knowledge of ourselves and our relation with the universe in which we live. We can't see the colour of the blue jay by microscopic examination of its feathers, and we shan't discover the fundamentals of the psychic experience by twisting Zener cards, lying down with senses blotted out, or bending cutlery. Only by drawing back and studying the experience from the inside and the outside can parapsychology become a progressive field of study. It may be that the 'forbidden knowledge of what psi is all about is there, in front of our eyes, our inner eyes, right now. Unless parapsychologists have the courage to examine, and experiment with, that inner eye, the experience, parapsychology itself, will continue to languish like an ancient raft in the doldrums with its timbers rotting and becoming ever more waterlogged with each windless day – although it is true that parapsychology is not short of wind, it is just markedly bereft of motive power.

Or is that prospect a touch too unorthodox?

I wanted to finish this book with a deep, meaningful statement about why, after two decades of poking and prodding the paranormal, I'm still going on, feeling that same thrill of excitement when something seems to appear on the horizon. Instead, I'll leave the last word to a fictional character, David Morris, played by Frank Windsor in the BBC Radio 4 play 'The House at Spook Corner', about a fictional poltergeist case:

I've been looking at Spook Corner and things like it for twenty years now. Every single one of them just falls apart once you start looking at what's really going on, all the evidence for the real thing seems to be around the next corner.

So I go around the corner, and the one after that, and the next, and I'll keep doing it. Because one day maybe I'll walk around the right corner and there it will be.

Or maybe by then I'll be too old and decrepit to notice I've been there before.

It doesn't matter.

That's my hobgoblin, too. The thought that somewhere there is a crack in the mask of the real world and behind all the warts and pimples and halitosis there's something else...

There isn't that much difference between ignoring the monster and looking for the zips in the Godzilla suit.

NOTES

Introduction The Reluctant Sceptic

1. Rhine, J.B., *Extra-sensory Perception*, London: Faber, 1935. Also Rhine, *New Frontiers of the Mind*, London: Penguin Books, 1950.
2. *Proceedings of the Society for Psychical research*, 1882/3, I.
3. Blackburn, Douglas, *Daily News*, 1.9.11
4. Inglis, Brian,*The Paranormal*, London: Grafton Books, 1985.
5. correspondence, *Journal of the Society for Psychical Research*, 53 (802).
6. Hodgson, Richard, *Proceedings of the SPR*, 1892, VIII (XXII).

1 A Meeting with Uri Geller

1. Geller, Uri, *My Story*, London: Corgi, 1977.
2. Puharich, Andrija, *Uri*, London: W.H. Allen, 1974.
3. 'To Geller and back', 'Forbidden Knowledge', BBC Radio 4, 10.7.85.
4. Couttie, R.D., 'The magician and the Geller effect', Conference of the Society for Psychical Research, Cambridge, 7.9.86.
5. Randi, James, *The Magic of Uri Geller*, New York: Ballantine, 1975.
6. Delvin, Jack, *Delvin Deceptions*, author's publication, undated. Also Delvin, 'Face to face with Uri Geller', *Magic Circular*, 70 (769), 30.
7. Leslie, Leo, *Uri Geller*, Copenhagen: Samleres Forlag, 1974 (quoted in Panati, Charles (ed.), *The Geller Papers*, Boston: Houghton Mifflin, 1976).
8. Zorka, Arthur and Dickson, Abb, 'Official report', Society of American Magicians, Assembly 30, Atlanta, 1975 (quoted in Panati, *The Geller Papers*).
9. Herd, Richard, 'Uri's tricks by the folk who know him', *Daily Mail*, 15.1.74.
10. Fuller, Uriah, *Confessions of a Psychic*, New Jersey: Karl Fulves, 1975. Also anon, *The Secret Tricks of Bending Metal Objects*, San Francisco: Trade Winds Press, 1976. Also Harris, Ben, *Gellerism Revealed*, Alberta, Canada: Mickey Hades International, 1985.
11. Van Hatten, Margaret, 'A cost effective count of the spoons', *Financial Times*, 18.1.86.
12. *The Skeptic* 2.6.86, 6.
13. Hanlon, J., *New Scientist*, 17.10.74, 64, 919.
14. *Daily Mail*, 15.1.74.
15. Playfair, G.L. and Geller, U., *The Geller Effect*, London: Jonathan Cape, 1986.
16. Randi, *The Magic of Uri Geller*.
17. *Haolam Haze*, 20.2.74.
18. Randi, James, 'New evidence in the Uri Geller matter', in Frazier, Kendrick (ed.) *Paranormal Borderlands of Science*, New York: Promethus Books, 1981.

19. *Daily Mail*, 15.1.74.
20. Berendt, H.C., 'Uri Geller – pŗo and con', *Journal of the Society for Psychical Research*, 47 (762), 475 – 84.
21. Inglis, Brian, *The Hidden Power*, London: Jonathan Cape, 1986.
22. Puthoff, Harold E. and Targ, Russell, 'Information transmission under conditions of sensory shielding', *Nature* 18.10.74, 252 (5476), 602 – 7. Also Puthoff and Targ, 'The record: eight days with Uri Geller', in Panati, *The Geller Papers*, 55 – 9.
23. 'Experiments with Uri Geller', in Panati, *The Geller Papers* .
24. Hawke, Ronald S. 'Magnetic pattern erasure: a proposed method of scientific study', in Panati, *The Geller Papers*.
25. *New York Times*, 3.8.77.

2 The Evidence of Science

1. Freud, Mathew, *Radio Times*, 3.8.85.
2. Panati, Charles (ed.), *The Geller Papers*, Boston: Houghton Mifflin, 1976.
3. 'To Geller and back', 'Forbidden Knowledge', BBC Radio 4, 10.7.85.
4. Puthoff, Harold E. and Targ, Russell, 'Information transmission under conditions of sensory shielding', *Nature*, 252 (5476), 602 – 7, 18.10.74.
5. Randi, James, *The Magic of Uri Geller*, New York: Ballantine,1975. Also Randi, *Flim-Flam*, New York: Prometheus Books, 1982. Also Hansel, C.E.M., *ESP and Parapsychology – A Critical Re-Evaluation*, New York: Prometheus Books, 1980.
6. Puthoff, Harold E. and Targ, Russell, 'The record: eight days with Uri Geller, in Panati, *The Geller Papers*, 53–9.
7. Panati, *The Geller Papers*, 39.
8. ibid., 55.
9. Geller, Uri, *My Story*, London: Corgi, 1977, 237.
10. Panati, *The Geller Papers*, 58.
11. ibido, 42.
12. ibid., 66.
13. Wagner, Herbert J. and Jackson, Curtis M., 'Nitinol doesn't forget', *Battelle Research Outlook*, 2 (1), 18 – 20.
14. 'What you can do with that 'memory' alloy', *Materials Engineering*, October 1969. Also '60 Nitinol alloys', US Naval Ordnance Laboratory, White Oak, Maryland undated. Also Jackson, Curtis M. '55 - Nitinol – 'the alloy with a memory': its characteristics and potential applications in the natural gas industry'. Proceedings of the First Conference on Natural Gas Research and Technology, Institute of Gas Research and Technology and American Gas Association, Chicago, 1971.
15. Gardner, M., 'Geller, gulls and Nitinol', *The Humanist*, May/June 1977, 25 – 32.
16. Byrd, Eldon, 'Uri Geller's influence on the metal alloy Nitinol'. in Panati, *The Geller Papers*.
17. *Battelle Research Outlook*, 1970, 2 (1).
18. ibid. Wagner and Jackson actually say: 'You can use your little piece of wire at parties from now until doomsday, if you don't bend it sharply.' Also personal communication with Renate Siebrasse. She writes: 'Do not deform the wire more than about 6% in tension or in bending (outer fibre strain).'
19. Taylor, John, *Superminds*, New York: Warner Books, 1975. Also Taylor, *Science and the Supernatural*, New York: E.P. Dutton, 1980.
20. Hasted, John B., Bohm, David, Bastin, Edward, O'Regan and Brendan, 'Experiments on psychokinetic phenomena', *Nature*, 10.4.75, 254. Also Panati, *The Geller Papers*, 184 – 96.
21. Berendt, H.C., 'Uri Geller – pro and con, *Journal of the Society for Psychical Research*, 47 (762), 475 – 84.

22. Mackenzie, Andrew, review – '*Uri* by Andrija Puharich', *JSPR*, 47 (762) 515.
23. Geller, *My Story*, 86.
24. Welfare, Simon and Fairley, Peter, *Arthur C. Clarke's World of Strange Powers*, London: Collins, 1984, 11.
25. Sarfatti, Jack, *Science News*, 6.12.75.
26. Cox, William, 'On the issue of Uri Geller and his claims', in Panati, *The Geller Papers*, 151 – 6.
27. 'A preliminary scrutiny of Uri Geller', *Journal of Parapsychology*, December 1974, 38, 408 – 11.
28. Puharich, Andrija, *Uri*, London: W.H. Allen, 1974.

3 Medium-not-very-rare

1. 'Mediums and their message', 'Forbidden Knowledge', BBC Radio 4, 17.7.85.
2. *New York Times*, 27.2.26. Also 69th Congress, HR8989, 26.2.26 – 21.5.26.
3. Houdini, Harry and Dunniger, Joseph, *Magic and Mystery*, New York: Weathervane Books, 1967,28.
4. Charney, David, *Magic: The Great Illusions Revealed and Explained*, London: Robert Hale, 1976.
5. Dunniger, Joseph, *Inside the Medium's Cabinet*, New York: Kemp, 1935.
6. Doyle, Sir Arthur Conan, *The Edge of the Unknown*, London: Murray, 1930.
7. Gibson, Walter B., Houdini, H. and Young, Morris N., *Houdini on Magic*, New York: Dover, 1953.
8. 'Medium's and their message'. Also Inglis, Brian, *The Hidden Power*, London: Jonathan Cape, 1986.
9. Houdini, H., *A Magician among the Spirits*, New York, Harper, 1924; reprinted New York, Arnos Press, 1972.
10. Prince, Walter Franklin, *The Enchanted Boundary*, Boston, 1930; reprinted Salem, N.H.: Ayer Company, 1975.
11. Keene, M. Lamar, *The Psychic Mafia*, New York: St Martin's press, 1976.
12. Eysenck, Hans J. and Sargent, Carl, *Explaining the Unexplained*, London: Book Club Associates, 1982
13. Quoted by Lynn Picknett, in Brookesmith, Peter (ed.), *The Unexplained*, 1982, 2 (!&), 331.
14. Hall, Trevor H., *The Enigma of daniel Home*, New York: Prometheus Books, 1984.
15. Davies, Rev. C.M., *Mystic London*, London: Tinsley, 1875.
16. Quoted in Lamb, Geoffrey, *Victorian Magic*, London: Routledge and Kegan Paul, 1976, 59.
17. Sladek, John, *The New Apocrypha*, London: Panther, 1978.
18. Jarman, Archie, High jinks on a low level, in Edmunds, Simeon (ed.), *Spiritulasim: A Critical Survey*, London: Aquarian Press, 1966, 195 – 204.
19. Christopher, Milbourne, *The Illustrated History of Magic*, New York: Thomas Y. Cromwell, 1973.
20. *Journal of the Society for Psychical Research*, May 1903, 274 – 88 (quoted in Hall, *The Enigma of Daniel Home*).
21. 'Mediums and their message'.

4 Seance and Magic

1. Davey, S.J., Hodgson, R., 'The possibilities of mal-observation and lapse of memory from a practical point of view', *Proceedings of the Society for Psychical Research*, IV, 381 – 404.
2. Correspondence, *Journal of the Society for Psychical Research* March 1891.
3. Inglis, Brian, *The Hidden Power*, London: Jonathan Cape, 1986.

4. Hodgson, Richard, 'Mr Davey's imitations by conjuring of phenomena sometimes attributed to spirit agencies', *Proceedings of the SPR*, 1892, 253 – 310.
5. Besterman, Theodore, 'The psychology of testimony in relation to paraphysical phenomena', *Proceedings of the SPR*, 1932, 1363 – 87.

5 Mediums and their Message

1. Driscoll, Margaret, *Daily Mirror*, 16.6.83.
2. Foxcroft, Sydney and Murphy, Frank, 'The face of the Ripper', *The People*, 1.7.79.
3. 'The happy medium', '40 Minutes', BBC2, 8.11.84.
4. Kenny, Mary, 'Doris raises the spirits', *Daily Mail*, 9.11.84.
5. Recorded 'Forbidden Knowledge' interview.
6. Carr, Jean, 'Battle of the psychic superstars', *Sunday Mirror*, 12.5.85.
7. Dearsley, Linda and Stokes, Doris, *Voices in my Ear*, London: Futura, 1980.
8. Letter, 17.9.80.
9. Letter, 1.10.80.
10. Note from James Randi to Mike Hutchinson.
11. *Los Angeles Times*, 16.6.79.
12. ibid., 18.6.79.
13. ibid., 19.6.79.
14. ibid., 20.6.79.
15. *Psychic News*, 11.12.82.
16. Letter, 3.5.83.
17. Hutchinson, Diana, 'Is there anyone there?' *Daily Mail*,21.5.84.

6 Misdetection

1. Frazier, Kendrick and Randi, James, 'Prediction after the fact: lessons of the Tamara Rand hoax', *Skeptical Enquirer*, 6 (1), 4 – 7.
2. Art Petacque and Hugh Hough, quoted in MacDougall, Curtis D., *Superstition and the Press*, New York: Prometheus Books, 1983.
3. Harris, Melvin, *Sorry you've been duped!*, Weidenfeld and Nicolson, 1986.
4. Undated press handout.
5. Martin, Zak, 'ESP development course', promotional literature.
6. Taped interview with the author.
7. 'The unknown factor', *Daily Mirror*, 9.5.83 – 13.5.83.
8. Taped telephone interview.
9. Sladek, John, *The New Apocrypha*, London: Granada, 1974.
10. MacDougall, *Superstition and the Press*.
11. Hoebens, Piet Hein, 'Gerard Croiset: investigation of the Mozart of 'Psychic Sleuths', *Skeptical Enquirer*, 6 (1), 17 – 27.
12. Pollack, Jack Harrison, *Croiset the Clairvoyant*, New Nork: Doubleday, 1964.
13. Roosmalen, Th. van, 'Ervaringen met paranosten en die zich zo noemen', *Algemeen Politieblad*, 109, 3 – 9.
14. Brink, Filippus, 'Parapsychology and criminal investigation', *International Police Review*, January 1960, 134.
15. Brian Inglis, taped interview for 'Mediums and their message', 'Forbidden Knowledge', BBC Radio 4, 17.7.85.

7 The Psychic Playground

1. Doyle, Sir Arthur Conan, *The Coming of the Fairies*, London: Hodder and Stoughton, 1921.
2. 'Frances takes fairy photo secret to the spirit world', *Psychic News*, 26.7.86. 4.
3. 'The psychic playground', 'Forbidden Knowledge', BBC Radio 4, 24.7.85.
4. Randi, James, 'The Columbus poltergeist case', *Skeptical Enquirer*, 4. 3.
5. Allan, Schiff, *H. & G. Kramer: Falsche Geister, Echte Schwindler*, Hamburg: Zsolnay Verlag, 1969.
6. Hovelmann, Gerd H., personal communication, 12.5.86.
7. Bender, H., 'Der Rosenheimer Spuk – ein Fall spontaner Psychokinese. Ein vorläufiger Bericht', *Zeitschrift fur Parapsychologie und Grenzgebiete der Psychologie*, 1968, 11.
8. Bender, H., 'Spuk – Täuschungen und Tatsachen', in Bauer, E. and von Lucadou, E. (eds), *Psi – was verbirgt sich dahinter?*, Freiburg: Herder Verlag, 1984.
9. Playfair, Guy Lyon, *This House is Haunted*, London: Sphere Books, 1981.
10. Letter published in *Radio Times*.
11. John Hasted, in 'Forbidden Knowledge' interview.
12. Gregory, Anita, correspondence, *Journal of the Society for Psychical Research*, 52 (793), 95.

8 Starlight and Moonshine

1. 'Night lawyer, all things will be revealed, but when, is the question, *UK Press Gazette*, 25.12.84, 15. Also Dean, G. and Mather, A. (eds), *Recent Advances in Natal Astrology*, Western Australia: Analogic, 1977.
2. Frazier, Kendrick, 'CSICOP's call for a disclaimer on newspaper astrology columns', *Skeptical Enquirer*, 4 (3), 194 – 6.
3. Elliot Roger, 'Sun Day', 29.12.85.

9 History, Science and the Stars

1. Dean, G. and Mather, A. (eds), *Recent Advances in Natal Astrology*, Western Australia: Analogic, 1977.
2. Quoted in Morris, Ralph W., 'Moon madness no myth,' *Science Digest*, March 1981. Also Skolnick, A., 'Moon madness at *Science Digest*, *Skeptical Enquirer*, 5 (4), 7 – 8.
3. Sanduleak, N., 'The moon is acquitted of murder in Cleveland', *Skeptical Enquirer*, 9 (3), 236 – 42.
4. Lieber, A.L., *The Lunar Effect: Biological Tides and Human Emotions*, New York: Anchor Press/ Doubleday, 1978.
5. Pokorny, A.D., 'Moon phases, suicide and homicide', *American Journal of Psychiatry*, 1964, 121, 66 – 7. Also Pokorny, A.D. and Jachimezyk, J., 'The questionable relationship between homicides and the lunar cycle', *American Journal of Psychiatry*, 1974, 131, 827 – 9. Also Lester, D., 'Temporal variation in suicide and homicide', *American Journal of Epidemiology*, 1979, 109, 517 – 20.
6. Abell, G.O. and Greenspan, B., 'The moon and the maternity ward', *Skeptical Enquirer*, 3 (4), 17 – 25.
7. Andrews, E.J., 'The cyclic periodicity of postoperative hemorrhage', *Journal of the Florida Medical Association*, 1960, 45, 1362 – 6.
8. Menaker, W.D. and Menaker, A., 'Lunar periodicity in human reproduction: a likely unit of biological time', *American Journal of Obstetrics and Gynecology*, 1959, 77, 905 – 14. Also Menaker, W.D., 'Lunar periodicity with reference to live births', *American Journal of Obstetrics and Gynecology*, 1967, 98, 1002 – 4.

9. Osley, M., Summerville, D. and Borst, L.B., 'Natality and the moon', *American Journal of Obstetrics and Gynecology*, 1973, 117, 413 – 15.
10. Rippmann, E.T., 'The moon and the birth rate', *American Journal of Obstetrics and Gynecology*, 1957, 74, 148 – 50.

10 Does Astrology Work?

1. Arouri, James, 'The Houdini birth research committee's report', *Magico Magazine*, 1972.
2. Addey, J.M., 'Churchill's time of birth', *The Astrological Journal*, 9 (1), 2 – 4.
   A.P.N., 'Rectification of Queen Elizabeth II's birth chart', *Spica*, 4, 2 to 5, 2.
4. Randi, James, 'A small-scale test of an astrological claim, *Skeptical Enquirer*, 7, 4, 6 8
5. Ianna, Philip A. and Tolbert, Charles R. 'A retest of astrologer John McCall', *Skeptical Enquirer*, 9 (2), 167 – 270.
6. Clark, V. 'Experimental astrology', *Aquarian Agent*, 1 (9), 22 – 3.
7. Dean, G. and Mather, A. (eds) *Recent Advances in Natal Astrology*, Western Australia: Analogic, 1977.
8. Gauquelin, M., 'L'Astrologue pafe de l'IBM', *Science et Vie*, 611.
9. Snyder, C.R., Shenkel, R.J. and Lowery, C.R., 'Acceptance of personality interpretations', *Journal of Consulting and Clinical Psychology*, 45, 104 – 14.
10. Lackey, Douglas P. 'A controlled test of perceived horoscope accuracy', *Skeptical Enquirer*, 6 (1), 29 – 31.
11. Bastedo, Ralph W., 'An empirical test of popular astrology', in Frazier, Kendrick (ed.), *Paranormal Borderlines of Science*, New York: Prometheus Books, 1981, 241 – 62.
12. Gauquelin, M., 'Zodiac and personality: an empirical study', *Skeptical Enquirer*, 6 (3), 57 – 65.
13. Mayo, J., White, O. and Eysenck, H.J., 'An empirical study of the relation between astrological factors and personality', *Journal of Social Psychology*, 105, 229 – 36.
14. Kelly, I.W. and Saklofske, D.H., 'Alernative explanations in science: the extroversion – introversion astrological effect', *Skeptical Enquirer*, 5 (4), 33 – 7.
15. Eysenck, H.J., 'Astrology – science or superstition?', *Encounter*, December 1979.
16. Robinchaud, G. and Kent, C., 'Action time', 13.7.50 (quoted in MacDougall, Curtis D., *Superstition and the Press*, New York: Prometheus Books, 1983, 54).
17. Quoted by C.P. Tobey in *American Astrology*, June 1937, 30 – 1.
18. Silverman, B.I., 'Studies of astrology', *Journal of Psychology*, 1971, 77, 141 – 9.
19. Gauquelin, M., *Astrology and Science*, trans. J. Hughes, London: Mayflower, 1970.
20. McGervey, J.D., in Frazier, *Paranormal Borderlands of Science*.
21. Smithers, A., 'The *Guardian* astrology test', 19 – 22.3.84.
22. Wyatt, J., Posey, A., Welker, W. and Seamonds, C., 'Natural levels of similarities between identical twins and between unrelated people', *Skeptical Enquirer*, 1984, 9 (1), 62 – 6.
23. Gauquelin, M., *The Spheres of Destiny*, London: J.M. Dent, 1980.
24. *The Cosmic Clocks*, London: Paladin, 1973.
25. Rawlins, Dennis, 'Report on the US test of the Gauquelins' "Mars Effect"', *Skeptical Enquirer*, 4 (2), 26 – 31.
26. Gauquelin, M., 'The Mars Effect: a response from M. Gauquelin', *Skeptical Enquirer*, 4 (4), 58 – 62.
27. Rawlins, Dennis, 'sTarbaby', *Fate*, October 1981.
28. 'Remus extremus', Skeptical Enquirer, 6 (2), 65.

11 Things Unseen

1. Couttie, R.D., 'Dowsing expectancy', *Psychology News*, 1984, 38, 7 – 8.
2. Randi, James, *Flim-Flam*, New York: Prometheus Books, 1982.

3. Smith, David, 'Two tests of divining in Australia', *Skeptical Enquirer*, 6 (4), 34 – 7.
4. Quoted in Sladek, John, *The New Apocrypha*, London: Panther, 1978.
5. Quoted in Ackerman, A.S.E., *Popular Fallacies*, London: Westminster Press, 1950.
6. Foulkes, R.A., 'Dowsing experiments', *Nature*, 1971, 229.
7. Ellis, K., *Prediction and Prophecy*, London: Wayland, 1973. Also Welfare, Simon and Fairley, Peter, *Arthur C. Clarke's World of Strange Powers*, London: Collins, 1984.

12 A Twitch in Time

1. Barrett, Sir W. and Besterman, T., *The Divining Rod*, London: 1926.
2. 'Divining the truth', 'Forbidden Knowledge', BBC Radio 4, July 1985.
3. Fairley, Peter and Welfare, Simon, *Arthur C. Clarke's World of Strange Powers*, London: Collins, 1984.
4. Briggs H.D., Cambridge E., and Bailey R.N., 'A new approach to church archaelogy', *Archaeologia Aeliana* 1983, 5th ser., XI, 89 – 100.
5. Bailey R. N., 'Dowsing for medieval churches', *Popular Archaeology*, February 1983, 33 – 7.
6. Tretwell, F., letter in *Popular Archaeology* November 1983.
7. Bailey, R.N., correspondence, 2.3.83.
8. Blakemore, R.P. and Frankel, R.B., *Scientific American*, 12 (58), 245.
9. Orstan, Aydin,'Patterns of communication in nature', *Skeptical Enquirer*, 9 (3), 276 – 283.
10. BBC Radio Features Archives.
11. Lewis, D.M., 'Why the scientist doubts the dowser', in Thompson, C. (ed.), *Site and Survey Dowsing*, 1980.
12. Vogt, E.S. and Hyman, R., *Water Witching USA*, New York: 1959.

13 The Scientists' Quadrille

1. Inglis, Brian, 'The unknown factor', *Daily Mirror*, 9.3.83.
2. Quoted in Crowther, J.G., *A Short History of Science*, London: Methuen, 1969.
3. Johnston, Alva, 'Scientist and mob idol', *New Yorker*, 1933.
4. Interview for 'The scientists', 'Forbidden Knowledge', BBC Radio 4.
5. Rhine, J.B., *New Frontiers of the Mind*, London: Penquin Books, 1950. Also Rhine, *Extra-Sensory Perception*, Boston: Bruce Humphries, 1964.
6. Sheldrake, Rupert., *A New Science of Life*, London: Blond and Briggs, 1981.
7. Quoted in Dixon, B., *What is Science for?*, London: Collins, 1973.
8. Eysenck, H.J. and Sargent, C., *Explaining the Unexplained*, London: Book Club Associates, 1982.
9. Quoted in Frazier, Kendrick, 'Ganzfeld studies: first detailed appraisal finds serious flaws, no evidence of psi', *Skeptical Enquirer*, 10 (1), 2 – 7.
10. Marks, D. and Kamman, R., *The Psychology of the Psychic*, New York: Prometheus Books, 1980.
11. Randi, James, 'The Project Alpha experiment: part 1', *Skeptical Enquirer*, 7 (4), 24 – 33, cont. in 8 (1), 36 – 45.
12. Rhine, *New Frontiers of the Mind*.
13. Hearne, K.M.T., 'A survey of reported premonitions and of those who have them', *Journal of the Society for Psychical Research*, 52 (796), 261 – 70.
14. Harris, Melvin, *Sorry, You've Been Duped*, London: Weidenfeld and Nicolson, 1986.
15. Hansel, C.M., *ESP: A Scientific Evaluation*, London: McGibbon and Kee, 1966. Also, Hansel, *ESP: A Scientific Re- Evaluation*, New York: Prometheus Books, 1980.
16. Quoted in Inglis, Brian, *The Hidden Power*, London: Jonathan Cape, 1986.

14 Faith and Fantasy

1. Evan, C., *Cults of Unreason*, London: Panther, 1974. Also Vosper, Cyril., *The Mind Benders*, London: Mayflower, 1973.
2. Schmeidler, G. and McConnell, R.A., *ESP and Personality Patterns*, Westport, CT: Greenwood Press, 1958.
3. No specific references but hard-line sceptical literature such as Randi and the *Skeptical Enquirer* do seem to display an almost religious fervour of disbelief at least equal to, say, Brian Inglis' fervour of belief.
4. Singer, B. and Bernassi, V.A., 'Occult beliefs', *American Scientist*, 1981, 69, 49 – 55. Also *The Times*, 20.12.80.
5. Blackley, S.R., *As In Adam All Die...*, Lewes, Sussex: The Book Guild, 1986.
6. Blackmore, S. and Troscianko, T., 'Belief in the paranormal: probability judgements, illusory control, and the "chance baseline shift"', *British Journal of Psychology*, 1985, 76, 459 – 68.

15 Madness, Mystics and Shamans

1. Lévi-Strauss, C., *Structural Anthropology*, London: Peregrine, 1977 .
2. Lewis, I.M., *Ecstatic Religion*, London: Penguin Books, 1971.
3. Hearne, K. M.T., 'A survey of reported premonitions and of those who have them, *Journal of the Society for Psychical Research*, 52 (796), 261 – 70.
4. Messing, S.' 'Group therapy and social status in the Zar cult of Ethiopia', *American Anthropologist*, 1958, 60.
5. Nicolas, J.' 'Les juments des dieux: rites de possession et conditions feminines en Pays Hausa, Niger', *Etudes Nigériennes*, 1967, 21.
6. Mischel, W. and Mischel, F.' 'Psychological aspects of spirit possession in Trinidad', *American Anthropologist*, 1958, 60.

16 The Evidence of Experience

1. Singer, B. and Bernassi, V.A., 'Occult beliefs', *American Scientist*, 1981, 69, 49 – 55.
2. Inglis, Brian, *The Hidden Power*, London: Jonathan Cape, 1986.
3. Brown, J.A.C., *Techniques of Persuasion: From Propaganda to Brainwashing*, London: Penguin Books, 1963.
4. E. Kinkead, quoted in Brown, *Techniques of Persuasion*.
5. Marks, D., 'Why people believe', Conference of the Committee for the Scientific Investigation of Claims of the Paranormal, 1985, issued on audio cassette.
6. Wyatt, D.F. and Campbell, D.T., 'On the liability of the stereotype or hypothesis', *Journal of Abnormal and Social Psychology*, 46, 496.
7. Cited in Marks, D. and Kamman, R., *The Psychology of the Psychic*, New York: Prometheus Books, 1980.
8. Hearne, K.M.T., 'A survey of premonitions and those who have them', *Journal of the Society for Psychical Research*, 52 (796), 261 – 70.
9. 'An ostensible precognition of the 1974 Flixborough disaster', *JSPR*, 51 (790), 210 – 13.
10. Welfare, Simon and Fairley, Peter, *Arthur C. Clarke's World of Strange Powers*, London: Collins, 1984.
11. 'The Flixborough disaster', report of the court of inquiry, HMSO, 1975.
12. Bruner, J.S. and Minturn, A.L., 'Perceptual identification and perceptual organisation', *Journal of General Psychology*, 1953, 53, 21.
13. Dallenbach, K.M., 'The "range of attention "', *Psychology Bulletin*, 1928, 25, 153.
14. Sherif, M., *The Psychology of Social Norms*, New York: Harper, 1936.

15. Vernon, M.D., *The Psychology of Perception*, London: Penguin Books, 1962.

16. Dingwall, E.J., 'Gilbert Murray's experiments: telepathy or hyperaesthesia?', *Proceedings of the Society for Phsychical Research*, 1973, 56, 209.

17. Dodds, E.R., 'Gilbert Murray's last experiment', *Proceedings of the S P R*, 1972, 55, 206.

18. Miller, J.G., 'Discrimination without awareness', *American Journal of Psychology*, 1939, 52, 562. Also Wilcott, R.C., 'Subliminal stimulation v. psychophysical thresholds', *Perceptual Motor Skills*. 1957, 7, 29.

19. Goldstein, M.E., 'Subliminal perception with optical illusions', *Journal of General Psychology*, 1960, 62, 89.

20. Roney-Dougal, 'Subliminal and psi perception: a review of the literature', *JSPR*, 53 (805), 405 – 34.

21. Cited by R. Falk in 'On coincidence', *Skeptical Enquirer*, 6 (2), 18 – 31.

22. Koestler, Arthur, *The Roots of Coincidence*, London: Hutchinson, 1972.